Contextualising Narrative Inquiry

Narrative inquiry is growing in popularity as a research methodology in the social sciences, medicine and the humanities. In narrative inquiry, the transparency of interactions between researcher and research participants, together with rich, contextual descriptions, help to shape and structure research texts rendering them engaging and readable.

Contextualising Narrative Inquiry argues that all researchers should foreground the importance of the context in which research takes place and develop methodological approaches that are grounded in their local contexts. To do so, they need to pay attention to how knowledge is constructed, shared and understood in those contexts. This is particularly important when contexts have been subjugated historically through colonialism and when local, indigenous ways of knowing have been ignored or dismissed.

The contributors to this edited collection have all used narrative inquiry for a range of topics and in a range of contexts, including:

- Leadership styles of Asian women
- The deaf community in the UK
- Voluntary celibacy in Malta
- Administrators in Ghanaian higher education
- Multiculturalism in primary education in Cyprus
- Teacher identities in Hong Kong
- The reflective practitioner in higher education in Malaysia.

The diversity of the topics illuminates the potential for narrative inquiry to be used to investigate a broad range of issues in many contexts by people with a wide range of backgrounds. A common thread throughout is a reflexive discussion of how each contributor used narrative inquiry as a methodological approach; highlighting not only its affordances, but also the complexities of using it in specific cultural, social and historical contexts.

Sheila Trahar is Reader in International Higher Education in the Graduate School of Education, University of Bristol, UK.

Contextualising Narrative Inquiry

Developing methodological approaches for local contexts

Edited by Sheila Trahar

LONDON AND NEW YORK

First published 2013
by Routledge
2 Park Square, Milton Park, Abingdon, Oxon OX14 4RN

Simultaneously published in the USA and Canada
by Routledge
711 Third Avenue, New York, NY 10017

Routledge is an imprint of the Taylor & Francis Group, an informa business

British Library Cataloguing in Publication Data
A catalogue record for this book is available from the British Library

Library of Congress Cataloging in Publication Data
p. cm.
1. Narrative inquiry (Research method)--Cross-cultural studies. I. Trahar, Sheila.
H61.295C68 2013
001.4'2--dc23
2012028478

ISBN: 978-0-415-53637-0 (hbk)
ISBN: 978-0-415-53638-7 (pbk)
ISBN: 978-0-203-07170-0 (ebk)

Typeset in Galliard
by Fakenham Prepress Solutions, Fakenham, Norfolk NR21 8NN

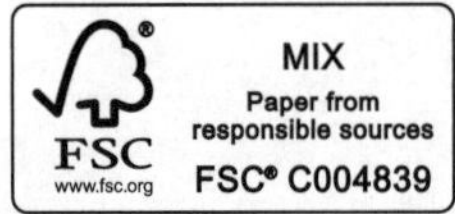

Printed and bound in Great Britain by
TJ International Ltd, Padstow, Cornwall

Contents

Contributors

Janetta Sika Akoto is an Assistant Registrar, Office of the Registrar in charge of the University Council Secretariat, University of Cape Coast, Ghana. She also has oversight responsibility of the Inter-Faculty Committee on Institutional Affiliation (IFCIA) Secretariat. IFCIA deals with issues of institutional affiliation and mentoring of affiliated university colleges in Ghana. Sika holds a PhD in Education from the University of Bristol.

Mary Baker is affiliated to a Higher Educational institution in the UK and has worked in the sector for more than fifteen years as both a lecturer and a manager. She has studied workplace bullying for over ten years and is particularly interested in the long term effects suffered by victims. Mary Baker is a pseudonym.

Pam Bennett is a doctoral researcher at the Graduate School of Education, University of Bristol. Her research interest is adult literacy and education.

Jane Horan is an EdD candidate with the University of Bristol. Her research focuses on Asian Women Leaders. Jane is a consultant helping organizations build inclusive and engaged work environments. She has lived in Asia for two decades and previously worked for Kraft, The Walt Disney Company and CNBC in organizational, leadership and talent management roles.

Jenny Knibb enjoyed extensive teaching experience in a wide range of educational settings prior to qualifying as a British Association for Counselling and Psychotherapy accredited senior counsellor. She currently teaches on the Master of Education programme at the University of Bristol, UK. Her research interests are focussed on the experiences of mothers who have a child with some kind of Special Need and the role that narrative research can play in enhancing society's understanding of their situation.

Verónica Larrain is Associate Professor in the Department of Teaching and Learning and Educational Organization at the University of Barcelona, Spain. She is a mother of two children and enjoys spending time outdoors. She is also a member of ESBRINA http://www.ub.edu/esbrina/index-en.html, a Catalonian consolidate research group dedicated to the study of the conditions and current changes in education. She is particularly interested in using and teaching reflexive narrative research methodologies in educational contexts.

Dione Mifsud is Head of the Department of Counselling at the University of Malta and President of the International Association for Counselling (IAC). He is a former Head of the University of Malta Counselling Unit and past President of the Malta Association for the Counselling Profession (MACP). Dione is a former Social Studies and guidance teacher and has been a counsellor for the past 17 years.

Evgenia Partasi holds a bachelor's degree in Primary Education (University of Cyprus), a Master's in Language, Ethnicity and Education (King's College, University of London) and a PhD in Education (University of Bristol). Her thesis focused on multiculturalism in primary schools in Cyprus through a narrative inquiry. Her research interests include multiculturalism and multicultural education, practices in multicultural and multilingual environments and identity construction in divided societies. She has published in academic journals and presented her work at international conferences.

Narina A. Samah is a Senior Lecturer in the Faculty of Education at the Universiti Teknologi Malaysia (UTM). She teaches educational foundation courses and educational psychology courses for both undergraduate and postgraduate programmes. Considering herself to be a practitioner researcher, Narina continues to venture into narrative inquiry as a means of exploratory research on transformative learning and continuing professional development among teachers and academics, across disciplines and specialisations, within the Malaysian context.

Sheila Trahar is Reader in International Higher Education in the Graduate School of Education, University of Bristol. She has published widely in the area of international higher education and intercultural learning and teaching. Her work foregrounds the value of narrative inquiry and autoethnography in research in these fields. Her book *Developing Cultural Capability in International Higher Education: A Narrative Inquiry* was published by Routledge in 2010 and her edited book, The *Learning and Teaching of Narrative Inquiry: Travelling in the Borderlands, was* published by John Benjamins in July 2011. Her edited book *Narrative Research on Learning: Comparative and International Perspectives,* published in 2006, continues to be one of the few texts to focus on narrative in international and comparative education. She teaches on the Doctor of Education in both Bristol and Hong Kong, the MSc Educational Research in Bristol and has taught on the Master of Education programme in Hong Kong for several years, leading the programme there since 2008.

Donna West is a postdoctoral researcher and teacher at the Graduate School of Education, University of Bristol. A former teacher of deaf children, she earned her PhD, a narrative inquiry into deafhearing family life, in 2009. She is part of a team of researchers collecting and analyzing sign-language poetry and teaches on the Narrative pathway, both within the Graduate School of Education.

Christina Yip Pui Lin is an experienced secondary teacher of English in Hong Kong. She obtained her doctoral degree in education from the University of Bristol. She has interests in developing creative teaching approaches of English Language and exploring research methodologies in education.

Preface

Sheila Trahar

Narrative inquiry recognizes and works with the idea that storytelling is a universal practice. A persuasive narrative inquiry enables its audience to see transparently how interactions between researcher and research participants help to shape and structure research texts rendering them engaging and readable. The context (s), within which those interactions occur, is/are, therefore, a crucial dimension of this methodological approach. A rich description of the context (s) needs to be to the fore in all narrative inquiry accounts so that '*narrative reality* in any local context – what does and doesn't get said, about what, why, how, and to whom' (Chase 2011: 422, emphasis in original) – can be understood. Yet such rich descriptions are all too often absent from texts, thus making it difficult for the reader to understand the 'narrative realities' that are being re-presented. This book foregrounds the importance of the influences of the context in which narrative inquiry takes place and, in doing so, critiques its appropriateness in contexts that may not necessarily privilege its discourses. In addition, each chapter demonstrates creatively and accessibly, ways of using narrative inquiry as a methodological approach for a broad range of topics.

> Stories don't fall from the sky (or emerge from the innermost 'self'), they are composed and received in contexts – interactional, historical, institutional and discursive – to name a few.
>
> (Riessman 2008: 105)

Consider Riessman's words; 'composed and received' are key. All stories are composed in a context, replete with history and with culture. Within that context, certain stories may be favoured over others and will be told in ways congruent with the context. The person/s hearing, 'receiving' the stories may be in or from a different context. As the reader, you may or not be familiar with the contexts from which the narrative inquiries in this book originate. Even if you are familiar with the geographical context, you may know little about deaf culture or bullying in higher education. If you are a teacher educator, you may not be aware of the significance of educational reforms in Hong Kong or the effects of the economic crisis in Spain on teachers. Narratives are developed in contexts; therefore, for the listener/researcher and then, subsequently, wider audiences to understand, to make sense of those narratives and why the writer/researcher has re-presented them in the ways that she or he has, a rich description of the context/s within which the stories were narrated – and of the relationship between narrator and listener – is necessary. One could argue that such descriptions should be visible in any research account – but they are rare – and we can be left musing about the researcher; why she or he wanted to do the research; how the research affected him/her/the participants; how the meanings of the narratives emerged. Bearing in mind the title – and the purposes – of this book, all contributors were asked to ensure that descriptions of their contexts were articulated as clearly as they needed to be, rather than assume that their audience would be familiar with them.

I have been conducting research using narrative inquiry and autoethnography for several years and have supervized the research of others using these methodological approaches at Masters and doctoral level, in the UK and Hong Kong. Narrative inquiry attracted me, not only for the importance placed on gathering stories respectfully – a practice very familiar to me as a counsellor – but also for its emphasis on reflexivity and on the researcher not being 'bracketed off' from the research. Such elements contribute to the potential to construct engaging texts that resonate with readers so that they reflect on their own lives, their own values and beliefs. I have been wary, however, of embracing narrative inquiry without reflecting carefully on its relevance and appropriateness for different contexts. I started to question whether narrative inquiry was in danger of becoming another form of 'paradigm fundamentalism' (Tomaselli, Dyll and Francis 2008: 357) if it were not interrogated critically and those researchers using it were not to consider its affordances and any factors mitigating against its use, in their context. I mused on whether I had brushed aside carelessly the cautious laments of those for whom narrative was unknown – or relatively unknown – in their context. Had I been too cavalier towards their concerns that using narrative inquiry would be risky – or even revolutionary? Moreover, 'narrative inquirers frequently find themselves crossing cultural discourses, ideologies and institutional boundaries' (Clandinin and Rosiek 2007: 59), yet these cultural discourses and ideologies, such as postmodernism and poststructuralism, remain rooted in European thought. They, too, need to be critiqued for their particular views of the world that may differ from, or be a challenge to, local knowledge in other contexts.

Composing the Preface, inevitably I reflect on how this book came about. And the preceding stories are important. I have been privileged to work alongside many of the book's contributors, in their research, in their first encounters with, and subsequent embrace of, narrative inquiry. I have also urged many of them to critique its methods and its suitability for their context and its local discourses. I have, therefore, orchestrated this book to gather specific types of contributions. But its seeds were sown a few years ago when Evgenia Partasi told me, when seeking the permission of the Ministry of Education in Cyprus to conduct her study, that using the term 'narrative inquiry' would not gain their consent. When

Sika Akoto told me about her research participants' resistance to her narrative interviews in Ghana and that narrative inquiry would be 'revolutionary' in that context. When Mary Baker and I realized the risks that she was taking in using narrative and autoethnography to write about her experiences of being bullied in her higher education context. As I suggested earlier in this Preface, not all narrative inquirers describe how they use it, how they make it their own, how they worked with the data, and the ethical complexities of the approach. I did not want this book to be a 'how to do narrative inquiry' text, but nonetheless all of the contributors were asked to address their use of the methodology and the complexities of using it, including any contextual limitations. I wanted to illuminate the value of narrative inquiry for myriad topics. I wanted the book to be an exemplar of what skilfully executed narrative inquiry can achieve – to engage the reader in ways that much social science writing does not do. Academic texts can be scholarly and yet still resonate with readers. In inviting these researchers to contribute to this book, I knew that I would get different writing styles and creative uses of literary devices to create compelling texts. Texts of this type create their own challenges. Would Sika Akoto's Ghanaian cloths retain their vibrancy when reproduced in black and white? Would Donna West's signs have prominence on the page so that readers, unfamiliar with working with deaf people could understand them? How would readers react to Verónica Larrain's use of a Carrefoc rap? Would the publisher agree to text reproduced in two columns as in Jenny Knibb's conversation with Special Needs? These creative and aesthetic dimensions of narrative inquiry add to the transparency of textual re-presentation, enabling the reader to understand and resonate with the meanings of the experiences described.

Many of the contributors to this book are not writing in their first language yet need to write in English because of the international readership. English continues to dominate academic texts and I have written elsewhere (Trahar 2008: 2011a, b) of how that dominance needs to be challenged. But, in this book, there are examples of other linguistic hegemonies. The deafhearing families in Donna West's chapter were not using spoken language. One of the Jamaican women in Pam Bennett's chapter is speaking in a form of English that Bennett considers needs to be translated for the reader. Jane Horan is humbled by the different meanings that an English word can carry when used by speakers of other languages and in different contexts. In each of these chapters – and in all of the book's chapters – the writers are navigating between languages, cultures and contexts where the placing of words on a page is a delicate and reflexive act.

The Chapters

'What *does* narrative inquiry help us to learn about our phenomenon that other theories or methods do not'? (Clandinin and Connelly 2000: 123, original emphasis). Donna West's and Jenny Knibb's chapters demonstrate how narrative inquiry can be used to think 'with' people whose lives are often dictated to by those who consider themselves to be wiser. West and Knibb want us to understand the meanings of the experiences of the deafhearing families and the mothers of children with special needs, rather than be presented with the theoretical dilution of those meanings. Narrative inquirers are not atheoretical but they recognize that people and their stories do not always 'fit' the theory. Theoretical labels can be constraining and difficult to loosen and, most importantly, 'must always be open to reexamination and change' (Tomaselli, Dyll and Francis 2008: 350), in particular, to take account of the context – social, professional, cultural – of researchers and researched.

A much proffered reason for using narrative inquiry is that it supports silenced voices to be heard and that it has an overtly political purpose – to challenge or trouble established ways of thinking. Donna West in her account of narrative inquiry with deafhearing families uses the term 'the visually oriented signing body' to explain the complexities of 'transforming speech and sign "acts" into a text-and-paper artefact'. Every stage of this act of transformation/translation was undertaken collaboratively with the families, which places issues of 'power, representation, cultural translation and conceptual equivalence firmly in the spotlight'. In this act of collaboration, West offered her own stories so that the interactions were a continuous and reflexive exchange of ideas and questions. Through the vignettes used to illustrate her ways of re-presenting the stories, she reproduces the signs used by the narrators so that, as readers, we are drawn into the original storytelling process. These vignettes communicate, vividly, the lived experience of people who have been – and continue to be – marginalized and misunderstood by wider society. The account of Bella, the 10 year old girl who is less interested in West's poetic transformations of her story than correcting the text so that 'people would not think she was stupid or illiterate' is a poignant illustration of this marginalization. Bella uses the metaphor of a switchable dial on her chest to 'show' powerfully how she wishes she could 'switch' between a deaf and a hearing identity. Had West limited her re-telling of this narrative to words, she would lose the power conveyed by the text wrapped around the dial. By accompanying the text with visual images, she invites us in to the narratives in different ways. Throughout her chapter, West foregrounds a tension in any research text, that of being fixed in time and of the consequent danger that we read the accounts and experience the life of the person as static and unchanging, which is totally disingenuous. West claims that narrative inquiry's methods allow the stories to live on in different forms to unknown and unimagined readers; the evidence for such claims in this chapter is powerful.

Jenny Knibb used narrative inquiry in her research with mothers of children with special needs and she foregrounds the tensions inherent in conducting research with people with whom one has had a counselling relationship. Knibb locates her study within the dominant models of disability in the UK – the medical model, with its emphasis on cure and mitigation of disability – and the social model, which locates disability within the organisation of society. Her clear accounts of how the mothers are positioned by the establishment as being unable to make decisions about their children are powerful and moving. Knibb, by juxtaposing extracts from the interview conversations with her own reflections, demonstrates how these mothers construct their identities while disputing how their lives are 'interpreted and edited' by others. She describes the challenges of the narrative interview and of the analysis of the narratives, explaining how she used both thematic and performative analysis, contextualising the narratives within broader societal frameworks. In doing so, she constructs a theoretical argument about disability within her text, an argument that questions and challenges the dominant models that she has previously described. Knibb, too, is concerned to articulate the tensions between enabling the mothers' stories to be heard and not fixing them on the page and thus in the reader's mind. She explains that the accounts encapsulate moments in time. They are partial truths. In the latter part of the chapter Knibb portrays a fictionalized conversation with 'Special Needs', a creative device that is used as a vehicle not only to challenge 'it', but also to illustrate how, through the process of the narrative inquiry, she has come to 'see' Special Needs 'differently'.

A narrative inquiry often begins with an incident from the researcher's life associated with the 'research puzzle'. Dione Mifsud, in his account of the Mużew society, a Maltese Christian lay society whose members commit themselves to a life of chastity, reveals how, as a younger man, he had contemplated becoming a Mużew member. Mifsud's memories of being spellbound by celibacy led him to seek out Xandru, a man who had chosen that life, to interview for his research. Following extracts from their conversation, Mifsud writes what he refers to as 'autoethnographic fiction' to imagine how his life might have been had he followed his earlier desires. His writing is located within the context of Malta, a Mediterranean island that has been colonized consistently until its freedom in 1964. Mifsud refers to Maltese people as being 'compulsive storytellers', attributing this trait to excessive colonization. In spite of this compulsion for storytelling, he claims that his chapter will be considered transgressive in his context, an observation indicative of how contexts permit some stories to be told, but not others. By telling his transgressive story, Mifsud gives a rich and multi-layered account of the continuing importance – and influence – of Catholicism in Malta. Delamont, (2009: 61) is critical of autoethnography, considering that it 'is an abrogation of the honourable trade of the scholar'. A different perspective is that, executed skilfully, that is by being 'self-luminous' rather than being 'self-indulgent' (Sparkes 2002: 214), the portraitist's life story gives clarity and authenticity to the text. Reading that Mifsud himself harboured desires to enter the Mużew brotherhood, enables the meaning of this sect to be crystallized and brought to life through his own contemplations.

Mary Baker foregrounds the use of autoethnography to research her experiences of being bullied in a UK higher education institution. Bullying in UK higher education is now a significant problem and Baker draws on research that attributes the increase in this phenomenon to the changes that have taken place in that context over the past 20 years or so, changes that make very different demands of academic staff. These different demands can lead to insecurity and, regrettably, the destructive practice of bullying. Research into bullying has tended to be quantitative and, while valuable for identifying the causes of bullying and the need for anti-bullying policies, the lived experiences of the bullied remain invisible. Baker's chapter is an account of the complexities of using autoethnography in her context and for this topic, foregrounding the methodological and ethical dilemmas that she encountered. Believing at first that, in autoethnography, as the 'researcher, researched', she could use a range of creative and literary devices to disguise the identities of the perpetrator and the institution, gradually she realized that this was impossible. 'In the end I had to consider whether this story was entirely mine to tell'. In narrative inquiry and autoethnography, narratives are co-constructed and mediated by their context. To speak of ownership of a story is complex, and, as indicated by other writers in this book, addressed in various ways such as collaboration with participants at all stages in the research process to produce joint accounts. After much deliberation and consultation, Baker decided to write her chapter using a pseudonym. In making this decision, she raises some of the ethical complexities inherent in narrative inquiry and, in particular, in autoethnography. Employing autoethnography has enabled her story to be told and witnessed by a wider audience but the use of a pseudonym renders her powerless to some extent, thus the bully and the institution may be seen to continue to exert their power over her.

Janetta Sika Akoto was seduced by narrative inquiry when she first encountered it in her doctoral research training programme. Her background in theatre drew her to the performative dimensions of narrative and she appreciated it as a methodological approach that would give her the freedom to incorporate her local ways of storytelling into her research into female administrators in Ghanaian higher education. In addition, she was able to challenge what she considered to be the 'Western' academic tradition of accounting for one's perspective by locating it within other texts. Akoto reflects on the educational context of Ghana and the remnants of colonization, citing African scholars who claim that 'Western academics' insistence that they draw on research from the West while seldom drawing on research conducted in Africa is another form of colonization. Akoto tells of how she came to value her local knowledge and to find ways of bringing it into her research. Gradually, she develops the confidence to question and to blend her Akan tribal myths and stories into her writing. Her use of the metaphor 'the teeth and the tongue' to illustrate how the teeth and the tongue may come into conflict in the mouth but work together for the common good is a powerful illustration of how she blends knowledge from different contexts. She writes of using a methodological approach that is almost unknown in Ghana and that rendered her vulnerable to criticism yet, as she indicates towards the end of the chapter, may ensure that her research is read much more widely than it might otherwise be. Akoto describes the narrative interviews with the women in her research and how this method of interviewing that encourages collaboration was alien to her participants, resulting in Akoto feeling diminished by the experience. The women's expectations, located within a context dominated by more positivist perspectives, call for a need to critique the narrative interview and to recognize that a research method that may be powerful and valuable in one context may have very different effects in another.

Narina A. Samah, also entranced by narrative inquiry, questioned, eventually, how its philosophical leanings towards postmodernism could coexist with her Islamic faith, and how postmodernism's challenges to certainty could sit alongside the certainty that her faith prescribes. A. Samah used narrative inquiry to research her own practice as a lecturer in a Malaysian university. Her text is replete with twists and turns as she moves backwards and forwards in time and space, grappling with many tensions. Tensions that arise between her exposure to different learning and teaching approaches in her British university; tensions between narrative inquiry and her previous exposures to research and finally tensions between philosophical perspectives and her faith. Her exposition of how she ultimately reconciles – and celebrates – these differences is powerful yet renders her vulnerable. It leads her into questioning her taken for granted assumptions that student-centred approaches to learning and teaching are to be preferred over other pedagogical approaches. In addition, it causes her to reflect much more deeply about the nuances within her own multicultural context. Such reflections, together with listening to Nur's and Aswad's stories enable her to recognize that, in striving to implement student-centred approaches in her teaching in Malaysia, she was transferring, uncritically, approaches developed in one context to another without considering the concepts – and values and beliefs – informing those approaches. She describes vividly how she slips back into her traditional lecture style, then bravely introduces a more active style yet continues to receive contradictory feedback from the students. It is not until she realizes the importance of being sensitive to the ramifications of her context that she begins to understand how to use ideas that attract her but that need to be considered sensitively and respectfully in order for them to be successful in that context.

Evgenia Partasi's chapter is the first of three concerned with teacher identities. It describes her narrative inquiry in primary education classrooms on the divided island of Cyprus, a context that has changed from the 'myth of a monocultural Greek Cypriot society' to one now populated by 21.4 per cent 'non-Cypriots'. Like Mifsud's Malta, the strategic position of Cyprus has attracted myriad colonizers, all of whom have left their footprints. Problems of racism and xenophobia are increasing, however, attributed to immigration by people from Asia and the former eastern bloc. Partasi makes her case for the value of narrative inquiry, unknown in Cyprus, in researching such a complex environment, in particular because its interactive nature enabled her to 'face and discuss' her own 'assumptions, fears and prejudices' when witnessing the discriminatory attitudes and behaviours in her participants. Previous research in Cyprus indicates the education system to be 'ethnocentric and nationalistic' and the lack of attention paid to the increasingly diverse population leads her to feel pessimistic about what she might encounter in her own study. Pleasantly surprised by a much more inclusive atmosphere in the classroom than she expected, Partasi moved to the opposite end of the spectrum, seeing the situation through rose-tinted spectacles. Finally, she was able to understand both the positive and negative attitudes and behaviours she encountered, not only through dialogue with the teachers and the children but also through her reflexivity that allowed her to understand her own prejudices and the reasons she held them. Like Larrain in Chapter Nine, Partasi writes about the complexities inherent in the roles performed in narrative inquiry, focusing on how she as a teacher, would react in similar circumstances, and on the discomfort she felt in criticizing her own people for their racist attitudes. Her discussion of how the different ways in which 'black' is perceived and used in Cyprus, the UK and the USA enables her powerful realization that participants mirrored many of her own stereotypical and discriminatory attitudes.

Christina Yip's context of a postcolonial Hong Kong is also populated with accounts of using a methodological approach still relatively unknown in this context, a context in which researchers are hindered from attempting to use 'alternate and unconventional methodologies' for several reasons. Yip locates her research on teacher identities during a period of intensive educational reform in a Hong Kong that is influenced, significantly, by Confucianism. The moral overtones of Confucianism make it difficult for teachers to express their resistance to the reforms and Yip, by conducting her research using narrative inquiry, enables her teacher participants' voices to be heard. At the heart of this chapter is Yip's story of her visit to Ah Leung, her masseur. Using the Chinese tradition of massage, she tells of a fictionalized conversation with Ah Leung where he is positioned as the voice of her doubts about her methodological approach. As she slumbers on the massage bed, lulled into sleep by his expert fingers massaging her body, she articulates what she finds complex about narrative inquiry and how she is struggling with it. Ah Leung is clearly her more traditional researcher voice as he questions her. Why doesn't she write a book? What is different about this approach? As the conversation progresses, we read of how she struggles to move away from a 'linear approach' to what she refers to as a 'kind of messiness in writing'. Ah Leung focuses on having 'a plan' and assumes that she is conducting interviews with a recorder and a microphone. Then, he slips in the revealing phrase, 'But I don't really follow all the steps in the prescribed sequence', as he describes to her how he has developed as a skilled masseur; a phrase that gives her permission to be more flexible in her approach to her research. This flexibility is revealed throughout the text as she explains how she gathered the teachers' narratives, integrating her own experiences as learner and teacher, to co-construct ways in which teachers in Hong Kong negotiate their professional identities in this changing environment.

The third chapter about teacher identities is by Verónica Larrain. The context is Spain, a country beset by economic crisis since 2008, where the welfare state is being dismantled and the reduction in education budgets is affecting classrooms and teacher employment. Larrain and Nuria, a Catalan teacher, take a feminist poststructuralist perspective on their narrative inquiry, wanting to explore the possibilities to disrupt identity categories and to 'produce a narrative that shows the conditions in which it was produced'. They use a range of writing practices, *scenes*, songs, anecdotes and fictional dialogues to subvert the authority that a research experience acquires in the text. The use of *scenes* is offered as a way of accounting for the difficulties in describing complex situations 'from the outside' when the observer's – in this case Larrain's – perspective is always incomplete. The examples of *scenes* provide vivid illustrations of this incomplete perspective together with the difficulties in managing the feelings that arise when observing another as a method of research. Larrain reflects on her Chilean upbringing in the Locating the Vulnerable Researcher *scene*, sharing how it informed her positioning of Nuria as a 'bad teacher'. Jordi Plays the Fool is an example of how an anecdote needs to be re-read for the theoretical insights afforded. One of Larrain's objectives for the fictional dialogue constructed from conversations between herself and Nuria following the Locating the Vulnerable Researcher *scene*, was to increase Nuria's presence as author of the interpretation. Generating narratives that reflect on the production and editing process provides Larrain with the rationale for conducting her research in the ways that she did and, like Donna West, displays how attending to our 'rituals of speaking' can alter what we assume to be natural and unquestionable. The final writing strategy used is the *Correfoc rap*, translated literally as 'fire run', a Catalonian tradition and a musical poem written by Nuria to narrate the relationships with her students and how they give identity meaning to her teaching. In the deconstructive deployment of the *Correfoc*, Nuria and Larrain were 'attentive to how splits and overlaps can … play with, dominate, frame … and change ourselves'.

Pam Bennett's chapter is located within her work in adult literacy in the UK. Bennett communicates both engagement with, and scepticism for, narrative inquiry. Towards the end of her chapter she writes of how she is 'drawn to the very elements that a positivist might wish to establish' as well as the unexpectedness of the emotions that she encountered in the process of the research and that contributed to ethical and methodological challenges for her. The chapter revolves around conversations with two Jamaican women. One is a revisiting of a conversation with Annie, conducted before Bennett had encountered narrative inquiry and the second is a narrative interview with Ellouise. Bennett focuses closely on the geographical contexts of Bristol, in the UK and Jamaica. Bristol is notorious for its connections with the slave trade, and, although Bennett articulates her struggle to suppress the similarities between the two women and herself, preferring to foreground the differences in order to create her 'own version of objectivity', it is hard for her, the daughter of Jamaican immigrants, to suppress the very powerful memories of her own upbringing and of child shifting, common to their three stories. Child shifting, children being raised by people other than their parents, continues to be common in Jamaica and the conversation extracts reveal the women's different experiences of this practice. Caught between the tensions of a book that will be read by an international audience and her desire to be faithful to the speech of her narrators, Bennett feels the need to 'translate' Annie's spoken words, assuming that readers will struggle to understand the Jamaican patois as she takes us through her process of dialogic/performance analysis.

Jane Horan, in the final chapter, uses narrative inquiry to explore and explicate complex layers of 'culture' in her work with Asian women leaders. Horan is a North American woman who has lived and worked in the Asia Pacific Region for 20 years. A Mandarin speaker, she writes poignantly of how she perceived herself to be an insider in the communities that she was researching, not only because of the length of time that she has lived in Asia, but also because of her work in global organizations. Horan writes about the challenges of using 'cross cultural narrative inquiry' to gather narratives from the women from Bangladesh, Japan, Singapore and Taiwan. She imagined that these women would relate to her as one of them, even though her physical appearance differed from theirs. To her disappointment, it became clear to her that she was being categorized as American. In her Chapter, Horan describes how the 'overabundance of cross-cultural theory' and her belief that she 'knew about culture' hindered her ability to recognize and value the individual experiences of the women she interviewed. Such insights highlight another tension. It can be helpful to develop understanding of contexts and cultures that we perceive to differ from our own, yet they are still composed of individuals. Balancing an individual's story with broader, contextual ones can be slippery. Horan focuses in particular on the concept of 'face' and of how she was bewildered by the word 'failure'. From her North American perspective 'failure' can be positive, an opportunity to learn, thus, when one of her participants told her that she had never failed at anything, she was puzzled and sceptical. Intense reflection on her responses to this incident, enable her to write 'I should have realized a question about failure would elicit such a response' and to acknowledge that, in spite of her many years of living in the Asia Pacific, she still had much to learn.

'The path is made by walking on it'

In writing this Preface, it is inevitable that my perspectives on narrative inquiry, its affordances and limitations are foregrounded. I have attempted to whet the appetite of the reader, through my summaries of the chapters, and to persuade you to delve into each one. We read about the uncertainty with which some of the writers embarked on their journeys. We engage with their curiosity, their desire to make sense of other people's stories and to communicate their understanding and knowledge gained in creative ways. In their attempts to communicate their insights to others, they write of how they risk misunderstanding, dismissal, scepticism and yet each one displays the compulsion to ground their research process in their own stories of discovery as a moral and transparent act.

> The daunting task of uncovering how narratives acquire their meaning within the context of asymmetrical cultural practices still needs to be done
>
> (Bhatia 2011: 351)

I am cautious about making claims that may seem to be exaggerated, but, in this book, each writer has grasped the nettle of a 'daunting task' in her or his context (s) of 'asymmetrical cultural practices' and made their paths by walking upon them. As the reader, you, too, will make your path by walking in the local contexts that are described so richly. Narrative inquiry is rigorous, creative and political. Enjoy your journey of discovering it.

References

Bhatia, S. (2011) Narrative inquiry as cultural psychology: Meaning-making in a contested global world. *Narrative Inquiry*, 21 (2), 303–310.

Chase, S. (2011) 'Narrative inquiry: Still a field in the making'. In N. Denzin and Y. Lincoln (eds), *The Sage Handbook of Qualitative Research*, 4th edn. Thousand Oaks, CA: Sage, pp. 421–434.

Delamont, S. (2009) The only honest thing: autoethnography, reflexivity and small crizes in fieldwork. *Ethnography and Education*, 4 (1), 51–63.

Riessman, C.K. (2008) *Narrative Methods for the Human Sciences*. Thousand Oaks, CA: Sage.

Sparkes, A. C. (2002) 'Autoethnography, self-indulgence or something more?' In A. Bochner and C.Ellis (eds) *Ethnographically Speaking: Autoethnography, Literature and Aesthetics*. New York: Alta Mira Press, pp. 209–32.

Tomaselli, K. G., Dyll, L., and Francis, M. (2008) ' "Self" and "other": Auto-reflexive and indigenous ethnography'. In N. K. Denzin, Y. S. Lincoln and L. Tuhiwai Smith (eds) *Handbook of Critical and Indigenous Methodologies*. Thousand Oaks, Ca: Sage, pp. 347–372.

Trahar, S. (2008) It starts with once upon a time. Editorial in Special Issue of *Compare* Narrative Methodological Approaches: Their Contribution to Comparative and International Education 38 (3), 259–266.

—(2011a) *Developing Cultural Capability in International Higher Education: A Narrative Inquiry*. Abingdon, Oxon: Routledge.

—(2011b) (ed.) *Learning and Teaching Narrative Inquiry: Travelling in the Borderlands*. Amsterdam: John Benjamins.

Acknowledgements

Many thanks to all of the contributors for responding so positively to my idea for this book and then for working with me to make its publication possible. Special thanks to Donna West for her support and comments on my Preface. Thanks to Philip Mudd at Routledge and to Vicky Parting for her prompt and helpful responses to my emails. As ever, thanks to Barry, who has to live with the piles of paper that constitute editing a book – at least the way I do it!

Chapter 1

What's in a sign? Narrative inquiry and deaf storytellers

Donna West

Introduction

Deaf culture and storytelling go hand-in-hand. Deaf stories, jokes, poems and fables are passed down through the generations in sign language. They are not usually written down (unless linguists, researchers and historians decide to translate them): the sign language is the text. The research on which this chapter is based is a narrative inquiry with three deafhearing families[1] who told me their stories of family life. One of the major challenges of this type of inquiry is the need for culturally sensitive and appropriate re-presentation of stories that are told in British Sign Language and set down in written English. This involves not only negotiating the minefield of translation between languages and cultures, but also imaginative and creative rule-bending, where a text-based document becomes a visual artefact, and the gap between signs and words on the page is reduced. It also involves facing up to the fact that written English has severe limitations when translating hilarious, moving, mischievous and downright angry stories. Narrative inquiry, which foregrounds the 'voices' of participants (Chase 2005) and respects them as agentic and performative narrators is a particularly powerful methodology where the documenting of deaf life is concerned. This chapter tells a reflexive and tricky tale of how sign-language stories might make it faithfully to the page: one of the affordances of narrative inquiry when researching with members of the deaf community.

Locating myself within the inquiry

My name is Donna and I am hearing. I started learning British Sign Language (BSL) when I was 24 years old. I have taught deaf children and worked as a communication support worker with deaf college students. I have also engaged in research with deaf children and adults who use BSL as their first and preferred language. I am not an interpreter, nor have I any formal training in translation. I would somewhat reluctantly describe myself as bilingual in English and BSL. When I asked three deafhearing families to tell me their stories for my PhD research I already knew that, whether my narrators were deaf or hearing, whether they spoke or signed, I was expected to produce a written thesis. That is to say, I would be transcribing their signs and words; I would be transforming speech and sign 'acts' into a text-and-paper artefact in order to fulfil the requirements of my university examiners. Rather than struggle with this process in isolation, as a 'responsible and able' doctoral student, I chose to treat the production of narrative transcripts and re-presentations as an integral and affirming part of the research collaboration between me and the families.

My early research experience – as a Master's student and junior research assistant – with members of the deaf community followed a largely critical-ethnographic tradition of participant observation and interviewing. Informants' signed 'data' were translated, analyzed and documented. While 'voice', reflexivity and representation were central to the work, and while the principle of respondent validation (Lather 1986) informed my practice, data in the form of interviews and journal notes were mostly sorted and organized thematically and as such, I would argue, rendered several-steps-removed from the original positioned, temporal, contingent, signed performance. Moreover, re-located 'chunks' of translated text often appeared so distant and transformed from the original telling that they risked becoming unfamiliar, unrecognizable and disconnected from deaf people's experiences and constructions.

Documenting the stories (and the story of the stories, West 2012) therefore became integral to this inquiry; deaf family-members specifically were invited into the translation/representation act, as editors, critics, theorists and authors. While not solely the remit, nor the exclusive domain of narrative methods, I suggest that such a democratic process, based on genuine curiosity and respect for each others' translation views, abilities and insights, offers collaborative opportunities that continue up to the moment of the Final Print. This is not to suggest that such intentions are always greeted with enthusiasm, willingness or interest, but that the spirit of the intention often opens doors to new ways of seeing and understanding, when (hearing) researchers and (deaf) participants come together in the re-presentation of their narrated lives.

Narrative concepts

Our inquiry (see West 2012) was loosely framed as a narrative inquiry. At its heart, it was about telling stories; about recovering and discovering memories, about remembering and forgetting, about sharing, recalling and explaining, about scripting, repairing and crafting. Through the inquiry, we learned about each other, we disputed, we surprised, we got lost, we connected. I offered back my own stories. The process of learning about deafhearing family life was 'thickened' through a continuous, reflexive exchange of ideas, questions and emerging theories; through email, or face-to-face discussions, beyond what might be termed the formal research conversation (Martin 2011). What developed from a simple question – *What's the story of your family?* – was a relational, back-and-forth research experience, where understanding of family-life-experience, of deafness, of relationships, love, care and resilience was enhanced through the telling of, and attendance to, stories.

Arthur Frank (2008) once counselled a group of workshop participants; 'Stories are like books, the narrative is the library.' I found it helpful to think of stories as That Which People Tell, and narratives as the recognized, co-constructed, politicized collection; the specialist library. I found myself drawn to the idea that a narrative inquiry embraces not only the meanings that are constructed, felt, known and told (Richardson 1997), but also the very phenomena of the telling: to paraphrase Bruner (1987); the life that is lived, the life that is experienced and the life that is told. Stories – memories, observations, anecdotes, performances and reflections, be they signed, spoken or written – are the *things* we tell each other. I recognized them as located at the intersection of biography, history, culture and society (Riessman 2001) and we – the families and I – worked together in order to *co*-construct and *re*-present them, based on our emerging, familiar and new understanding.

In the spirit of a postmodern, post-structuralist tradition, where knowledge and understanding of family life is realized as discursively, historically and culturally situated (Davies and Gannon 2006) and narratively constructed (Richardson 2003), what I hoped for, and what the families joined me in, was a troubling of a hegemonic, 'established way of thinking' (Trinh 1992: 125) about deaf and hearing lives, about parenthood, about cultural negotiation and migration, about language and communication. I wanted to engage in an inquiry that explored and embraced different ways of knowing while acknowledging the ways in which the personal, the social, the cultural and the political are integral and inextricably linked in terms of meaning, experience and belief (see Domosh 2003).

Deaf culture and storytelling go hand-in-hand. Deaf stories, jokes, poems and fables are passed down through the generations in sign language. Narrative inquiry acknowledges, respects and taps into the storytelling lifeline of an often-marginalized and historically misunderstood community of signing deaf people (see Branson and Miller 2002). It draws on and foregrounds the performative act of telling stories as a way to transmit wisdom, experience and memory through the visually orientated, signing body. It also permits the creation of spaces wherein a hearing researcher can learn about the intimate, culturally specific meaning-making processes of deaf people and be trusted to write them down.

Narrative time and performance

> Most of us comprehend … human actions as being organized in time.
>
> (McAdams 1997: 30)

Throughout the inquiry, I reflected a great deal on the ways in which stories become fixed in the moment of the printing, the binding. This is not necessarily problematic: while Huber and Clandinin (2002) comment on the ways that the freezing-in-time of stories obscures or limits our abilities to perceive them in a wider, temporal context, perhaps it is the setting down of stories that serves as a reminder of the very temporality of the narrative act (Ricoeur 1984; Vigouroux 2007). Our work together, then, could be understood through a temporal lens as a convergence and simultaneity of pasts, presents and futures (St Pierre 1997). The three-dimensional space of our inquiry embraced not only a moving-about-in-time (Brockmeier 2000), but also the historicality of the cultural, social, relational and geographical. That is to say, while narrators tell remembered stories – offering performances of memory and anticipation (Genette 1980; Keats 2009) – their narratives also lie at, and circle or spiral through, the fluid convergence of other plotlines, histories and lifespans.

By looking at the situated performances of stories as they are told within a narrative inquiry, we can begin to understand the (deaf) narrator's historical position(ing) in relation to various cultural and moral discourses and resources (Schrauf 2000; Drewery 2005; Hole 2008). The choosing subject (Davies and Harré 1990) takes responsibility for her storyline, and makes choices about the crafting of that story (Denzin 1994; Bamberg 1997) and the construction or repair of her identities, in reference/resistance to various (medical, pedagogical, cultural) canonical scripts (Butler 1990; Ochs and Capps 1996). The theatrical metaphor is extended beyond the telling of one's story by looking at ways in which the subjective narrator not only positions herself within a storyline, but also assigns, scripts and directs other roles and parts (Kraus 2006) in order to render her actions meaningful and intelligible (van Langenhove and Harré 1999; Rudd 2009). Stories, say, of visits to audiology clinics, of genetics counsellors and of school parents' evenings are re-visioned when invited and performed as deaf-centred *counter*-narratives (Andrews 2004). Medical and educational experts are wickedly recast, and we are invited to witness and think *with* (Frank 1995) a young deaf mother, for example, whose life is constantly interrupted by health visitors, teachers and doctors telling her how to parent, how to manage, how to cope, when all she wants to do is find her own way, trust her instincts and enjoy bringing up her deaf children.

The negotiation of relations

> The between. The realm of the between. That reality which we feel, and which is going on, between us. Between you and me. Between this part of me and that part of me ... It is intangible, invisible, moving, disappearing, expanding, softening, hardening, opening, welcoming, freezing over, clamming shut ... it concerns entering inside relationships, inside whatever is going on, and is sensed as going on, between us.
>
> (Mair 1989: 65)

Miller Mair's interpretation of spaces-between informs the nature of the relational space between families, between each other, between them and me. It casts light on the spatial distance between narrator and author, between narrator and protagonist/antagonist, between narrator and audience, author and audience, author and actor. This spatial distance, according to Currie (2007), can be physical in terms of point of view, temporal in terms of the telling and the listening/watching, and moral in terms of judgement and interpretation. I became interested in the intimate, private, interrelational spaces of research conversations, and the ways in which the temporal and interpretive spaces are played out – between deaf and hearing, sign and speech, performance and writing, telling and re-presenting – as connections, understandings, sense-making and politics move precariously and messily beyond private 'inter-view' to the wider, imagined audience.

Trans-scriptions

> The tape recordings, the transcriptions thereof, and notes written at the time of the recording constitute a primary record that is accurate in the literal sense: they set down what has been said and what has been seen. The finished stories are accurate in a secondary sense, not as facsimiles of the transcripts, but as literary depictions of the ebbs and flows in the lives that created the transcripts.
>
> (Kotre 1996: 32)

When stories are told or performed in sign language, many complex issues arise in relation to the moving between the visual-spatial (non-written) modality of sign, and the traditional, linear written form of text (Temple and Young 2004; West 2009). In addition to issues concerning the production of translation, the recording and re-presentation (by a hearing person) of stories told by, for and about, deaf people – whose history is arguably largely one of discrimination and marginalization – is a methodological, epistemological and political minefield. It places issues of power, representation, cultural translation and conceptual equivalence firmly in the spotlight (Simon 1996; Stone and West 2012). Much has been written about transcribing as a situated, interpretive and political act (Duranti and Goodwin 1992; Edwards and Lampert 1993; Green, Franquiz and Dixon 1997). This is compounded when navigating deaf and hearing cultures, signs and words, community and academy, histories and meanings. Within the created, relational narrative space – one that respects and acknowledges the act of narration and all that converges on that moment of telling – is the recognition of the ephemerality and transience of 'orality'. Narrative inquiry foregrounds not only what is told, but how it is constructed, made sense of and re-told. Writing down, or documenting, signed stories becomes an inherently political act. The performance transfers to the page. The concept of authorship is troubled. A deaf readership is imagined, invited, addressed. The following vignettes illustrate some of the ways in which deaf stories, narrative inquiry, language, culture, signs and writing bump up against each other, and how these bumps can be sidestepped, traversed or embraced.

Vignette: Sign language as temporal-spatial

Georgina, who has traced her deaf heritage back at least seven generations, is a deaf mother with four deaf children and one hearing son. Some time after her fifth child, Thomas, was born, he had a hearing test. Georgina was told that Thomas was 'fine'. She instinctively thought this meant that he was deaf.

> G: … but when Thomas went-for hearing test, they said he hearing, my mum burst into tears! My mum! She cried when they said Nick deaf and she cried when they said Thomas hearing! (laughs). She said, 'He should (be) deaf!' 'I know!!'… I remember they handed Thomas back (to me) I looked-at him I couldn't-see Thomas, I just see h-e-a-r-i-n-g (label across his chest in big letters) … er … right, so what do? Y'know, should I sign with him? (In) my work I tell parents they must sign with their deaf child, means I should <voice> (with) him? Also I had-to think-about him and family and what <happy> all-of-us and what <happy> him (look down to baby) <you hearing world will give-you-back hearing world> you hearing world but you also my child … so I will sign …

Georgina and I are sitting in her living room; she on the sofa, me on a chair, the videocamera somewhere off to the right, quietly recording her stories. As I recall, it was getting dark; late afternoon, January 2008. Within the space of our conversation, Georgina's hands, face and body recreate and navigate the remembered spaces of the hospital audiology department and of her kitchen where her (deaf) mother was waiting for her daughter and baby grandson to come home. These are layered with her 'work' spaces of other people's homes – hearing parents with deaf children – and with the intimate, signing spaces of her family life, the private spaces of her 'conversation' with Thomas, and the abstract spaces of, and between, deaf home and hearing world. Georgina places them all metaphorically in different signing spaces in front of her body. In one minute, she draws together temporal, spatial and relational spaces that span 30 years of direct experience and that cast, direct and position several actors. Below is a suggested re-presentation that acknowledges these layered spaces where identities (deaf mother/deaf daughter), sensory orientation (visual/aural) and meanings (culture/disability) intersect and collide.

But
    when Thomas went for hearing test
    they said he hearing

my mum burst into tears!
My mum!

She cried when they said Nick deaf
she cried when they said Thomas hearing! (laughs)
She said, 'He should be deaf!'
'I know!!'

I remember they handed Thomas back to me
I looked-at him I couldn't-see Thomas
I just see h-e-a-r-i-n-g label across his chest in big letters

Right, so what do?
Y'know, should I sign with him?

In my work
I tell parents they must sign with their
deaf child

means I should <voice> (with) him?

Also I had-to think-about him and family
and what <happy> for all-of-us and
what <happy> him

<you hearing world will give-you-back hearing world>
you hearing world but you also my child
so I will sign …

Vignette: At the threshold of the untranslatable[2]

Bella is ten. She has one hearing brother and one deaf brother. She told me about how her mum found out her daughter was deaf.

B: Also, like … when … in past, when … when me born … so me born my mum felt me deaf **but** everyone like no silly crazy she hearing! **But** my mum look at them she sure me deaf… **but** my dad said <fee> she definitely hearing … no deaf in my family … so anyway my mum say nothing get-on-with-things then me about 15 months we went see dad his friend … and one friend look-at me he think me deaf 'I think she deaf' and my mum like *see*! And she said my dad 'I think she deaf' … so my mum took me hospital test and they <find-find-find-find-find-find> and right! <fant> Mum right! Me deaf!

Like Georgina, Bella blends several temporal and relational spaces into this short story: her birth, the audiology clinic, the house of her father's friend. She also shifts role, becoming her mother, her father, his friend and the audiologist. The first-draft transcript closely follows Bella's particular ways of signing; her idiosyncratic sequence markers (also, so, but, and), her BSL sign order, the lip-pattern 'me' when referring to herself where in English we would expect to see 'I', and what we might consider strange, unfamiliar and untranslatable BSL signs, enclosed <thus>. Here is a suggested re-working of the original text.

Also
Like
When
in past
When I was born

So
When I was born
My mum felt I was deaf
But
Everyone was like 'No that's silly crazy, she is hearing!'
But my mum looked at them
She was sure I was deaf
But my dad said <fee>
'She is definitely hearing'
There are no deaf in my family

So
Anyway my mum said nothing just get on with things

Then
When I was about 15 months
We went to see my dad's friend
And
One friend looked at me he thought I was deaf 'I think she's deaf'
And my mum was like 'See!'
And she said to my dad 'I think she's deaf'

So my mum took me to hospital for tests
And they <find-find-find-find-find>
and right! <fant>
Mum was right!
Me deaf!

During our discussions, Bella and I made editorial changes to her story. We talked in particular about ways of translating BSL into English. She casually appreciated the poetic transformations, but concentrated her efforts more on making corrections to the text, 'improving the English' so that people would not think she was stupid or illiterate. We decided, somewhat mischievously, to retain certain BSL features (<fee> <fant> and <find-find-find-find-find>) as our attempts to translate these were wholly unsatisfactory, weak or long-winded, and anyway she quite liked the idea that we both knew what she meant and if other people did not, they should 'go learn BSL.'[3]

Vignette: Poetics

Maisie, who is deaf, and her hearing sister, Harper, together signed their story to me. They took turns, they gave each other space, they invited, they interrupted, they questioned and they teased. Here, they were trying to recall the moment they realized that Maisie was deaf and Harper was hearing:

M: Really … I never remember actually realizing huh she hearing and me deaf … no … more like (oh) deaf hearing <fant> deaf hearing <fant> signing speaking communicating … never she i.s. hearing I a.m. deaf means w.e. different … never thought-about *that* … (so) never remember sudden realize <penny-drop> nothing like *that* …

H: (Mmm) … no … I don't-remember thinking-about us being different … but I do remember point where … it felt like a more *integrated* life. Made-up of different parts. Do you remember, learning sign or all-of-us learning, teaching each other?

M: Don't-remember Formally Teaching You … more like teaching you natural … I sign she pick up natural, we just sign-to-each-other, natural way really, that what I feel …

The meter, the rhythms and repetitions of Maisie's and Harper's signing fell as words on to the page almost effortlessly:

Really
I never remember
actually realizing
huh
  she's hearing
  and I'm deaf
no
more like
Oh!
deaf hearing <fant>
deaf hearing <fant>

signing
  speaking
    communicating
never
  She Is Hearing
  I Am Deaf
  means We Are Different
I never thought about *that*
So
I never remember suddenly realize
<penny-drop>
  Nothing like *that*

Mmm
No
I don't remember thinking
about Us Being Different
but I do remember a point where
it felt like a More Integrated Life
made up of different parts

Do you remember
learning to sign
or all of us learning
teaching each other?

I don't remember
Formally Teaching You
more like teaching you naturally
  I would sign
  she would pick it up naturally
Just signed to each other
Just a natural way really

  That's what I feel …

Vignettes: Playing with text

Deaf narrators, whatever their age, often appear effortlessly to weave complex, metaphorical, highly visual, profound, hilarious and moving expressions into their narratives. Even with at best 'adequate' word-for-sign equivalence, there is a constant, nagging doubt concerning the extent to which stories get lost on the page in the translation/transcription act. Facial expression, modification of signs (i.e. change of speed, size), selection of particular, visually powerful signs, and the switch to fingerspelling in place of a sign enrich a narrative performance by drawing on knowledge of deaf cultural-historical worlds beyond the reach of standard word-processed English.

Georgina told me once about a battle she had with her local education authority (LEA) over Thomas's education:

> G: Thomas applied to specialist college, went-for interview, offered place <eyeball pop> ... So I thought, it suddenly hit me, I realized, the LEA had failed Thomas, so I thought, well you can pay for him to go to college, so fine, fine, I filled-out forms, very positive and then I got email saying LEA *agreed* to fund!! <eyeball pop out on to floor> ...

Bella observed the way her hearing brother's school experiences are different (better, more varied and challenging) than hers:

> B: Sometimes wish me have <dial on chest> means can switch me hearing or deaf wish ... maybe hearing school more better higher than deaf so <switch-to hearing> <head fill-up> <switch-to deaf> that's better! Means can switch between both, can deaf and hearing can.

Toni remembered conversations with her deaf grandfather when she was little:

> T: ... I went chat with my grandfather but, he didn't sign ... he fingerspelled everything! I remember one time I ask-him tell-me story I remember something to-do-with wartime but he fingerspelled whole thing! I was only seven eight maybe ... I was still learning English I was still building-up my understanding. So I had to try link each spelling to word to sentence and put-it-all-together I could understand individual words but couldn't put-it-together sentences you know and at-the-end I had-to think, so what that story about? That my grandfather his way fingerspelling that how he absolutely his ...

While translation from the spatial, non-written source language (BSL) to the linear, written target language (English) is fraught with political, linguistic and semantic difficulties, we can perhaps think more in terms of exploiting the visuality of signs and seeing how creative and artistic play with notions of text can be used to restitute, or breathe life back into sign language narratives, through font, diacritics and image. For speech transcription, Tedlock (1990) for example recommends full stops for drops in intonation and commas for gentler dips. Loudness can be **emboldened**, quiet speech can be written in smaller fonts, and a slow precision can be s p a c e d o u t.

In Georgina's story about the LEA, she modifies her signs to match the emotions and actions of the story, but then demonstrates her total shock through an almost cartoon-like sign, literally translated as, 'My eyes popped out of my head!' followed soon after by, 'My eyes popped out of my head and rolled across the floor!'

T h o m a s
applied to specialist college
went for interview
was offered a place <eyeball p—o—p>
So I thought
it s u d d e n l y **hit me**
I realized the LEA had **failed** Thomas
So I thought
well you can pay for him to go to college

so fine fine
I f i l l e d o u t t h e f o r m s very positive
and **then** I got email saying
LEA ***agreed*** to fund!!

<eyeball p O p r~o~l~l~o~n~t~o~f~l~o~o~r>

In the next excerpt, Bella's desire to be able to switch between a deaf and a hearing identity is symbolized by an imagined dial on her chest. With this, she could switch to become a hearing schoolgirl and fill her head up with lots of knowledge, and then switch back to being deaf again. The metaphor of a switchable dial on her chest is powerful and adds a moving, philosophical depth to her musings about deaf and hearing life.

S o m e t i m e s . . .
I wish I have a <dial on chest>
Means I can switch to hearing or deaf
Wish!
Maybe hearing school more better
↖higher
than
deaf
so <switch-to hearing>
<head fill-up>
<switch-to deaf>
that's better!
Means I can switch between both
I can be deaf
and hearing

Finally, Toni's memories of conversations with her deaf grandfather, who did not use BSL signs but spelled his stories out, letter by letter, on his fingers, captures, relives and replays a snapshot of a passing older deaf generation.

I went to chat with my grandfather
But he didn't sign
he  e v e r y t h i n g!

I remember one time
I asked him to tell me a story
I remember something to do with 
but he  the w h o l e t h i n g!
I was only seven or eight maybe
I was still learning English
I was still b/u/i/l/d/i/n/g up my understanding
So I had to try link each 
to word
to sentence
and put-it-all-together
I could understand individual words
but couldn't put-it-together sentences you know?

and at the end I had to think
soooo *what that story about?*

That was my grandfather's way

that's how
absolutely **his**

Vignette: Cultural meanings and referents

Georgina's four deaf children all went away to a residential school for deaf children. I asked Georgina to tell me what that meant for her and her family. She had mixed feelings.

G: I remember one time ... I dropped Wes off at Mary Hare ... and we stand there chatting, and Wes (behave strange facial expression not right) 'You all right?' bit strange ... then later, Wes home for half term, I-ask-him about that ... he told-me and <blew my top> because Wes told me as we stand there chat to each other, care worker walk by said 'Wesley use your voice!' and Wes felt, he didn't-know what do! And Wes told me, when he said that, he wanted cry 'I'm talking-to my mum!' In our language!

As Georgina recalled this memory of dropping her son off at school, she had tears in her eyes. She had transported herself back to a time when, as a young, deaf sign-language-using mother, she unwittingly placed her deaf son in a difficult position. The reader may or may not know what Mary Hare is. The audience may or may not be able to appreciate the significance of the phrase, 'Use your voice.' In re-presenting this story, Georgina and I had to make decisions about what to explain or contextualise, and what to leave to hang in the air. This short story is laced with so much poignancy, sadness, bitterness and regret it is hard to know how to begin the migration to paper. We started with the title.

BECAUSE WE SIGN

I r e m e m b e r one time
I dropped Wes off at Mary Hare
And
we stood there c-h-a-t-t-i-n-g
And
Wes (behave strange . . . facial expression not right)
'You all right?' (bit strange)
Then
L a t e r
Wes came home for half term
I asked him about *that*
And
he told me
And I <blew my top>
because
Wes told me as we stood there chatting to each other
A care worker walked by and said
'Wesley use your voice!'
And Wes felt
he didn't-know what do!
And Wes told me
when he said that
he wanted to cryyyyy

'I'm talking-to my mum!'

In **our** language!

Reflections

The examples offered in this chapter are suggestions of ways to not only read more deeply into the cultural, social and historical semantics of deaf people's narratives, but also to consider how we might trouble accepted, or more traditional ways of re-presenting stories that began as signed performances, anecdotes, memories, acts of repair and celebration. These issues are, of course, not exclusive to sign language, neither to narrative inquiry nor to research with deaf people. Any conversation or interview, in any language, that is recorded, documented, annotated or transcribed, is transformed (*inter alia* Mishler 1991; Green et al. 1997; Lapadat and Lindsay 1999). The inquiry described in this chapter, for example, also involved hearing narrators, whose words went through very similar processes to the signs of my deaf narrators; the deaf-hearing family narratives all found their way to the page via colour, image, font and poetics and through many discussions about re-presentation, aesthetics, meaning and message.

When I first approached the families to ask them if they would tell me their stories, we embarked on a project together that took trust as one of its central, guiding tenets. Trust opened doors to mutual discovery, construction and understanding of each other's stories, philosophies and beliefs, of each other's analyses and interpretations of deaf-and-hearing family life, and of deaf-and-hearing biographies, worlds, languages and cultures. This collaborative, dialogical way of working with stories shed light on concepts and experiences and created spaces for us to uncover, recover and discover memories, thoughts, beliefs and hopes.

To close the door on our collaboration and return to my office alone to construct their narratives would, I suggest, have trampled over, crushed or rendered meaningless and superficial our dialogical ways of working together. To return 'home' from the 'field' armed with notes, tapes and transcripts and to write it all down in isolation would not only feel pointless, but would also set in place the idea that it was now up to me to author other people's lives. To translate the signs of members of a marginalized minority community into words for the academy without due care, attention and respect for that community and its relationship with social scientists would simply reinscribe and reinforce the hearing/deaf power imbalance that historically has represented much of academia's interest in deaf people, and deaf people's experiences of 'being researched' (Young and Ackerman 2001).

Having worked together so intensely on the 'telling', we would continue to have dialogue on the 'showing.' A narrative inquiry, guided by principles of feminist and culturally appropriate research methods (Bloom 1998; Kahakalau 2004, Tuhiwai Smith 2005) and ethical mindfulness (Bond 2000), affords the extension of collaborative ways of working together where the re-presentation of the sign-language narratives of deaf adults and children is negotiated, contested, explored and agreed upon by the authors (deaf narrators) and the writer (hearing researcher). Translation, transcription, artistry, aesthetics, cultural equivalence, textual resonance, meaning, understanding and communication are some of the elements of this migratory process where languages, cultures, performance and narrative purpose are the 'sticking points' from which we either risk becoming lost or submerged, or we somehow reach a place where we feel we have achieved something purposeful and persuasive with our stories.

I should confess however that much of the research writing *was* done in isolation. It was my responsibility to write a thesis and to defend it as 'my' work. There were periods where I had little contact with the families. We did not collaborate on the content, writing or presentation of several of the thesis chapters. That was my job (and one or two of them told me as much). I must also confess that, at times, my narrators did not necessarily *wish* to collaborate, and writing decisions were initially made by me, to be edited later through consultation and conversation. Bella was keen to talk about translations and anonymity but sometimes less forthcoming about artistic choices (she wanted to check I had got her story right, and that she recognized her voice). Toni let me work on poetic re-presentation and commented/edited once I had set down a draft of her story. Some of her own drawings and photographs were woven into her text. Georgina was keen and willing to read through everything I wrote, from first draft to final rendering, actively guiding the editorial process and voicing concerns about how deaf people might (not) engage with the re-presentation of her deaf narrative. Maisie also liked to reflect and comment on cultural concepts, (e.g. definitions of deaf and hearing identities, and how they might (not) translate to the page). Overall, a significant amount of time was devoted to the sharing of ideas, of making sense of signs, of capturing and keeping alive the emotions, the power, the historical resonances and the meanings behind the meanings of these intimate, local and grand stories. As Georgina told me one evening in the pub as she read through my first attempts to follow her wishes and turn her stories into poetic texts: 'I like the way you've done this. I like the poetry. Help me remember. Pictures playing in my head.'

The committing of stories to print is risky. Words and pictures set in ink on a page are open and vulnerable to a multitude of misunderstandings and misinterpretations. They also become set in stone, fixed in time, almost instantly out of date, a remnant of the past as the temporal trajectories of the storied life and the lived life diverge.[4] Negotiating agreement with deaf narrators about how they wish their narratives to play out in text goes some way perhaps to mitigate those risks if they feel satisfied that there exists a link, a thread, a resonance between the meanings behind the telling and the meanings performed on the page. Narrative methods that allow for a caring, respectful and ethically mindful way of sharing stories and meanings both permit *and charge* us to pay the same respect and care for the ways in which those stories might live on, albeit in different forms, to unknown and imagined readers.

References

Andrews, M. (2004) 'Counter-narratives and the power to oppose', in M. Bamberg and M. Andrews (eds) *Considering Counter-Narratives: Narrating, Resisting, Making Sense*, Amsterdam: John Benjamins Publishing Company, pp. 1–6.

Bamberg, M. (1997) Positioning between structure and performance, *Journal of Narrative and Life History*, 7: 335–42.

Bloom, L. R. (1998) *Under the Sign of Hope: Feminist Methodology and Narrative Interpretation*, New York, NY: State University of New York Press.

Bond, T. (2000) Standards and Ethics for Counselling in Practice, 2nd edn, London: Sage.

Branson, J. and Miller, D. (2002) *Damned for their Difference: The Cultural Construction of Deaf People as Disabled*, Washington, DC: Gallaudet University Press.

Brockmeier, J. (2000) Autobiographical time, *Narrative Inquiry*, 10 (1): 51–73.

Bruner, J. (1987) 'Life as narrative', *Social Research*, 54 (1): 11–32.

Butler, J. (1990) *Gender Trouble: Feminism and the Subversion of Identity*, New York, NY: Routledge.

Chase, S. E. (2005) 'Narrative inquiry: Multiple lenses, approaches, voices' in N. K. Denzin and Y. S. Lincoln (eds) *The Sage Handbook of Qualitative Research*, 3rd edn, Thousand Oaks, CA: Sage Publications, pp. 651–680.

Currie, M. (2007) *About time: Narrative, Fiction and the Philosophy of Time*, Edinburgh: Edinburgh University Press.

Davies, B., and Gannon, S. (2006) 'The practices of collective biography', in B. Davies and S. Gannon (eds) *Doing Collective Biography*, Buckingham: Open University Press, pp. 1–15.

Davies, B., and Harré, R. (1990) Positioning: The discursive production of selves, *Journal for the Theory of Social Behaviour*, 19 (4): 43–63.

Denzin, N. K. (1994) 'The art and politics of interpretation', in N. K. Denzin and Y. S. Lincoln (eds) *Handbook of Qualitative Research*, Thousand Oaks, CA: Sage Publications, pp. 500–515.

Domosh, M. (2003) Toward a more fully reciprocal feminist inquiry, *ACME: An International E-journal for Critical Geographies*, 2 (1): 107–11.

Drewery, W. (2005) Why we should watch what we say: Position calls, everyday speech and the production of relational subjectivity, *Theory and Psychology*, 15 (3): 305–24.

Duranti, A. and Goodwin, C. (1992) *Rethinking Context*, New York, NY: Cambridge University Press.

Edwards, J. A., and Lampert, M. D. (1993) 'Principles and contrasting systems of discourse transcription', in J. A. Edwards and M. D. Lampert (eds) *Talking Data: Transcription and Coding in Discourse Research*, Hillsdale, NJ: Erlbaum, pp. 3–32.

Frank, A. W. (1995) *The Wounded Storyteller: Body, Illness and Ethics*, Chicago, IL: University of Chicago Press.

—(2008) *Narrative Analysis Workshop*, School of Health Studies, University of Bradford, 11–13 April.

Genette, G. (1980) *Narrative Discourse*, trans. J. Lewin, Oxford: Basil Blackwell.

Green, J., Franquiz, M., and Dixon, C. (1997) The myth of the objective transcript: Transcribing as situated act, *TESOL Quarterly*, 31 (1): 172–6.

Hole, R. (2008) Narratives of identity: A poststructural analysis of three deaf women's life stories, *Narrative Inquiry*, 17 (2): 259–78.

Huber, J., and Clandinin, D. J. (2002) Ethical dilemmas in relational narrative inquiry with children, *Qualitative Inquiry*, 8(6): 785-803.

Kahakalau, K. (2004) Indigenous heuristic action research: Bridging western and indigenous research methodologies, *Hülili: Multidisciplinary Research on Hawaiian Well-Being*, 1 (1): 19–33.

Keats, P. A. (2009) Multiple text analysis in narrative research: Visual, written, and spoken stories of experience, *Qualitative Research*, 9 (2): 181–95.

Khatibi, A. (1990) *Love in Two Languages (Amour bilingue)* trans. R. Howard, Minneapolis, MN: University of Minnesota Press.
Kotre, J. (1996) *Outliving the self: How We Live On in Future Generations*, New York, NY: W. W. Norton and Co.
Kraus, W. (2006) The narrative negotiation of identity and belonging, *Narrative Inquiry*, 16 (1): 103–11.
van Langenhove, L. and Harré, R. (1999) 'Introducing positioning theory', in R. Harré and L. van Langenhove (eds) *Positioning Theory: Moral Contexts of Intentional Action*, Oxford: Blackwell, pp. 14–31.
Lapadat, J. C., and Lindsay, A. C. (1999) Transcription in research and practice: From standardization of technique to interpretive positionings *Qualitative Inquiry*, 5 (1): 64–86.
Lather, P. (1986) Research as praxis, *Harvard Educational Review*, 56 (3): 257–77.
Mair, M. (1989) *Between Psychology and Psychotherapy: A Poetics of Experience*, London: Routledge.
Martin, V. (2011) *Developing a Narrative Approach to Healthcare Research*, Oxford: Radcliffe Publishing.
McAdams, D. P. (1997) *The stories we live by: Personal Myths and the Making of the Self*, New York, NY: The Guilford Press.
Mishler, E. G. (1991) Representing discourse: The rhetoric of transcription, *Journal of Narrative and Life History*, 1 (4): 255–80.
Ochs, E., and Capps, L. (1996) Narrating the self, *Annual Review of Anthropology*, 25: 19–43.
Richardson, L. (1997) *Fields of Play*, New Brunswick, NJ: Rutgers University Press.
—(2003) 'Poetic representation of interviews', in J. F. Gubrium and J. A. Holstein (eds) *Postmodern Interviewing*, Thousand Oaks, CA: Sage Publications, pp. 187–202.
Ricoeur, P. (1984) *Time and Narrative: Vol I*, Chicago, IL: University of Chicago Press.
Riessman, C. K. (2001) 'Analysis of personal narratives', in J. F. Gubrium and J. A. Holstein (eds) *Handbook of Interview Research: Context and Method*, Thousand Oaks, CA: Sage Publications, pp. 695–710.
Rudd, A. (2009) In defence of narrative, *European Journal of Philosophy*, 17: 60–75.
Schrauf, R. W. (2000) Narrative repair of threatened identity. *Narrative Inquiry*, 10 (1): 127–45.
Simon, S. (1996) *Gender in Translation: Cultural Identity and the Politics of Transmission*, London: Routledge.
Stone, C. and West, D. (2012) Translation, representation and the deaf voice, *Qualitative Research*, doi:10.1177/1468794111433087.
St Pierre, E. (1997) Nomadic inquiry in the smooth spaces of the field: A preface, *Qualitative Studies in Education*, 10 (3): 365–83.
Tedlock, D. (1990) From voice and ear to hand and eye, *The Journal of American Folklore*, 103 (408): 133–56.
Temple, B., and Young, A. M. (2004) Qualitative research and translation dilemmas, *Qualitative Research*, 4 (2): 161–78.
Trinh, T. M.-H. (1992) *Framer Framed*, New York, NY: Routledge.
Tuhiwai-Smith, L. (2005) 'On tricky ground: Researching the native in the age of uncertainty', in N. K. Denzin and Y. S. Lincoln (eds) *The Sage Handbook of Qualitative Research*, 3rd edn, Thousand Oaks, CA: Sage Publications, pp. 85–108.

Vigouroux, C. B. (2007) Trans-scription as a social activity, *Ethnography*, 8 (1): 61–97.

West, D. (2009) '"Strong together": Poetic representations of a deaf-hearing family narrative', in M. Prendergast, C. Leggo and P. Sameshima (eds) *Poetic Inquiry: Vibrant Voices in the Social Sciences*, Rotterdam: Sense, pp. 333–54.

—(2012) *Signs of Hope: Deafhearing Family Life*, Newcastle-upon-Tyne: Cambridge Scholars Publishing.

Young, A. M., and Ackerman, J. (2001) Reflections on validity and epistemology in a study of working relations between deaf and hearing professionals, *Qualitative Health Research*, 11 (2): 179–89.

Notes

1 The three families, all bilingual (in English and British Sign Language) have deaf and hearing members.

2 Khatibi (1991).

3 We spent a long time together trying to work out how to translate the signs transcribed here as <fee> and <fant>. In the context of this particular snippet of Bella's story, and because Bella does not really mind if I explain, <fee> represents the lip-pattern accompanying a sign where two fingers are flicked from a loosely closed fist towards the upper-left (if you are right-handed) chest area and may be translated *here* as, 'Don't be ridiculous!' Likewise, <fant> (formed on the lips) accompanies a sign where the same two fingers, facing forwards away from the body are flicked downwards in a fast sweeping motion (rather like playing with a yo-yo) and could be translated as, 'Huh/well I never/can't believe it!' Finally <find-find-find-find-find> was kept unchanged as it not only respectfully and affectionately echoes Bella's signs, but also expressively conveys her 10-year-old-understanding of a hearing test; that the audiologist really had to do a lot of intense searching in order to discover that she was a deaf baby.

4 Digital technologies are opening up more and more possibilities for sign-language texts to exist, for sharing, for interpretation, for academic exploration (see e.g. http://dsdj.gallaudet.edu/). While this addresses the issues concerning translation from BSL to English, sign-language texts are still fixed in time. The life as told, whether in BSL or translated into English, is differently positioned in time to the life as lived and experienced.

Chapter 2

Private lives, public property

Narrating the lives of mothers whose children have significant Special Needs

Jenny Knibb

Introduction

'When my daughter was diagnosed with significant Special Needs her life became public property and so did mine,' reflected Danielle. 'My whole life is turned upside down.'

This chapter focuses on the lives of mothers such as Danielle and shows how narrative inquiry can be used to challenge dominant discourses of mothering a child who has been classed in some way as different from the norm. The data were gathered from unstructured interviews with six mothers who volunteered to speak of the topics that were important to them. I then demonstrate the value of using narrative inquiry in research of this kind, for these conversations were used not only to narrate mothers' lives but also to produce a text that allowed others to speak, including Special Needs itself. Creative, engaging and informative devices are used throughout to demonstrate the practical application of the narrative approach and to invite the reader to consider the position of mothers of disabled children within the current cultural, social and economic climate in the UK in the twenty-first century.

A landscape of Special Needs

I drive slowly along the narrow lane, carefully avoiding a group of Down's syndrome adults enthusiastically collecting their gardening tools and park alongside an attractive stone building signed:

Jack and Jill welcomes special families

Apprehensively, I push open the door. I am about to begin work as the counsellor here, but what understanding do I have of Special Needs children? What do I know of their families' lives? How will I work with mothers who dwell in the terrain of Childhood Special Needs?

I smile uncertainly at a small boy whose head lolls uncontrollably over his mother's shoulder; there is no response. She explains, 'He can't see you.'

I move closer. The child chuckles, his hand waves with wild abandon and my spectacles are no more. Amidst the ensuing laughter I sense both the difference and the sameness of children here, and in the bare earth of my unknowing the seeds of research are sown.

Why narrative?

As a counsellor I listened as mothers spoke of complexity of lives so unexpectedly interrupted. Alice, whose child had cerebral palsy said, 'People just don't get it. We need someone to write our stories so that people will start to think about what it is like for us. Can't you do it?'

I began to read widely about childhood disability and also gathered information from listening to mothers' stories in the counselling room and beyond, and from conversations with family, friends and professionals who were involved in this landscape of difference. Eventually I gathered stories more formally as recorded interviews, and started to look at them in greater depth.

I was interested to read that professional advice offered to mothers of children who have been diagnosed with significant Special Needs is generally predicated on research into children's development and experiences; the impact of such a diagnosis on the manner in which mothers perform their role has often been neglected. I was concerned with the identity of such women:

> ... as a social achievement, contingent on audience, culture, history, memory and agency.
>
> (Speedy 2008: 45)

Teresa's younger son has severe cerebral palsy and learning difficulties and is also registered as partially sighted. She told me:

> I took the news really well though, because I had to. I didn't even have time to sit down and shed a tear because I also had a little boy who was just over a year; I had Peter as well.
>
> Now Dave [husband] and I go out together occasionally, as Mum and Dad will offer to have them, but I don't actually want to go out because I am quite happy with my lot. I'm alright as long as the children are alright. That's my main aim, and if Dave's alright, then so am I. We do get a chance to do things together, but I've got to be honest with you, it is few and far between. We don't even get a chance to watch the TV, not really, but I always try not to separate us off. I say, 'Look we'll do that together with Henry and Peter.'

> We always go swimming as a family. We never go separate. I don't like to split us up in any which way. I don't like that. I'm like any other mum running a family. No different than I ever was before.

After the initial diagnosis, Teresa was clearly determined to live within the story of her mothering self unchanged by disability; she was still essentially a mother like any other. Such stories, which emerged over time as I listened to mothers talking, enabled me to construct research texts that facilitated my theoretical focus of researching how mothers of Special Needs children construe their personal identity and simultaneously challenge ways in which their lives are interpreted and edited by others.

McAdams (1993) supports my view that in creating narrative we attempt to make sense of our lives and the lives of those around us, and my research methodology emerged at the confluence of numerous ideas and ways of understanding. My interest grew from stories told in the counselling context, and I felt that I needed a research approach based on a pragmatic ontology that treats lived experience as both the beginning and ending points of inquiry, that uses narrative as an object of investigation and narrative thinking as a key form of experience and of writing about it. If I wished to understand mothers' lives, I needed to listen to their stories with both heart and mind, for I agree with Etherington that:

> Narratives are particularly suited for portraying how people experience their position in relation to a culture. The richness of the narrative helps us to understand how they understand themselves, their strategies for living and how they make theoretical sense of their lives.
>
> (Etherington 2004: 31)

I too, was concerned with how mothers understand their lives and negotiate their position in the wider social sphere. I was not seeking to generate positivist, factual, logico-scientific data, but rather to pursue the subjective narrative knowing that is predicated on the postmodern, post-structuralist view of knowledge as socially constructed and created through the stories we tell (Bruner 1986).

Danielle spoke movingly about the time she felt medical discourse changed her identity forever:

> In talking about an identity as a parent, or as a woman with a child with Special Needs, I think one of the first things that has always struck me, because of not knowing about Alexandra's Special Needs till she was developing in her first year, was that the first thing you have to do is get a medical opinion. As soon as you get that, whether you get it at birth or, like us, eight to twelve months afterwards, to everybody else you've moved on, you've now *got it, you've absorbed it and you're now ready.* It's as if you've started a

> new job already, like it's keyed in. But you haven't, because actually that's when your world falls apart, because you then start thinking, 'Well, what does this all mean?'
>
> It's very hard to listen and talk about things without crying or getting really upset, which then means people say lots of things like, 'It will be alright' and 'Oh, you must be really stressed by this' rather than accepting it's a natural kind of grieving process to go through. It never even crosses your mind that your child will have Special Needs; you believe all these things happen to other people.

Mothers generally acknowledged that a diagnosis of significant Special Needs identified them as 'other' and separated them from mothers whose children were free from impairment. When mother and disabled child are treated as one unit, the mother, although not actually disabled herself, often feels that she has acquired a stigma of disablement that appears to position her within an oppressive ideology.

Collecting the data

Although I gathered much information in the course of my work as a counsellor, I also needed to collect data more formally. I advertised for participants and chose the first six people who volunteered. This was demonstrably fair and transparent, and although I knew that I would have too much data, I needed to allow for participants withdrawing from the study. Circumstances change and mothers of very sick children live precarious lives.

I did not provide interviewees with a list of questions beforehand because I wished to know what was important *to them in the moment.* I viewed the research interview as a collaborative endeavour and aimed to use counselling skills to enable me to walk alongside the mothers as they narrated their lives. My primary purpose was to elicit information and understanding about the lives of mothers of Special Needs children, which would add to an existing body of knowledge. I did not assume that the process would create adequate answers, but rather that it would unearth subjugated knowledge that had previously been submerged beneath dominant discourses.

I was focused on the individual construction of identity in the face of societal norms that often present disability as undesirable whilst simultaneously viewing mothers of flawed children as self-sacrificing, heroic and especially loving of those children (Gregory 2002). In my research, I aimed to deconstruct such dominant discourses and challenge accepted ways of knowing. I noticed that mothers often appeared to tell stories that simultaneously served to represent, constitute and shape their lives, and in so doing *became reality.* Michelle, a mother of two autistic children said ruefully, 'The more we live with it and talk about it, somehow the more autistic we *all* seem to become.'

When children have Special Needs, parental roles are performed within competing discourses of disability which must be negotiated with care. Knowledge can often be equated with power, especially when it is withheld and mothers frequently fear that power struggles with authority may adversely affect services offered to themselves and their children. This is particularly pertinent given the nature of my research. There exist many conceptual models of disability, but knowledge and understanding of disability in the UK has tended to become polarized. In the positivist medical model, disabled people are seen as 'the problem'. The emphasis is on cure or mitigation of disability to help the disabled person to change and adapt to circumstances in the world around them. The alternative social model, developed by disabled people, positions the cause of disability within the organization of a society that discriminates against people with impairments and excludes them from involvement and participation. Disability is therefore defined in terms of social oppression rather than a category of impairment (Linton, 1998).

These opposing concepts accord with the view that knowledge and reality are social constructions. Narrative methodology can demonstrate how mothers might seek to understand their situation within competing views of reality rather than in accordance with different perspectives on their situation. Five-year-old John is on the Autistic Spectrum, and his mother Louise often felt judged guilty of poor parenting because of this. She told me:

> You have to develop a very thick skin which I haven't developed yet. People in supermarkets tell you to look after your child better, or say that you shouldn't bring your child into the supermarket if it's going to behave like that. People shout right in your face about your child in a playground. Everyone has their opinion. Even if they're not being rude everyone has an opinion, everyone's an expert about my child. To those people who say, 'Just give him half an hour with me and he'll be alright. I'll knock some sense into him' I would like to say, 'Well here you are, I'll be back later.'
>
> The problem is they all think it's a behavioural problem, rather than the fact that his brain's seeing the world in a different way. I think it is harder with a brain development issue because it's not visible. John looks like a happy smiley sweetie really. He's just difficult to handle.
>
> It does get you down. I am quite, well stroppy is not the right word but people can say what they like and on the face of it, it's water off my back. But of course you do go home, after one shuts one's door and comfort yourself, for people shouting right in your face is very distressing and you do try to explain it. Many people don't know what Autism is and other mums have actually said, 'I don't care what he's got, he shouldn't be doing that!'

Such stories represent local knowledge and are formulated within the discourses available to the narrators. I was also aware that, within the context of the narrative inquiry interview, I would position myself as a reflexive researcher and that my own fluid experiences would impact on both process of storytelling and end product (Vice 1997); I was 'contextually negotiating and narrating the fluidity of my identity as a narrative inquirer' (Etherington 2004: 31). Throughout my project, I heard stories from numerous sources and each time I was challenged to consider different ways of thinking, as I encountered not just alternative perspectives, but diverse views of reality that reflect a depth of confusion that is part of the human condition.

From theory to practice

My concerns turned to the difficulties of converting theoretical concepts of narrative inquiry into practical reality. What exactly is a narrative interview? What are the rules? How am I going to get my data? Will I get enough to enable me to complete this project? And will it be the 'right' data? I have a long history of wanting to 'get it right' and now I was embarking on a project that demanded not that I 'get it right' but that I 'get it differently'. I had to contend with the notion that there is no such thing as 'right', just what *is*, what *emerges*. Yes, I had my own ideas, my preconceived notions. That was inevitable, for without them I would not have been led to this topic initially, but I needed to engage in research, in having another look and another and another; in an educative process of discovering new and alternative ways of seeing.

I had had many casual interactions with mothers of disabled children, in which we might be said to have jointly produced data, but there was more formality in asking to record a conversation for a particular purpose. How, I wondered, was I going to conduct interviews? How formalistic, almost pre-determined seemed the term 'interview process', with its sense of searching for an objective truth. I gained some feeling of reassurance from Laurel Richardson's notion of connecting with my participants in a united endeavour to construct text, with myself positioned as a facilitator (Richardson 1997). This sounded challenging, but I was more comfortable with a sense of the interview as a discourse between two active participants working together within a creative liminal space to examine old views and to generate alternative ways of understanding.

A counsellor/researcher

The edges between my research and my counselling work were fuzzy, and I was conscious of my responsibility to be ethically vigilant, to respect professional and personal boundaries and be ever mindful of participants' welfare. I prepared to engage in following the speakers' lead and in listening for what was *not* said in the spaces between the words. In both roles, my aim was to understand and facilitate the telling of a story, for in my counselling work I attempt to walk alongside clients on part of their life's journey. I openly acknowledge that I cannot know what it is like to parent a child with a disability; I can only seek to understand more about the meaning of this for any particular client. I am frequently told that my most useful intervention is when I acknowledge that I do not, and cannot, fully understand their experience. It is from this place that I would be listening as a narrative inquirer. I heard Annie, whose son had a brain tumour, cry, 'I get *so angry* with people who tell me that they *know* how I must feel. How can they, but *they could listen and learn a bit about my life ... gain some understanding.*'

I was aware of the slippery, ever changing nature of the data that I would be collecting. The stories I heard would not represent direct experience, but would be *stories about that experience.* As those stories intersected with others over time, differing power formations would be shaped, both by my expectations and those of the narrators as they chose which stories to tell; I would be listening for what is said, and how it is said (Gubrium and Holstein 1995), and also to gain a sense of what might be being omitted both intentionally and unintentionally. I wanted to know what was *important to these mothers* and what *they wanted people to know about their lives.* What would guide their choice, I wondered? How would the knowledge they offered be shaped and from what position would I hear it, for I was aware that the interview process itself fundamentally shapes the structure and nature of the data.

Slippery stories, multiple meanings

My research participants had identified a number of motives for taking part, including a desire to support me, a wish that their story might help someone else and a feeling that it would provide a chance to say what they really think without the need to protect themselves from authority. I prepared to listen as a researcher, a woman in her sixties, a mother, a wife and a counsellor. Similarly, the mothers would also be speaking from the complexities of multiple roles within their lives. Together we would be constructing meanings from myriad pathways of experience that we have traversed during our lives, from the present but ever changing situations in which we find ourselves and from our hopes and concerns for the future, all set against the backdrop of societal norms and pressures prevalent in the UK in the twenty-first century.

I hoped the conversations would proceed as a collaborative partnership, for I believed that the women with whom I would be working all had something important to say about their roles as mothers, although my experience from working alongside them suggested that they did not always recognize it. I wished to elicit both the story of what was happening in mothers' lives and how they made meaning of these events. The value of data collected in this way lies in the construction of meaning rather than in its 'truth', and this fitted with my research question about how mothers construe their identity.

Narrative identity

Narrative identity rests on the premise that: '... intertwining of experience and story lies at the core of individual life and psychological understanding' (Widdershoven 1993: 3).

I believe that the stories that we tell simultaneously narrate *and* shape that experience. As Marina, a counselling client whose child had severe learning difficulties told me, '*Nothing really changes but I can talk about how it really is in here and then somehow it feels different when I get outside.*'

Narrative identity research does not view identity as positioned within any grand theory of motivation, but rather emphasizes the individual's need to find a balance between autonomy and relationship (McAdams 1993). It assumes that narrative coherence underpins the ways in which people actually live their lives and make meaning of their identity, and 'Self and identity therefore are not viewed as essential properties of the person but as phenomena that are contextually shaped in talk and particularly in social practice' (Bamberg et al. 2007: 1). I too was not espousing the idea that identity is an intrinsic characteristic of the person, but rather that it is construed through the stories mothers tell and their ways of being in the world, for 'To understand the identity formation process is to understand how individuals craft narratives from experience, tell these stories internally and to others, and ultimately apply these stories to knowledge of self, others and the world in general' (Singer 2004: 438).

Decision time

The interview process was lengthy, interesting and stimulating. I had heard many of the stories before, but as Teresa said, 'Telling it all like this is different somehow.'

Although therapy was not the primary purpose of the interview, most interviewees reported a therapeutic element, probably because the eventual research findings showed they often felt it was difficult to make their voices heard.

My research journey began with stories, as I believe does all research, for stories are the seeds from which research questions grow. In turn, those emergent questions determine the nature of the data collected but, whether that is qualitative or quantitative, the original story remains. My own story/ies of myself as a counsellor working with parents of Special Needs children led me to wonder, '*What is it really like to be the mother of a child with Special Needs?* Not '*What are the dominant narratives, created by others?*' but '*What are individual mothers' unique experiences?*'

I gathered a plethora of information and faced the problem of how to use it, for how I viewed such data would profoundly affect and might actually determine my interpretation of it (Sorsoli 2007). The stories that had been transcribed beckoned me emotionally against a background of previously acquired factual knowledge, and were 'complicated, nuanced and non-transparent' (ibid p.311).

I read for multilayered meanings, returning again and again to the data, and how distancing and impersonal the word 'data' seemed. Each time I was moved afresh, as passionate as ever about wanting to understand more about the lives of 'implicitly disabled' mothers[1]. Their narratives spoke directly to me, and I sensed the value of allowing them to stand alone, for they had the power to stir hearts and minds, undiminished by authorial analysis (Goodley et al. 2004).

However, I also appreciated the value of thinking alongside the stories and accepted that they could only represent a partial truth encapsulating a moment of time in the presentation of a life. I had no wish to subject them to a reductionist, analytic process of excavating for a skeletal, core meaning. My intention was rather to strengthen them by contextualising them within a wider personal and societal framework, to assist readers in constructing their personal understanding, especially with regard to the theoretical significance of these narratives of difference (Goodley 2000).

This led me to consider anew how these research texts have been shaped. They are not impartial for:

> Each interview is a product of the mutual interaction between speaker and listener. Narrators do not simply reproduce prefabricated stories regardless of the interactional situation, but rather create their stories within the social process of mutual orientation according to their definition of the interview situation.
>
> (Rosenthal 1993: 64)

I was also positioned as an insider-researcher for my research participants knew me within the family support organization, where I was primarily situated as a counsellor who empathically listened to stories of difficulties and disempowerment. This may well have influenced their choice of narratives and the manner of the telling. I notice that they all emphasized their difficulties, and that may partly be because they naturally brought their problems into the counselling room. Maybe my dual roles of researcher/counsellor encouraged them to speak more freely of their difficulties, but it has also meant that ethically I needed to maintain clear boundaries both during the conversations and in the writing up of the research.

The texts were then subjected to further modification as they were transferred from spoken to written form, for there can be no neutral transcription. For practical reasons I chose to have the recordings professionally transcribed and then, with my research question in mind, I reorganized the texts around various topics to produce stories complete with settings, plots and events. In my initial readings, I noticed that I became very aware of themes that were emerging in the narratives. This drew me towards thematic analysis as a suitable analytic tool.

Thematic analysis

As thematic analysis is concerned with *what* is said rather than *how* and *to whom,* it seemed a good starting point. At this stage I was concerned with content, as I was curious as to the ways in which mothers narratively construct their identities within the disruption to their life pattern caused by the birth of a disabled child. I was looking for possible interpretations of 'the nature and function of the presentation in the interview and not the biographical details themselves' (Rosenthal 1993: 70).

I was also interested in the different aspects of mothers' lives that they choose to portray in relation to their maternal identities as they '[Wove] together themes of achievement, of family obligations, personal development, love lives, children's welfare and friends' (Gergen and Gergen 1993: 191).

What internal narratives did they draw upon in order to present their identity to the world? What discourses informed their choices? How did their private worlds intersect with externally constructed narratives which bestowed identities upon them? A story-centred, thematic approach that maintained the integral structure of the stories with regard to sequence, detail, time and place would enable me to search for theoretical argument within the texts, rather than evaluate them for their representational significance (Riessman 2008). In this way, I could move beyond a simplistic interpretation of meaning towards more nuanced and alternative readings of the text. Thematic analysis would also enable me to locate themes across the different stories. Although I was not seeking the generalizablity and certainty that more positivist research methods may appear to offer, I noted with interest, for example, that grappling with designated authority, especially in the world of medicine, is a recurrent topic of discussion. How do such tales serve to reinforce dominant discourses about privilege and power? And how do they serve to challenge specific and established ways of knowing?

Performative and dialogic analysis

I then moved to consider performative and dialogic approaches, which would enable me to develop thematic analysis further by including historical and cultural contexts. Such approaches adopt an ontological distinction between performance as an 'act' (doing) and an 'enactment' (representation of doing), and are predicated on the notion that as human beings we are social actors, constantly engaged in staging performances of our desirable selves. Davies and Harre (1990) note that conversations embody an intrinsic social dimension that causes people to position themselves in relation to one another in ways that have traditionally been defined as 'roles', and as such, they 'produce' themselves and others as 'social beings'. Bamberg (1997) emphasizes the performance aspect of the telling and views the act of narrating as intervening between the story and the experience. What is *actually being said* is only one of many different performance features employed by the speaker to achieve her goals. Using the performative analytical approach would enable me to examine the narratives for content, and also to understand how the narrator attempts to evaluate past events. I also needed to consider the role of audience, mindful that 'In constructing the content and one's audience in terms of role participants the narrator transcends the question of "How do I want to be understood by you the audience?" and constructs a [local] answer to the question "Who am I?"'(Bamberg 1997: 37).

The positioning of audience was important in my work for I hoped that 'As the reader passes through the various perspectives offered by the text, and relates the different patterns to one another, he (sic) sets the work in motion and so sets himself (sic) in motion too' (Izer 1980: 106).

I also needed to consider the role of language in context as mothers narrate identities constructed (and lost) in the face of public policy, dominant discourses and the hidden dimensions of power. By engaging with the interplay between structure, content and interpretation, I sought further understandings (my own and others) of how mothers are able to make the presence of a disabled child meaningful in their lives. I was curious about the various discourses of power between mothers and established authority, particularly the medical profession. It is in bearing witness to such struggles that I have gained greater knowledge and understanding both of an emotional process of parenting a child with Special Needs and of the constantly shifting power balance between the mothers' enactment of their private lives and the public bodies with which they need to engage. Performative analysis is concerned with 'the functional and pragmatic aspects of the narrative and how characters are positioned in relation to themselves, the audience and to other characters in the story' (Petraki et al. 2007: 108).

How did the mothers who talked to me perform their identities? What rhetorical devices did they employ to draw me into their world and signify a feeling that I was on their side? My researcher self sought manifold meanings in the multilayered text, whilst the counsellor within listened for the music that lends emotion to the words. I noticed that I said very little in the conversations, therefore much of what we produced may not be construed so much as dialogue, but more as 'a form of meaning making that looks like dialogue' (Vice 1997: 52). My role was often that of helping along a performative monologue in which no replies were expected (Bakhtin 1984) but, in spite of this monologic nature of our discourse, we were engaged in telling stories *with* each other (Vice 1997). Together we jointly constructed a multilayered text that is a source of knowledge about living with a disabled child, and I subsequently analyzed those narratives within a thematic, discursive and performative framework in order to demonstrate ways in which mothers may seek to make their lives meaningful whilst simultaneously reconstructing their identity within an alternative maternal landscape (Gergen and Gergen 1986).

Unique children, exceptional mothers: A conversation with Special Needs

'But what did you discover,' do I hear you ask? 'What *use* is your research?'

In reply, I invite you to eavesdrop on part of my conversation with Special Needs itself. Special Needs has been present implicitly throughout the research, but I felt that its voice should be made more explicit so, on a warm June morning, I welcomed it to my office, whilst simultaneously remaining uncomfortably aware of my guilty relief that it was only making a temporary visit rather than taking up a long-term tenancy in my life. When it arrived I was somewhat taken aback, for it wasn't what I had expected. Should I offer coffee? Would a normal cup be suitable? Was my office about to be wrecked by unpredictable behaviour? *Was it toilet trained?* I took a deep breath, smiled uncertainly and began. (My words are on the left, those of Special Needs on the right.)

Thank you for coming to see me, Special Needs. I do appreciate this opportunity for us to speak directly with one another.

Thank you for inviting me, for invitations are rare. Even you have left me until last. Although we have had many informal encounters.

I have watched with interest your work about my influence on mothers.

(*Deep sigh*)

It is really hard. We live in an imperfect world so I have to reside somewhere. I cannot wander homeless forever. General ignorance on healthcare matters used to make it easier for me to find a home but now accommodation is becoming increasingly scarce.

I haven't invited you before because I am not interested in you as an entity, but in how mothers might make sense of their lives when you move in. I notice that the first thing you mention is the world of medicine. All my research participants chose to talk about that too, and how they often felt disempowered by the medical profession. Are you saying that your power is being slowly eroded too?

Well, my ***presence*** is slowly being eroded or mitigated by medical knowledge, and as knowledge and power are often bedfellows then I suppose my power has also been reduced in certain areas, but that doesn't mean mothers are in the ascendancy. Often power has passed from me to the medical profession and my effect on mothers' identities is just differently situated. Your inquiry shows that mothers often feel an immense time pressure as they become embroiled in complex battles between me and the medical profession.

But Jenny, you are staring at me in such a strange way. Is something wrong?

I'm sorry but I am puzzled by your appearance. You look so very different from the last time we met.

I have the ability to metamorphose into an infinite number of forms. What you see isn't necessarily what you get.

That is true, and I have been concerned about how individual mothers view you.

As I watched the creature was transformed before my very eyes. It ballooned in all directions and changed from perilous pink to bilious green.

You have changed again.

Ah! Have I changed? Or are you just seeing me differently? Or both? I think that your work has made you view me differently and I suspect it will make others do the same.

Well yes, but that can't be the whole story.

In these postmodern times there never *is* a *whole* story.

In times past, my companion and I were often abandoned in institutions and left to our own devices. The mother construed her identity in my shadow but we were not forced to reside together. If she chose to live with me then she had to struggle without much help, but that also meant she suffered minimal outside interference. I'm not saying that even that was the whole story, but it seemed that it was more complete than it is now.

I have been the star of a great deal of research positioned within the social discourse of a deficit model of assessment of child and family, which draws critically on medical theory, developmental educational theory and individual need within the current socio-political discourse of the Welfare State. Why did you choose narrative inquiry as your methodology? I think it is a narcissistic reflection of your personal interest.

I take issue with you there. Narrative inquiry has allowed me to add to understanding about mothers' identity in ways that would not be possible in other ways. I have also linked my own interests to those of the mothers, to other researchers in the field and to the wider social context that shapes personal lives and public policy in Britain today. My research adds to cumulative knowledge.

So what have you discovered?

My work has shown me that mothers of Special Needs children are generally doing the best they can in the circumstances in which they find themselves. Like most mothers, they are often ambitious for their children to reach their full potential, however limited that might be. They also perform all the usual maternal functions, but there is an added layer to their mothering caused by your presence, Special Needs.

You mean that I need care too?

Well, many mothers place their children's welfare above their own, but it appears that you often cause great tension by demanding top priority. You expect individual attention, which creates hassle for mother and child, along with extra responsibilities that can be time consuming and expensive. Also, all the mothers highlighted your restrictive presence in many areas of their lives. These difficulties can, of course, be linked to lack of resources particularly for respite care, and for day-to-day living needs, like changing facilities and suitable wheelchairs.

I guess that you are going to recommend that mothers and I would benefit from more resources?

I certainly think that would help and fit with my beliefs

about a just and equitable society that should be prepared to support our most vulnerable children. For me, that means also supporting their mothers, although I know that view is not universal. Louise asked for help but was told that assistance depended on the child's needs and not on those of the mother.

You do need to be realistic though, for you are concluding this research when Europe is facing a severe economic crisis and the British coalition government is intent on cutting £6.3bn from public spending. Politicians and economists are warning us all that we must tighten our belts. I do appreciate that mothers with Special Needs children tend to be among the poorest in our community but you have aligned yourself with this group. All groups tend to feel that that, as theirs is a just cause, then their members should be spared. Your research might well be positioned as small and local, but it is also situated within a wider public domain. You can't escape this. More resources for your group mean less for others.

I do agree with you Special Needs, but I think that again you have to search for the less visible aspects of the situation and consider the bigger picture. If help is cut, you don't go away, do you? The extra effort that you require is done as unpaid labour, often by mothers who are deprived of choice about how to live their lives. They are disadvantaged compared with their peers whose children do not know you.

So if more resources were allocated then where would you target them?

That is a huge question. Such detail is not the purpose of this project but all the mothers have highlighted their lack of choice as important in their identity formation. I suggest therefore, that service providers should emphasize flexibility alongside concern for *individual needs*, which may perhaps be determined objectively, and for *individual preferences*, which may be more subjective. I would like to see more resources available for flexible respite care to enable mothers to exercise choice about work/home life balance and develop aspects of their identity separate from you. This may help to release those whom you are imprisoning in a poverty trap, mitigate against loneliness and isolation and improve mothers' autonomy, in line with the current social discourse of valuing individuality. So increased economic resources, based on rights rather than 'charity' or mothers' unpaid work, could help improve many mothers' lives, but my research also indicates that improvements need not require additional resources.

I am inclined to agree with you. Many problems you have highlighted arise because people define me as a medical problem that resides within the child and engage in a battle to destroy me, or at least to beat me into some kind of submission. I suspect that many mothers' lives could be altered by changing societal perceptions of me.

By fitting you into a more social model?

Mmm. I would cause a lot less disruption if only people made more effort to accommodate me, both practically and in their hearts. It isn't just I who create problems, it's the society in which I live. Although physical provision for me has improved in recent years, I still suffer from misconceptions and negative attitudes.

We are back to the importance of listening with the heart for that which is essential, and I consider that is one of the most important outcomes of my research. All the mothers spoke of loneliness, isolation and of being positioned as 'other'. In the invisible layer of their lives, in that part so often termed 'the soul', they often felt disregarded and disempowered. I hope that studies like mine will remind professionals of the benefits of working within a climate of mutual respect. My professional power as a teacher was not eroded from working alongside parents; in fact, the reverse was often true.

And how does being a counsellor fit into this inquiry?

The effectiveness of counselling also rests on the quality of the relationship between counsellor and client, and in this work I have been concerned with the quality of the relationship a mother has with herself and with the external world.

I suggest greater attention be paid to a mother's individuality and the

uniqueness of her child.
There are many policies addressing 'partnerships', but *how those policies are implemented is crucial.*

And you found the mothers to whom you talked are not passive victims, but women who deserve respect. They accommodate me in many different ways by developing specialized knowledge; alternative ways of being and by becoming confident in their new roles, *but this can often mask something really essential.* They may appear to be coping, they often *are* coping, but the hidden costs, physical, psychological and emotional, can be immense and their identity is changed for ever.

It has been an interesting conversation but I must hasten away. I have important work to do.

Thank you for …

Too late! As Special Needs went crashing out into the corridor, I noticed that it was now wearing a T shirt emblazoned 'I AM AUTISTIC Please be patient'.

Conclusion: Not a designer label

The calm that followed seemed almost palpable. Special Needs had not been difficult, but its unpredictability had prevented me from relaxing and I had nervously remained vigilant throughout the interview. Designer T-shirts, printed with messages, are currently fashionable but this seemed altogether different.

Louise dressed her child in this way in the hope of eliciting sympathy and understanding. 'I don't care what the label is,' she declared. 'I just want people to give me a bit of slack.'

All mothers engaged with the problem of labels, which were often resented for being overly simplistic and patronizing, but were also accepted as a useful and necessary part of the process of getting extra help and resources. As I opened my computer to begin to transcribe my latest interview, I reflected on the links between labelling and narrative methodology, and my mind wandered to a grey winter day in a children's hospital.

Marianna's three-year-old son suffered from delayed development, but the cause remained a mystery until he was diagnosed with cancer and admitted to hospital for treatment. One morning Marianna was confronted by a world-renowned geneticist striding along the corridor flapping his papers and smiling excitedly. 'Good news,' he announced. 'I think your son is suffering from ... ... because that is characterized by cancers popping up all over the place.'

I don't know whether that mother ever told me the name, but if she did I certainly can't recall it. I can, however, remember that she returned to her hospital room and cried in desolation; she saw no reason to rejoice.

I recount that story because it represents tensions between the consultant's work and mine. As a medical scientist, the consultant aimed for quantifiable knowledge, a definitive naming of the problem and an ultimate solution. I collaborated with the mothers to produce knowledge of a more tenuous kind, based on the theory that we make sense of our lives through the stories we tell and that others tell about us.

Conrad told me, 'We have friends with a disabled child, the same age as ours, about ten. I read your work and thought that is just how it is for them. My wife's life and that of her friend have been very different. Life with a disabled child is so much the same but is also very different in many ways. It really set me thinking.'

This is one of the great strengths of narrative inquiry as a methodology for work in this area. Mothers frequently spoke of feeling marginalized, but most reported a feeling of greater sense of agency after they had told their stories. Subsequently I situated those stories within the collective, public, social, political, cultural and economic spheres of our national life, for I believe such contextualised knowledge should be a vital component of any policy decision-making process. Narrative inquiry also enabled me to present evocative and provocative texts which troubled dominant discourses of mothers of disabled children, and to actively engage readers with my work, challenging them to reflect on the life of the child wearing the T-shirt and the mother at that child's side.

References

Bakhtin, M. M. (1984) *Problems of Dovtoesky's Poetics,* Minneapolis, Minnesota: University of Minnesota Press.

Bamberg, M., Defina, A., and Schiffen, D. (2007) *Selves and Identities in Narrative and Discourse,* Amsterdam Philadelphia: John Benjamins Publishing Company.

Bruner, J. (1986) *Actual Minds, Possible Worlds*, Cambridge, MA: Harvard University Press.
—(2001) 'Self making and world making', in J. Brockmeier and D. Carbaugh (eds) *Narrative and Identity: Studies in Autobiography, self and culture*, Amsterdam: John Benjamins Publishing Company, pp. 25–37.
Etherington, K. (2004) *Becoming a Reflexive Researcher; Using Ourselves in Research*, London and Philadelphia: Jessica Kingsley Publishers.
Gergen, K. J., and Gergen, M. M. (1986) Narrative form and the construction of psychological science, in F. Steir (ed.) *Research and Reflexivity*, Newbury: Sage, pp. 22–44.
Gergen, M. M., and Gergen, K. J. (1993) 'Narratives of the Gendered Body in popular autobiography', in R. Josselson and A. Lieblich (eds) *The Narrative Study of Lives*, London: Sage, pp. 191–218.
Goodley, D. (2000) *Self-advocacy in the Lives of People with Learning Difficulties: The Politics of Resistance*, Buckingham: Open University Press.
Goodley, D., Lawthom, M., Clough, P., and Moore, M. (2004) *Researching Life Stories: Method, Theory and Analyses in a Biographical Age*, London, New York: Routledge-Falmer.
Gregory, S. (2002) *Bringing Up a Challenging Child When Love is Not Enoughi* London: Jessica Kingsley.
Gubrium, J. F., and Holstein, J. A. (1995) 'Biographical Work and New Ethnography', in R. Josselson and A. Lieblich (eds) *Narrative Study of Lives*. Newbury Park, CA: Sage, pp. 45–58.
Izer, W. (1980) *The Act of Reading: A Theory of Aesthetic Response*, Baltimore: Johns Hopkins University Press.
Linton, S. (1998) *Claiming Disability, Knowledge and Identity*, New York: New York University Press.
Mcadams, D. P. (1993) *Stories We Live By*, New York: William Morrow.
Petraki, E., Baker, C., and Emmison, M. (2007) '"Moral versions" of motherhood and daughterhood in Greek-Australian family narratives', in M. Bamberg, A. Defina, and D. Schiffen (eds.) *Selves and Identities in Narratives and Discourse*, Philadelphia, Amsterdam: John Benjamins Publishing Company, pp. 107–31.
Richardson, L. (1997) *Fields of Play: Constructing an Academic Life*, New Brunswick: Rutgers University Press.
Riessman, C. K. (2008) *Narrative Methods for the Human Sciences*, Thousand Oaks, CA: Sage Publications, Inc.
Rosenthal, G. (1993) 'Reconstruction of Life Stories: Principles of Selection in Generating Stories for Narrative Biographical Interviews', in R. Josselson and A. Lieblich (eds) *The Narrative Study of Lives*, London: Sage, pp. 59–91.
Singer, J. A. (2004) Narrative Identity and Meaning Making Across the Adult Lifespan: An Introduction, *Journal of Personality*, 72 (3): 437–59.
Sorsoli, L. (2007) 'Like Pieces in a puzzle: Working with layered methods of reading personal narratives', in M. Bamberg, A. Defina, and D. Schiffin (eds) *Selves and Identities in Narrative and Discourse*, Amsterdam, Philadelphia: John Benjamin Publishing Company, pp. 303–321.
Speedy, J. (2008) *Narrative Inquiry and Psychotherapy*, Basingstoke: Palgrave Macmillan.

Vice, S. (1997) *Introducing Bakhtin,* Manchester & New York: Manchester University Press.

Widdershoven, G. A. M. (1993) 'The Story of Life: Hermeneutic Perspectives on the Relationship Between Narrative and Life History', in R. Josselson and A. Lieblich (eds) *The Narrative Study of Lives*, London: Sage, pp. 1–24.

Note

1 I use the term 'implicitly disabled' because, although the mothers themselves are not disabled, my work has made me realize that they often feel treated as such because of the disability of their children.

Chapter 3

Looking down on the world from a wooden balcony

A narrative autoethnographic study of voluntary celibacy

Dione Mifsud

Introduction

This chapter sets out to explore voluntary celibacy through the narrative multilayered story of two men. The first part contains excerpts from an interview conversation with Xandru, a lay member of the Mużew Society. The second part is a piece of autoethnographic fiction on how living as a celibate would have been for me. The outcome is a rich and intricate narrative that contextualises the feelings, doubts and ambiguities surrounding male celibacy in Malta. The chapter ends by academic reflection on the value of narrative inquiry, for the topic and for the context.

I remember walking back from school every day in glorious sunshine and catching a glimpse of the wooden balcony as soon as I turned the corner. It was my grandmother's coop. She would always be there, looking down beneath her as the world went by every day of her life. Looking through the Persian blinds, she would see the neighbours gossiping, the children playing, the street vendors selling their wares from their donkey carts, devotees coming to pray to the niche of Our Lady that was on the side of her house. She was in the world and out of it at the same time, feeling part of it but not actually taking part in it. It was like a theatrical performance where the audience interacts with the actors but does not leave the auditorium to go up on the stage. It was as if she was taking leave of the world, sitting on the same chair in the same place fingering through her rosary beads and saying her prayers. As soon as I arrived, I would make tea for both of us, do my homework and then read to her.

*Then, at 5.30 p.m. it was time for me to go to '*Il-Mużew*' (The Museum). This is a Maltese Christian lay society dedicated to teaching Catholic Catechism to children and adolescents. Attendance is compulsory for children preparing themselves for their First Holy Communion and Confirmation. It becomes voluntary after Confirmation. At that stage, members of the Mużew start preparing themselves for actual membership, usually at age 18. Full members promise to live a life of chastity, poverty, humility and obedience, even though they remain lay persons engaging in brotherhood and teaching within the community.*

When I was15 years of age I was busy building my wooden balcony convinced that I was to become a celibate Mużew member...

The decision to choose voluntary celibacy, that is, to remain sexually inactive either within cloistered walls, or as in the case of the Mużew Society by continuing to live outside the protective walls of convents, has been of interest to me for many years. Etherington (2004) asserts that '...by allowing ourselves to be known and seen by others, we open up the possibility of learning more about our topic and about ourselves' (p. 25).

In this respect, I am aware that making voluntary celibacy the subject of this chapter is personally significant, having myself gone through the throes of such an important decision in my teens, when I had the option of either joining the lay *Mużew* Society, or a Seminary to prepare for the priesthood. In the end, I did not opt for voluntary celibacy at all. Now in my late forties and married with two children, I can look back at how my story developed. However, I remain fascinated with celibacy as a life choice, as well as with learning how persons who endorse it experience it. I feel the metaphor of looking down on the world from a wooden balcony describes the world of voluntary celibacy well, where people metaphorically (and sometimes even physically) shut themselves up inside, whilst still engaging at different levels with the world outside. Aged 48, my grandmother had shut herself up in her balcony following the death of her husband, a voluntary withdrawal from the world in which she had participated fully up to then. Voluntary celibacy requires the voluntary withdrawal into a metaphorical 'balcony' which acts as a barrier to sexual and physical intimacy whilst at the same time allowing a 'vista' into the world.

Autoethnography has been described as a 'balancing act' (p. 764) by Holman-Jones (2005) and as a 'boundary crosser' (p. 3) by Reed-Danahay (1997). Ellis and Bochner (2000) refer to it as 'an autobiographical genre of writing and research that displays multiple layers of consciousness, connecting the personal to the cultural' (p. 735).

Developments in qualitative research over the past three decades have given new importance to writing using the 'self' (Moustakas 1990) and reflexivity (Hertz 1997). In her seminal book *Final Negotiations*, Carolyn Ellis (1995) provides a magnificent example of an autoethnographic story in which she also suggests that 'In evocative writing, the story's validity can be judged by whether it evokes in you, the reader, a feeling that the experience described is authentic, that it is believable and possible' (p. 318). The two stories presented in this chapter re-present the personal experience of how two men construed meaning around their decision to live a celibate life, thereby sensitizing readers to the cultural experience of voluntary celibacy within a Maltese context.

The context and narratives

Malta is a small archipelago of islands in the central Mediterranean. Long colonized because of its strategic position, Malta acquired nationhood in 1964 and became a member of the European Union in 2004. Malta has a long tradition of Catholicism which is in direct competition with the secular and individualistic values as lived within Western Europe. Indeed questions about cultural identity including ethnicity, language, religion, cultural values and customs tend to be perennially discussed (Baldacchino 2002). In a context where people have been subjected to various colonial experiences, narratives tend to yield stories of folk heroes fighting mythical 'dragons' whilst brandishing a uniting tool like language and religion. Maltese ethnographer George Mifsud Chircop (2003) suggests that narrative can be described as a means of communication that involves stories, situations, descriptions or a series of events. Perhaps because of their colonial past, Maltese people tend to be compulsive storytellers. One way of making sense of the stories and experiences which I will be re-presenting is to attempt to use the research material to create order and construct a text that creates a meaningful story within a context (Polkinghorne 1988; Riessman 1993).

Comparing our balconies: A conversation with Xandru

The following three extracts are taken from a transcript of an interview conversation with Xandru who, besides being a celibate lay member of Mużew, is also a counsellor, as am I. In the conversation, Xandru speaks of his experiences around voluntary celibacy. In excerpt one, Xandru speaks of how he lives as a celibate. In excerpt two, he recounts his experiences and doubts as a celibate school counsellor. In excerpt three, he speaks about living in what I have termed a 'balcony': in his words, 'Being in the world but not of the world'.

Excerpt One

Dione: And if I may ask ... eh ... you do not feel the need for sexual intimacy with another person...

Xandru: No ... Not I do not feel the need ... eh ... I do feel it actually, but I try to ... I made a commitment ... a voluntary commitment ... eh ... I knew what I was going in for ... that I should not express genitally my sexuality ... eh ... I knew from the very beginning that there would be moments when things would be somewhat difficult ... eh ... but I think I have managed to live my vocation very positively. But these contacts with females ... they help me ... they could be sources of difficulty but I think they are more healthy than not.

Excerpt Two

Xandru: Somehow, sometimes when I stop and think even about my counselling practice, I have a large number of clients who used to be my clients when they were students here (University of Malta) or at Junior College, and now they are in a relationship, and some of them are now married, and somehow they introduced me to their partner, and invited me to their wedding, and they keep on inviting me every now and then to their home to discuss family and even sexual matters with me ... and then I say ... Am I the right person to help them? But since they invite me and since they keep their appointments with me I think they find something that is nourishing them probably.

Dione: So your experience has been one of being 'in' rather than 'out'. It's one of being 'with people' rather than 'looking at people.'

Xandru: Definitely. Definitely.

Excerpt 3

Xandru: Now our vocation, Dione, the Mużew vocation is not a cloistered one. Our founder wanted us ... eh ... to be in the world with our professions, with our jobs, living at home with parents ... with siblings ... but at the same time ... we say it in our Society 'being in the world, but not of the world'.

Dione: Yes.

Xandru: 'Being in the world', with the hectic life of the world, but at the same time not being of the world, sort of not letting money overwhelm us, letting success, honours, possessions come much less in our priorities. Issa (now) where to strike this balance is very delicate ... it is very delicate ...

Dione: ... Especially because you live a 'normal' life in the sense that you don't have any particular dress code like a priest or like a monk or like a nun, but at the same time you are bound by the vows that you have taken. Are they vows, Xandru?

Xandru: No, not exactly, because OK we promise to be humble, obedient, chaste, poor etcetera. But if we decide to leave the Society, we just write to the Superior General informing him we are quitting sort of. It's as easy as that! But that's the beauty of it.

Dione: Yes, because you're free to go in and to go out.

Looking through the persian blinds in my balcony

This piece of autoethnographic fiction is the result of a conversation I had with a colleague about voluntary celibacy in Malta and how as a youth I was close to taking it up as a life choice. She encouraged me to write a piece re-telling what could have happened had I joined the Mużew Society. The result is a narrative of reflexive writing which as Laurel Richardson (2000a: 931) states, attends to, '... Feelings, ambiguities, temporal sequences, blurred experiences, and so on; we struggle to find a textual place for ourselves and our doubts and uncertainties'.

I am aware that writing an autoethnographic and fictive piece can be seen as transgressive both within my culture and within traditional academia. What follows is not a factual account but a fictive piece of writing that animates the issues that I would have had to face had I embraced voluntary celibacy as a way of life. The story is grounded in my tacit knowledge of male celibacy within the Maltese cultural context.

Sitting on my single bed at six in the morning, I look at the small wooden cross I have held in my hand every morning at the same hour for the past 24 years. It is a simple cross made of a cheap wood with an upper black part which I have invariably kissed every morning since the day I joined Mużew. Memories flood back: the small upper chapel inside the Msida Qasam *(centre), all my colleagues beaming as I stepped up to the* Superjur *(superior) who handed me the cross devoid of a crucifix. 'This cross is your own', he whispered, 'and you will have to carry it for the rest of your life'. I was too overcome by the moment to understand fully what he meant by that. I turned to look at the congregation and caught a glimpse of my parents. My mother seemed to be smiling but my father, as always, was deep in thought. 'Are you sure you want to do this?' he had asked me a week before. My father had almost become a Society member, but had withdrawn a few weeks before taking the promise. 'I think I am, Pa!' I had said trembling with fear and doubt.*

I say my daily prayers from l-Arlogg Mużewmin *(The Museum Clock) as I wear my clothes in preparation for the daily Mass. There are prayers for every hour of the day with a special meditation at three p.m. As I walk the few metres to the church more memories come back. The first years had not been easy. I was reading for a degree in Education at university and at the same time was given a catechism class to teach at Mużew. My old issues regarding sexuality had come back to me, which I had tried to dismiss as 'temptations'. There was not much I could do. I was young and university was not an easy place to be a Mużew member with all those girls around. Mostly I kept to the promise, but there were a few times when I succumbed. What a can of worms of doubt and shame was opened every time I succumbed! And yet I had given my word and was supposed to keep to it. The only thing I looked forward to was the safety of the 'Qasam'. There, I could be myself, teaching catechism and meeting with my Mużew colleagues. There was very little time to think as university lectures finished at 5 p.m. and I was at Mużew by 6.15 leaving me only some time to grab a quick coffee at our house. Mum always grumbled about me not being 'there' at all. She still does. As the university course got into its final years and all my colleagues started coupling up, more questions came up. Everyone around me was settling down whereas I was still living with my parents and probably destined to continue to live there till the end of my days.*

Back home from Mass, I have a cup of tea and some toast as I prepare for another day at school as a counsellor with a church school. I became a school counsellor in 1996 after I sat for interviews for counsellor posts at the university, government schools and church schools. Becoming a church school counsellor had then seemed to be more appropriate than the more glamorous post at university. I had been chosen to be in the first batch of church school counsellors then. It was so different nine years ago: the issues the students discussed were so innocent. Now everything is more sexualized as life gets more Westernized and more complicated. And I dread counselling adolescents on their sexual issues as I immediately go back to my own days as a young person and realize that I have still not resolved some of those issues. Again I try not to think about them as I drive to work. My school is a medium sized girls' secondary school where I have been working for the past two years.

My working day starts inside the school staff room. Most of the teachers are married or on their way to forming a family. Being a school counsellor also means listening to the personal problems of the staff. I find myself being asked questions and asked to help deal with issues that leave lots of unanswered questions for me. In a way I relive the mixture of feelings I experience when I attend a marriage. It seems to be such a huge decision to promise to live alongside one person for the rest of one's life. My mind goes back to the marriage of my brother and sister, and to marriages of other close friends. Some have been successful in their married life, others have separated and are now adapting to a different lifestyle either with another partner or as single parents. And they come to me to discuss choices! I put on a brave face and try to listen to their questions: Should I stay? Should I leave? What will I think of myself? What will the others think of me? Where do I go from here? Will I still belong to the church if I go against its teachings? Should I forgive him? Like an ageless ritual I feel their questions melt and become my own as I go to the counselling room to start my day, a full day as usual. Twelve year-olds, 13 year-olds, 14 year-olds. These young persons are the right age to have been my children. Sometimes what they say makes me unhappy not to have had children of my own, other times I thank God for my decision to have chosen this life.

My first client is a twelve year-old girl experiencing the helpless pain of witnessing her parents going through a separation. She speaks of the scenes that she witnesses and narrates how she tries to drown the shrieks and the shouting by locking herself into her room and putting a pillow over her ears. We work on how to make the best out of a hopeless situation. We also work on accepting that life can turn out to be completely different from the one aspired to. When she leaves I feel my thought processes nagging: Making the best out of a hopeless situation; Accepting that life can be different to the one aspired to. How appropriate!

My second client is a 14-year-old girl who comes to the counselling room with her classmate. It is the classmate who speaks first, holding the client's hand. She narrates how her friend told her she had been going out with a married man 20 years her senior. They had also been having sex regularly and now her period was late by 14 days. I look at the girl and she bursts out crying. As I am about to mechanically start empathizing the girl says, 'Please do not say anything. I do not want to lose him'. Her friend butts in to say that she had already done two pregnancy tests and that both were positive. I can just imagine what it will be like for this girl in the next few days. She is afraid she will be thrown out of the house and asks whether I can tell the parents myself. I know it is the least I can do and dial the number. The usual alarmed questions from the other side as I try to placate fears subside when I ask the mother to come to school as soon as possible and hang up. I am aware it is only crisis management. I know I have not seen the last of this girl and her family. When the two girls leave, I think of how much young people can complicate their lives. I catch myself saying how simple my youth was, and understand that it was simple only because I had been trained to suppress my feelings. I am aware I still do that today…

My third client is a 15-year-old girl who comes to discuss her sexual orientation. She thinks she's lesbian and has been having a 'kind of relationship' with a classmate. She says she is very confused. She wants me to help her to 'come out of it'. She seems quite panicky and cries throughout the session which I use to calm her down and to assure her that there is nothing wrong with her. At the end of the session, I overhear myself saying that if she is really lesbian she will ultimately find that out for herself and will not need to 'come out of it'. I am aware I have said that statement in a church school and smile! At the end of the session, she seems relieved and wants to come another time…

So much pain, so much suffering…

At 7.30 p.m. I am sitting inside the Qasam enjoying a few moments of silence. What a day! The meeting with my second client's parents had been a vast exercise that really tested my communication skills. Witnessing all that pain, and in another way containing it, had really exhausted me. It's obviously not over. The girl needs all the help she can get. She will be undergoing various tests tomorrow, including some for STDs. After that ordeal I had gone back home, where I arrived at about three, said my three o' clock prayers and ate some 'minestra' *(vegetable soup) with my father. He always makes it a point to eat with me. He has done this ever since he retired ten years ago. Since then we have become real friends. At 5.30 I was at the Qasam, and at 6.30 gave my lesson for today. It was the passage about Samuel and Eli from Chapter 1 of the First Book of Samuel and focused on saying 'yes' to the Lord. I had spoken about choices and decisions being about saying 'yes' or 'no' and not 'maybe'. I feel the words I am uttering mocking me, laughing at me…*

'No maybes, eh?'

I am torn once again as I walk upstairs to the chapel for the evening meeting of the Society members. Has my life been full of maybes? My mind wanders back to my grandmother saying the rosary in the balcony, looking at life going on about her whilst she shuttles between connectedness and detachment. Do I want to continue looking at life from a balcony? Do I want to go out of the house? I put my hand on my lapel and feel for the Society badge. It's there as always. I look at the people inside the chapel: familiar faces, familiar chants, familiar walls…

This night I must decide as I have done so many times. Will it be a 'yes'? Will it be a 'no'? Or will it be another 'maybe'?

Reflections on a multi-layered narrative inquiry

Laurel Richardson (2000b), whilst declaring that 'The ethnographic life is not separate from the self' (p. 253), goes on to say that ethnography needs to be both scientific in that it needs to be true to a world that can be 'known through the empirical sense', as well as literary in the sense that the writer expresses him/herself evocatively. She also introduces the criteria she uses to evaluate ethnography, and these include substantive contribution, aesthetic merit, reflexivity, impact and whether the inquiry expresses reality. Other researchers, like Ellis (2000) and Clough (2000), though speaking about how they evaluate ethnographies, keep away from actually presenting a standardized evaluation tool. Thus, whilst embarking on this exercise of reflection, I understand that presenting my work in a particular form may not meet all the requirements put forward by different researchers. Denzin (2000) declares that 'writing is not an innocent practice' (p. 256) and proposes a 'utopian project where writing can be politically induced in favour of the construction of a free democratic society' (p. 257). On the other hand, I am also keeping in mind that Speedy (2005) points out that 'arts based research … illustrates and suggests but it does not explain and evaluate' (p. 64).

I firmly believe that the stories in this chapter are shaped by the social reality that Malta has gone through during the past 40 years. For many Maltese brought up in the sixties, within very traditional Catholic families and a society that had not yet started to 'taste' the different lifestyles introduced by incoming tourism, voluntary celibacy within the church was seen as a life choice that was honourable and 'blessed'. The church and Mużew were our second homes, and the priest and Mużew members were as familiar to us as members of our extended families.

Narrative inquiry may be shrouded in controversy over concerns about validity and generalizability (Polkinghorne 2007), but in this present context the use of narrative was useful to uncover the personal and social meanings that Xandru and I ascribe to our experiences of voluntary celibacy within the Maltese socio-cultural context. The narrative emerging out of the two stories helped me make sense of my own experience of voluntary celibacy. The use of autoethnography was appropriate because it 'make[s] the researcher's own experience a topic of investigation in its own right' (Ellis and Bochner 2000: 733) and enables a cultural understanding of oneself in relation to others. Autoethnography also has the propensity to give insight into issues and problems that are often overlooked in culture.

Research process

As I have already stated, and because of my own experience, I have been interested in the subject of voluntary celibacy for a long time, and put pen to paper immediately after the conversation with the colleague I mentioned earlier. I opted to do research involving a conversation with a person, Xandru, who has embraced voluntary celibacy. The interview subsequently took place in my office and was recorded and transcribed. The transcript was given to Xandru for his approval. Later, I met Xandru again and discussed the outcome of the interview with him. The conversations with Xandru also helped to inspire and in some ways inform the second part of the inquiry. 'Looking through the Persian Blinds in my Balcony' developed into a significant personal journey permeating into the realms of autoethnography (Bochner and Ellis 2001; Frank 1995) and auto-ethnographic fiction (Gray 2004; Sparkes 2002). In it, I really closed my eyes and reflected on how my life could have been had I gone into voluntary celibacy. I also included experiences that were narrated to me by some counselling clients who try to live a celibate life though not always succeeding. These experiences were completely re-shaped to respect anonymity and to fit with the narrative.

Ethical issues

Ethical issues revolved around the understanding that good intent does not necessarily lead to good outcomes unless there is persistent awareness to all ethical dimensions involved in the work (Bond and Mifsud 2006), as well as the management of consent (Duncombe and Jessop 2004). I also kept in mind the benefits and changes in the public's perceptions that emanate from the research of lives (Agronick and Helson 1996). Finally, Xandru provided valuable feedback on both the draft and the interview transcript before he finally approved the finished work.

The inquiry

My 'unfinished business' with regard to voluntary celibacy was the spark that reignited interest in the subject. At first, I was inclined to have just an interview with Xandru mainly because he represents the lifestyle I could have led had I entered into voluntary celibacy, as Xandru is a counsellor and involved in many voluntary circles. Reading through the interview many times and seeing how much Xandru's experiences resonated with mine in different ways, I was aware that using autoethnographic fiction was a powerful vehicle that could be used to describe the experiences of one whose doubts were stronger than his certainties. The piece also represents the experiences of a number of counselling clients who go through grave difficulties to keep to the promise of voluntary celibacy, and who, like I did, experience shame and guilt when they do not manage, as well as doubts over their choice of so many years ago.

Various researchers have written about interviews and interview conversations including Briggs (2003), Fontana and Frey (2000), Gubrium and Holstein (2003), Kvale (1996) and Mishler (1986). Gubrium and Holstein (2003) assert that in-depth interviewing helps not just to construct a subject, but takes the researcher directly to the heart of the experience being researched. The interview conversation with Xandru had this distinct flavour: it gave me the chance to hear a story of someone who is fully committed to living the experience of voluntary celibacy. It is a moving story of someone who chooses to live in an 'open balcony', permitting more permeation with the world. In a Maltese context, this world now makes it even more difficult for him to live within the 'balcony', and yet he withstands the onslaught. The interview conversation also gave me the chance to share the story of my inability to stay within the parameters of voluntary celibacy. In this way, we experienced 'reciprocity' in that we both entered the space of the story for the other (Frank 1995), as well as acknowledging our identity by our revelation to others (Lieblich, Tuval-Masiach and Zilber 1998).

Like Speedy (2004), 'I was intrigued' (p. 46) with Xandru's narrative and his experiences when we met for our conversation and spoke of our different experiences and retold our stories. Our interview took the form of a conversation which developed into what Mishler (1986: 52) terms a 'joint construction of meaning', especially with regard to the construction of the metaphor of voluntary celibacy as an act of being in a balcony, of participating in life and withdrawing from it at the same time. This is shown in the three excerpts chosen, especially in the first, where after some hesitation, Xandru admits to his feeling the need to express himself sexually with females, though refraining to express himself 'genitally' as he terms it. In the second excerpt, Xandru speaks of his doubts as to whether he is the right person to help couples when he lives in a 'balcony'. I feel this resonated with my fears of 25 years ago and comes out again in the autoethnographic piece. The third excerpt is about balance in life when one is celibate. Xandru says it is very 'delicate', almost like walking a tight rope. The word 'delicate' struck me as I understand that whoever chooses this kind of life has to be delicately balanced all the time.

I am aware that the interview conversation also focuses on relationships with bodies (Davies 2000), in this case the celibate body. In it, both Xandru and I speak about our experiences of celibacy and call on the reader to share in what Denzin (1997) calls an 'evocative epistemology' (p. 12) of our experience of growing up in a country steeped in Catholic traditions and values. The stories of how Xandru chose to stay in voluntary celibacy, while I did not, provided the ellipses that make up the landscape for the research. However, as I gradually immersed myself into the research, the metaphor of looking at life from a balcony became stronger. Gray (2004: 45) declares that: 'using stories to represent research can also resist premature closure on understanding conveying complexity and ambiguity and making space for alternative interpretations'.

The memory of my grandmother withdrawing from the 'world' into her 'balcony' made me ask what could have happened to me had I withdrawn into my 'balcony' so early in life. The image of my grandmother 'Looking through the Persian Blinds' tries to answer that question, by providing the other ellipsis of opening up what I had closed years gone by. Thus it provided what Gray (2004: 59) calls an 'entry-point into the themes' gleaned both from the interview and the personal questions that keep on nagging me. Denison and Rinehart (2000: 1–4) speak of ethnographic fiction as experiences grounded in 'everyday events', while Sparkes (2002) speaks on the importance given by ethnographers of being there as participant observers, in other words of seeing, hearing, smelling, tasting and feeling the experience. Keller-Cohen and Gordon (2003) speak of the importance of coherence within a narrative. They say that coherence:

> ... may arise out of an individual's analysis of events ... thus enabling an individual to consider alternative possibilities of interpretation, to contemplate the many ways in which events may be linked together and deemed coherent, and to weigh the consequences of these possible interpretations. (p. 2)

They continue to say that metaphor is one way of achieving coherence. In this respect, I feel there is a lot of coherence between the stories of my grandmother's balcony, Xandru's experience of being 'in the world' but not 'of the world' and my story of what could have happened had I constructed my own wooden balcony of voluntary celibacy.

The story can be described as a 'true fiction' (Clifford 1986: 6) in that the setting, people and experiences are authentic, as are the Mużew rituals described. My father, like me, almost embraced voluntary celibacy, and it seems I followed his footsteps. It is also true that I sat for an interview to become a church school counsellor, and, though successful, did not take up the job in order to follow an academic career at the University of Malta. The daily routine that is described is really the one followed by most Mużew members who are either teachers or counsellors. I still feel uneasy counselling adolescents on sexual issues, though I do feel that I can do it without going through psychological traumas. The doubts expressed with regard to voluntary celibacy belong to some of my counselling clients. They also belong to me. At 49, I can now state without feeling ashamed that closing the choice of 'voluntary celibacy' had more to do with the inability to suppress sexual desires than with 'lack of vocation'. Now that I have stated this and see it printed before me, like Bochner (2000) I can exclaim that 'narrative is our means of fashioning experience in language' (p. 270).

Finally, the story of the 'Persian Blinds' gave me the chance to use reflexivity (Hertz 1997; Etherington 2001) to the full. In it, as Gray (2004) states, I engage in a useful strategy to face and come to terms with 'personally and conceptually challenging issues' (p. 59). For me, these included traditional religious ethics, sexuality and sexual issues faced by adolescents and young adults, issues of shame and guilt and unfinished stories from my past.

Concluding comments

This story is personal, interpersonal and contextual. Re-presenting it in this way gave me the chance to paint it with the colours of the country I come from. It also gave me the chance to explore vocational celibacy, an issue which is often maligned and misinterpreted, from the eyes of two people who were (and are) somehow involved in it. My hope is that the reader may be transported to his/her own balcony and experience a few moments of what Xandru describes as:

> '...Being in the world, but not being of the world'.

Looking at a disused balcony: My story

Vague memories of a twelve-year-old,
Standing in the little Msida chapel
With a white lily held steadily in his hand.
'Dear Mary, I offer you the flower of my chastity.
Chastity ... What exactly does it mean?'

Vivid memories of a 16-year-old
Witnessing the promise of a new member in the Society
But thinking of that red head in yesterday's hike.
'Dear Mary, I am not sure any more I want to do this.
Girls! Why did you have to make them so attractive?'

Guilty memories of a 17-year-old
Struggling with the fact that his sexual desires are stronger
Than his will to be celibate. The shame of it!
'Dear Mary, please forgive me. I tried so hard,
And I do not want to let you down.'

Colourful memories of a 19-year-old
In love for the first time in his life,
With the promise of a bright and beautiful future.

'Dear Mary, I think I do not want to do this anymore.
Voluntary celibacy. What a bore!'

Blurred thoughts of a 42-year-old,
Hitting the keys of his computer keyboard
And struggling with the doubts of soft middle age.
'Dear Mary, I wonder how it might have been
Who knows! The sun has started to set now!'

References

Agonrick. G., and Helson, R. (1996) 'Who benefits from an examined life? Correlates of influence attributed to participation in a longitudinal study', in R. Josselson (ed.), *Ethics and Process in the Narrative Study of Lives*, Thousand Oaks, CA: Sage Publications, pp. 80–93.

Baldacchino, G. (2002) A nationless state? Malta, national identity and the EU, *West European Politics*, 25 (4), 191–206.

Bochner, A. (2000) Criteria against ourselves, *Qualitative Inquiry*, 6 (2): 266–72.

Bochner, A., and Ellis, C. (2001) *Ethnographically Speaking*, Walnut Creek, CA: Altamira Press.

Bond, T., and Mifsud, D. (2006) 'Narrative conversation between two cultures: a novel way to addressing an ethical concern', in S. Trahar (ed.) *Narrative Research on Learning: Comparative and International Perspectives*, Oxford: Symposium Books, pp. 239–51.

Briggs, C. L. (2003) 'Interviewing, power / knowledge and social inequality', in J. Gubrium and J. Holstein (eds) *Postmodern Interviewing*, London: Sage Publications, pp. 243–54.

Clifford, J. (1986) *Writing Culture*, Berkeley: University of California Press.

Clough, P. T. (2000) Comments on setting criteria for experimental writing, *Qualitative Inquiry*, 6 (2): 278–91.

Davies, B. (2000) *(In)scribing Body / Landscape Relations*, Walnut Creek, CA: Altamira Press.

Denison, J., and Rinehart, R. (2000) Introduction: Imagining sociological narratives, *Sociology of Sport Journal*, 17 (1): 1–4.

Denzin, N. K. (2000) Aesthetics and the practices of qualitative inquiry, *Qualitative Inquiry*, 6 (2): 256–65.

—(1997) *Interpretative Ethnography*, London: Sage Publications.

Duncombe, J., and Jessop, J. (2004) 'Doing rapport and the ethics of faking friendship', in M. Mauthner, M. Birch, J. Jessop and T. Miller (eds) *Ethics in Qualitative Research*, Thousand Oaks, CA: Sage Publications, pp. 107–22.

Ellis, C. (1995) *Final Negotiations: A Story of Love, Loss and Chronic Illness*, Philadelphia: Temple University Press.

—(2000) Creating criteria: An ethnographic short story, *Qualitative Inquiry*, 6 (2): 273–77.

Ellis, C., and Bochner, A. P. (2000) 'Autoethnography, personal narrative, reflexivity: Researcher as subject', in N. Denzin and Y Lincoln (eds) *Handbook of Qualitative Research*. Thousand Oaks, CA: Sage Publications, pp. 733–68.

Etherington, K. (2004) *Becoming a Reflexive Researcher*, London: Jessica Kingsley.
—(2001) Research with ex-clients: A celebration and extension of the therapeutic process, *British Journal of Guidance and Counselling*, 25 (1): 467–82.
Fontana, A., and Frey, J. (2000) 'The interview: From structural questions to negotiated text', in N. Denzin and Y. Lincoln (eds) *Handbook of Qualitative Research*, Thousand Oaks, CA: Sage Publications, pp. 645–672.
Frank, A. (1995) *The Wounded Storyteller: Body, Illness and Ethics*, London: University of Chicago Press.
Gubrium, J., and Holstein, J. (2003) 'From the individual interview to the interview society', in J. Gubrium and J. Holstein (eds) *Postmodern Interviewing*, Thousand Oaks, CA: Sage Publications, pp. 21–49.
Gray, R. (2004) No longer a man: Using ethnographic fiction to represent life history research, *Auto/Biography*, 12: 44–61.
Hertz, R. (1997) *Reflexivity and Voice*, London: Sage Publications.
Holman-Jones, S. (2005) 'Auto-ethnography: Making the personal political', in N. Denzin and Y. Lincoln (eds) *Handbook of Qualitative Research*, Thousand Oaks, CA: Sage Publications, pp. 763–91.
Keller-Cohen, D., and Gordon, C. (2003) On trial: Metaphor in telling the life story, *Narrative Inquiry*, 13 (1): 1–40.
Kvale, S. (1996) *InterViews: An Introduction to Qualitative Research Interviewing*, Thousand Oaks, CA: Sage Publications.
Lieblich, A., Tuval-Masiach, R., and Zilber, T. (1998) *Narrative Research: Reading, Analysis and Interpretation*, Thousand Oaks, CA: Sage Publications.
Mifsud Chircop, G. (2003) *Il-Folklor Malti*, Malta: Pin Publications.
Mishler, E. G. (1986) *Research Interviewing: Context and Narrative*, London: Harvard University Press.
Moustakas, C. (1990) *Heuristic Research Design: Methodology and Applications*, London: Sage Publications.
Polkinghorne, D. (1988) *Narrative Knowing and the Human Sciences*, Albany, NY: Suny Press.
—(2007) Validity issues in narrative research, *Qualitative Inquiry*, 13 (4): 471–86.
Reed-Danahay, D. (1997) 'Introduction', in D. Reed-Danahay (ed.) *Auto/Ethnography – Rewriting the Self and the Social*, Oxford: Berg, pp. 1–17.
Richardson, L. (2000a) 'Writing: A method of inquiry', in N. K. Denzin and Y. S. Lincoln (eds) *Handbook of Qualitative Research*, Thousand Oaks, CA: Sage Publications, pp. 923–948.
—(2000b) Evaluating ethnography, *Qualitative Inquiry*, 6 (2): 253–55.
Riessman, C. K. (1993) *Narrative Analysis*, Newbury Park, CA: Sage Publications.
Sparkes, A. C. (2002) *Telling Tales in Sport and Physical Activity. A Qualitative Journey*, Leeds: Human Kinetics Europe.
Speedy, J. (2005) Writing as inquiry: Some ideas, practices, opportunities and constraints, *Counselling and Psychotherapy Research*, 5 (1): 63–4.
Speedy, J. Thompson, G., and Anon (2004) Living a more peopled life: Definitional ceremony as inquiry into therapy outcomes, *International Journal of Narrative Therapy and Community Work*, 2004 (3): 43–53.

Chapter 4

Workplace bullying in higher education

A victim's perspective

Mary Baker

Introduction

The surge in the level of incidences of workplace bullying in recent years in the United Kingdom (UK) has been matched by an extraordinary intensification of interest in the topic and a dramatic increase in the number of studies taking place. Regardless of the plethora of criteria data already gathered on the subject, such as manifestation and coping strategies, there is still a lack of understanding of what can be truthfully described as *unnecessary hell* for the victim. In common with other forms of abuse, only those who have suffered it fully appreciate the sheer awfulness.

In the past, research into workplace bullying has been largely positivist in nature and there has been a lack of appreciation of the value of a narrative approach to research in this area. However, this chapter chooses to ignore the lingering influence of the earlier approaches to researching this phenomenon and instead examines workplace bullying in UK Higher Education (HE) from an autoethnographical perspective. It starts by outlining the driving forces that have resulted in workplace bullying emerging as a significant problem within HE, and continues with a discussion of autoethnography as a methodological approach to exploring workplace bullying within HE. An assessment is made of the strengths and weaknesses of autoethnography, in order to assess its potential for application within this specific context. The chapter continues with a post-experience appraisal of the methodology, highlighting the ways in which the approach benefitted the research, but also considering the limitations that emerged in the process, paying particular consideration to ethical concerns. Autoethnography has turned out to be a complex approach to research in this area and there have been some challenging stumbling blocks. However, it has added to my understanding of the problem at a more personal, subjective level with the hope that the silence and denial amongst both the bullied and the non-bullied will be overcome.

Driving forces

There is much evidence to support the fact that workplace bullying has become a significant problem within HE in the UK (Lewis 2004). Funding deficits and 'creeping commercialism' (Field 1996:12) have driven changes in policy and practice, and have created an environment where increasingly stringent quality standards, demanding student customers, cost-cutting programmes, staff rationalization exercizes and increasing workloads have become the norm. Academics, appointed to unfamiliar 'new management' roles where demands and responsibilities have changed significantly, have experienced insecurities of performance, and as a result workplace bullying has thrived (Field 1996; Adams 1992).

The formation of incorporated institutions, under the Further and Higher Education Act took place in 1992. This meant that HE institutions would be allowed to operate in a much more market-oriented manner and so benefit from the opportunity to compete in the open market in the same way as private sector companies. At first, it appeared that the newer universities (those who had originally operated as *polytechnics* and who were only just getting used to being able to award their own degrees) were going to bear the brunt of the pressure to adopt commercial practices, for national and local governments were starting to become increasingly involved in institutional activities to ensure that they were focusing on research and teaching activities that were of benefit to the economic needs of both region and nation. But at the same time, governments were also supporting the entrance of a new player into the tertiary education market – the private sector. So … with less support being offered by the state, and yet more and more levels of accountability being demanded (Rushton 2001), HE as a whole was being increasingly compelled to embrace the new commercialism. This had a significant impact on academics as they were forced out of their comfort zones by the new focus on the 'bottom line' and the resulting shift in the balance of power in universities from the academic *teacher and deliverer*, to the academic *line manager* (Hoel and Stalin 2003). Staff, who had little or no previous experience of traditional business operations, were being confronted with activities like target setting, increasing student numbers, penalties for student withdrawal and deficits – and all because of the reduction in government funding. Universities were becoming rivals, and where there had previously been little concern for productivity or corporate reputation, the increasingly 'cash poor' new universities now had little option but to accept the challenge of consumerism and competition in order to achieve greater market share and profits (De Vita and Case 2003) to try and stem the tide of funding deprivation. All of this seemed to indicate that universities were going to have to 'change more drastically than they [had] since they assumed their present form more than 300 years ago' when they reorganized themselves around the printed book (Drucker 1992: 97).

Nearly 20 years later, this metamorphosis is continuing at an ever increasing pace with changes in working practice and relationships being demanded of all universities. These universities with their blend of individuals from a variety of cultures, with different beliefs, values and attitudes are being required to work together in what is now a hyper-competitive, high stress environment: a workplace characterized by 'differences of opinions, competition for power and territoriality, jealousy, prejudice, envy and problematic group dynamics' (Luzio-Lockett 1995: 12; Thomas and Cornuel 2011). As conflict and dispute between vocational and managerial objectives continues – the knowledge-imparting raison d'etre of the conventional academic versus the position-of-power seeking ambitions of many of the new academic managers – it is hardly surprising that workplace bullying has emerged as a serious problem.

There is no doubt that the costs of workplace bullying are significant, whether viewed from an organizational or victim perspective. The failure to deal with incidents of bullying can undermine an organization's effectiveness (Einarsen et al 2003), not least through the loss of morale and high levels of absenteeism. The ensuing shortfalls in productivity and efficiency and ultimately higher levels of staff turnover mean that businesses experience higher financial expenditure because of the need for additional recruiting and retraining. As a result, work-related bullying is becoming acknowledged as a significant contributory factor to the financial ill health of organizations (Thomas 2005).

The effects of workplace bullying are also significant when examined from an individual/victim perspective, and the evidence is both physical and psychological. Physically, extended stress can evidence itself in a conglomeration of associated ailments: according to Kinchin (2005: 87), there are 'at least thirty four physical symptoms of stress which can result from bullying'. Psychologically it is common to experience hypervigilance, hypersensitivity, irritability, poor concentration and an impaired memory – just a few of the considerable number of the emotional symptoms associated with bullying (Kinchin 2005).

At a time when the health, well-being and support of employees is key to the survival of academic institutions, staff are being subjected to the distressing, disempowering, career stalling practice that is the lived experience of workplace bullying. Unchallenged, the phenomenon has resulted in nervous breakdown, heart attack, post-traumatic stress syndrome and even suicide (Tehrani 2004; Kinchin 2005).

A new research direction

In terms of research into the problem, narrative inquiry and autoethnography in particular have not previously been viewed as appropriate methodologies for the exploration of workplace bullying, for the approaches are in stark contrast to the 'outsider' standpoint which was preferred by many of the psychologists who were early researchers into this phenomenon. As positivists, they were looking to produce propositional knowledge about human behaviour that would be generalizable to specific populations (Ellis 2004) and their research projects focused largely on defining bullying behaviours, identifying the causes of bullying and highlighting the need for anti-bullying policies (Djurkovik and McCormack 2005). The empirical studies that have been carried out into the causes of workplace bullying have concentrated largely on the personality of the victim and psychosocial factors at work, with most of the studies viewing bullying holistically and not recognizing the different behaviours that are involved (Einarsen 1999). In addition, large scale incidence studies using postal questionnaires to assess the extent of the issue of bullying have formed a significant proportion of the research.

However, as the perspective widens as to what comprises bullying, deviating towards the acceptance of the perceptions of the victim, it is likely that the perception of what must be studied may widen also. This leaves open the opportunity for different methods to be employed. 'The quest for 'the truth' may be 'out there' (especially in a legal context), but researchers in this field are realising that they must work with different realities and perceptions as part of the process' (Rayner, Sheehan and Barker 1999: 13). This seems to indicate that researchers in this area may be becoming increasingly more accepting of the need for alternative approaches to developing knowledge of workplace bullying.

Therefore, although both 'insider' and 'outsider' approaches to researching workplace bullying (Stronach and Maclure 1997) have their merits in the context of HE, I believe that the representation of the unbelievable and, at times, personally shattering experience of workplace bullying can only be effectively achieved from an individual, 'insider' autoethnographical perspective. The advantage of sharing personal experiences of workplace bullying should help 'expose the facts and bring them to people's attention' (Orwell 1958: 103). It will push the boundaries of accepted knowledge about workplace bullying – not just for the researcher herself and for those going through similar experiences, but also for the 'others' who look on. Silverman, (1999: 199) is of the opinion that the value of this research approach lies in what some researchers have yet to be convinced of, 'the report(ing) people's exciting, gruesome or intimate experiences', and this gives me confidence that this is an appropriate approach for research into the phenomenon of workplace bullying. The account may be the subjective view of one person, but it represents and speaks for a more pervasive crisis (Marcus 1994), giving credence to the value of the information within a wider arena.

The narrative analysis paradigm that underpins this research supports the search for understanding in the meanings people attribute to the complexities of their life experiences (Josselson 2006, cited in Trahar 2009). Specifically, this means that I have sought to acquire knowledge as to why one member of staff would engage in deliberately destructive behaviours towards another without provocation and why witnesses to the maltreatment largely failed to intervene or offer their support to the target. However, my options in terms of gathering data have been constrained by the complexities of the phenomenon itself and by way of the current organizational climate in HE. My experience has shown that those who have viewed bullying incidents from the sidelines are largely reticent to speak up officially and so put themselves in the 'firing line.' The bully meanwhile is just as improbable a source of information, for it is unlikely that she or he will interpret her/his behaviour as harassment (Namie and Namie 2003, cited in Cowan 2012), let alone self-confess to engaging in bullying behaviour (Seigne et. al. 2007). Given these constraints, research into workplace bullying has largely ignored the activities of the perpetrator (Jenkins et al. 2011: 33) and relied instead 'on self-reports from victims and bystanders.' Recently, even the willingness to speak up has been hampered by political sensitivities currently affecting HE, as staff become increasingly reserved about sharing personally sensitive information for fear that their jobs might be put at risk should their comments be perceived as criticism by the organization.

However, valuable insights into the different realities of workplace bullying will come from the examination of the personal encounters, observations, sensing, actions and reactions of the victim. Knowledge will also emerge from the behaviours and vocalizations of the other participants, for it is in my kinaesthetic response to their physical and oral representations – their conduct – that my understanding of workplace bullying lies, viewed through the different lenses of the bully and the 'onlookers'. If I am to successfully circumvent the difficulties identified in approaching and obtaining information from both the bully and any 'onlookers' and move on from the predominance of the distanced, macro-lens currently focused on the phenomenon of workplace bullying, then it would seem that autoethnography is the answer: a route to knowledge 'less travelled' but no less valid (Ellis et. al. 2011).

Despite the apparent appropriateness of autoethnography within the context of this research, the methodology has nonetheless been subject to a significant amount of criticism. Coffey (1999, cited in Maguire 2006) condemns autoethnography for being self-indulgent, seeing its contribution as being restricted to the specifics of what one person has to say about a particular subject. Delamont (2007) agrees, arguing that autoethnography's lack of analytical outcomes (see also Atkinson 2006) is linked to such introspection. She protests that autoethnography is almost impossible to write and publish ethically and that it is extremely difficult to disguise and protect other actors. Citing Becker (1967: 239) and his classic question 'whose side are we on?', she further criticizes autoethnography for being biased: for focusing on the powerful in society and not the powerless. The wrong focus, according to Becker's premise. In the context of workplace bullying, however, and as the researcher, researched, I have come to a keen appreciation of my personal predicament. I believe myself to be more sinned against than sinning and above all I see myself as a victim: someone who is powerless to break away from the anguish of bullying. Will that perspective make me biased as I interact with other bullying realities in my story? Possibly. But if the objective of autoethnography is not to create universal truth, but to express the individual truth of the researcher through an engagement in 'intense and transparent reflection and questioning of (one's) own position, values and beliefs' (Trahar 2009 http://www.qualitative-research.net/index.php/fqs/article/view/1218/2654) then my truth is the truth. Therefore, the search for knowledge and understanding in the anguish of the powerless victim through autoethnography could result in empowerment ... for knowledge is power.

Whilst I concede that, in focusing purely on myself as the only data source in this exploration, the research might be considered 'too introspective and individualized' (Sparkes 2000: 15), introspection gives rise to individual life stories from which 'there is much to learn' and which 'reflect wider social and historical changes' (Andrews 2007: 491, cited in Trahar 2008: 262). Thus introspection can move the discipline forward in creating a greater understanding of bullying at both a personal and societal level. Similarly, recounting my experiences is likely to be a painful and emotional process (Smith 1999: 267) and I risk anguish and suffering as I allow others access to a previously hidden area of my life (Luft 1969). Yet the argument for a 'highly personalized and revealing text,' (Richardson 1994, cited in Sparkes 2002: 73), is compelling even though Delamont (2007) strongly believes that the most important questions are not about anguish. For as Vickers says, we should not be fearful and thus become 'enemies of new knowledge' (2008: 608) because the benefits have the potential to far outweigh the negative aspects of this form of research, for the readers' interpretation sheds light on what the victim has endured. And such introspection enables lived experience to become 'primary data' (Ellis 2004: xvii).

Traumatic times

My research has been achieved through personal reflections on remembered episodic incidents, experiences, outcomes and evaluations (Fournier 1990; Shank 1990). Such problematic experiences as bullying (when someone is confronted by a significant event or crisis) are termed epiphanies or moments of revelation (Denzin 1989). He defines epiphany as 'those interactional moments that leave positive and negative marks on people's lives' and suggests that it is by recording such experiences in detail that the researcher is able to shed light on those moments that 'have the potential for creating transformational experiences for the person' (Denzin 1989: 15). Therefore, by focusing on these epiphanies, I have produced stories that are composites of real events that have been previously experienced and observed. In trying to re-present these events accurately, I have endeavoured to show not only my personal involvement in the incidents, but also the ways in which the reader might identify with, reflect upon and interpret the occurrences. Polkinghorne (1983: 239) says that 'human science is largely ex post facto understanding' and 'inescapably historical', and it was in consideration of these factors that I have sought to create 'verisimilitude' in my commentary so that readers feel that either they have experienced or could experience the events being described (Denzin 1989). In the past, sociologists have been repelled or threatened by the seemingly unmanageable content of subjective experiences such as these (Katz 1988), but nowadays, sociologists generally recognize that emotional processes are crucial components of the social experience (Ellis and Flaherty 1992).

Before carrying out this research, I was aware that recounting my experiences of workplace bullying was likely to be a painful and emotional process (Smith 1999: 267) and also not without risk, for I would be allowing others access to a previously hidden area of my life (Luft 1969). There were issues with the sensitive, embarrassing and stigmatizing nature of the information that I would be sharing, as well as the stigma of being bullied, being labelled as a victim and the shame of being judged negatively (Lewis 2004) by others who did not have a proper understanding of what had been taking place. As an academic, those 'others' could include my students, my colleagues and, in the new 'regime', those external to the university with whom I might be developing commercial relationships. Writing my truth too frankly might also be unwise, for 'telling it like it is' can threaten the status quo (Tal 1996:7). There is, after all, the consideration that my organization is not going to be happy about me producing a defamatory polemic on its inefficiency and unfairness (Hannabuss 2000).

However as time has gone on, it has become increasingly difficult to 'expose the facts' and 'get a hearing' at work (Orwell 2004) with regard to the promulgating bullying activities for denial and ignorance of the impact and consequences have been rife. For my part, the constraints of professionalism, coupled with trying to treat people as I would wish to be treated myself, have meant that I have been frequently forced to work within self-imposed communication boundaries whilst at work (Plummer 1995), yet all the while being driven by the desire to give voice to the story of workplace bullying.

You would imagine that as this is the narrative of *my* personal lived experiences, it would not require permission and ethical clearance in the telling. However, in choosing to focus a 'scientific' gaze on these happenings, I have been faced with the dilemma as to what I can ethically portray. As a result, ethical considerations have presented a significant stumbling block in this research, which has chosen a more personalized, and hence more difficult to anonymize, perspective. Although from the beginning I had determined that it would be out of the question to name the perpetrator, I did not initially consider the extent to which harm was likely for the bully even given the anonymity preserved throughout the work. This, however, proved not to be the only ethical dilemma, and therefore in order to understand, navigate and make sense of the situations that I have encountered, the consideration of narrative ethics has been an important undertaking in this research (Adams 2008). The British Educational Research Association (BERA) was my initial information source when looking for direction as to how to approach this task ethically, and I discovered that their guidelines for ethical educational research (2004; 2011) encouraged confidentiality, informed consent and rights to privacy for all participants, with the objective of protecting them from harm. But, interesting as these recommendations were, they appeared to be more suited to a scenario where the research is being done with – or on – strangers with whom there are no prior relationships and where there is no plan for future interaction. There seemed to be a lack of specific rules and regulations to govern the ethical way forward in the many and varied situations that might occur in autoethnography. What seemed more appropriate was the advice given by Ellis (2007) in governing actions and activities within autoethnography, which is simply to adopt the generic principle of 'doing no harm.'

In this autoethnographical piece of work, I have no 'research participants' as such. The research is about me: my story, my perspective and my reactions. I am the 'vulnerable observer' (Behar 1996: 1) and I was confident at the outset that I was adequately prepared to deal with the potential consequences of my writing; my exposure. The reality of writing ethically about myself and my world however, turned out to be more challenging than I expected. As Chatham-Carpenter (2010: 38) said, 'how up-front and personal, in-your-face become the ethical questions, (the most important of all the questions) I think' – and she was right!

My first thoughts on what would be an ethical approach, centred not around the potential for ethical trespass upon the bully, but upon how I would protect *myself* in the process, for autoethnography is as much about protecting ourselves as protecting those implicated in our stories (Chatham-Carpenter 2010). Tolich (2010: 1608) tells researchers to 'treat any autoethnography as an inked tattoo by anticipating the author's future vulnerability', and I was planning to stamp *victim* on my forehead for all (potentially) to see! Telling my story could be detrimental to both my career and my health: career damage in terms of status and standing, and physical and psychological hurt as a result of the possibility of an escalation of abuse from the bully – so it was crucial to manage the level of the exposure contemplated. As the 'researcher, researched' in this narrative, I am faced by a paradox: a *pull towards* revealing a vulnerable, intimate, autoethnographic self versus a *pull away* from fear of the consequences. In choosing to resist the full potential of this methodology, I risk not achieving the therapy I am seeking, yet equally my openness may have profound implications for my future relationships and interactions with colleagues, management and students alike. And 'once a story is told, it cannot be called back. Once told, it is loose in the world' (King 2003: 10), and once entrusted to the permanency of print, writing can become a 'dangerous' practice because texts can be 'misappropriated and used against us' (Smith 1999: 36). I had to consider whether I was ready to be 'outed'; ready to risk the impact on my personal identity (Flemons and Green 2002: 93), given that 'few have considered (psychologically, physically, materially, or emotionally) the potential harm to researchers when we write about our experiences as we go about our work' (Vickers 2002: 612), I had to make sure that I took great care in navigating what was rapidly becoming a potentially complex and ethical minefield.

Still clinging to the conviction that I was the only participant in my research, I was quite certain at the time that if I were to ensure that the bully could not be recognized in my writing then I would be protected from harm. I firmly believed that my ethical obligations would be discharged as long as I did not identify the bully or our employing institution if I brought together my experiences in fictional format (Watson 2000; Clough 2002; Humphreys and Watson 2009).

However, as time has gone on, I have had to reconsider whether my intentions and behaviours with regard to telling my story have really addressed the issues here, for as I have *tried on* and *worn* my story (Brody 2002), what once seemed to be the ethical 'best fit' in terms of representing my experiences and confronting my issues (Brummett 1984, cited in Adams 2008) now seems less appropriate. Zylinska (2005, cited in Colclasure 2010: 60) encourages us to engage in 'permanent vigilance' – an 'ethics that calls for judgement *always anew*' – and I found myself challenged by the sort of questions that contemporary ethnographers ask themselves when they try to write up their 'data' about other people. Who might I be hurting? How do I balance 'fact' and 'fiction?' How do I write a 'true' ethnography of my experiences? I wanted to speak meaningfully and ethically about my experiences, but in the end I had to consider whether this story was entirely mine to tell. 'Self revelations always involve revelations about others' (Freadman 2004: 128), and as Ellis (2007) says, we do not have an inalienable right to tell the stories of others. Tolich (2010: 1599) expresses curiosity about how the 'rights of the "other" in autoethnography are weighted against the interests of the self when the starting point of the research is one's own sociological imagination and is likely to involve others.' He thinks that Clandinin and Connelly (2000) were right to question whether an author actually owns the story they are telling, for he believes that you cannot ignore the rights of others mentioned in the text.

It was becoming increasingly apparent to me that I needed to pay more attention to the bully's involvement and contribution to my story in the context of research participant. Perhaps I had been somewhat blinkered before by the label *auto*ethnography, but in accepting the bully in this new capacity there were consequences in the telling that I had not previously considered. Similar deliberations were emerging from the field, with autoethnographers such as Ellis moving towards the recognition and acceptance of the responsibilities we have towards those who are characters in our life stories. She described the predicament as 'a quagmire in ethnographic research' (2007: 4): a predicament I was now facing.

This autoethnographical research, which began as an examination of the experiences of a vulnerable self, had now to take into account the observation and revelation of the broader context of that experience. Having accepted that, in writing about myself, I was also writing about others, I could see how I was running the risk that the 'others' in my story might become recognizable to my readers, and that they had not consented to being portrayed in ways that would reveal their identity. Writing about others violates anonymity. Even if these 'others' do not know about the writing, it still violates their rights, for they have not given their permission and they do not have the right of withdrawal or refusal that informed consent provides (Morse 2002). I could understand if the university ethics committee might consider this as a situation where informed consent would be required from the researched. After all, their processes had long been set in place to ensure informed consent, confidentiality, rights to privacy, deception and protecting human subjects from harm where necessary (Johnson 2008). However, the relational issues I am facing here are not the normal focus of institutional ethics applications (Denzin 2003). Research Board and autoethnographers alike may continue to grapple with how to behave ethically towards everyone, but Buber (cited in Ellis 2007: 55) says that in the end it comes down to doing what is necessary to be 'true to one's character and responsible for one's actions and their consequences on others'; in other words, the practice of *relational ethics*. But relational ethics is about having and valuing mutual respect and dignity between researcher and researched (Lincoln 1995; Brooks 2006): it is about acknowledging interpersonal bonds with others and initiating and maintaining communication (Bergum 1998, cited in Ellis 2007; Slattery and Rapp 2003). The practice of workplace bullying meanwhile is at the other end of the spectrum and involves the 'abuse of power, intrusion of self, imposition of will and destruction of the individual' (Field 1996: 5). Criticism masquerades as communication, and the relationship between the bully and the victim is tense and anxious. This presents an inherent difficulty in honouring relational responsibilities and yet still endeavouring to present the lived experience of bullying in a complex and truthful way for readers (Ellis 2007).

Where does this leave me? How is this research affected? Well ... my writing may be seen as hazardous in that it requires a significant use of self-disclosure and honesty, which may be distressing or difficult for me, the researcher (Johnstone 1999). I could consider the option of 'mindful slippage' (Medford 2006: 853) and remove the highly personal and potentially harmful elements from my story, for qualitative research accounts are characterized by absences resulting from what cannot be repeated because it should not be stated (Rappert 2010). Frank says that the best way forward is to be open about the choices we have made and the priorities we have set, and to be receptive to people's responses to our 'moral maturity and emotional honesty' so that 'we engage in the unfinalized dialogue of seeking the good' (2004: 191). My self-narrative may pose a threat to my audience, where reading my story could result in uncomfortable feelings, identification or insights on the part of the reader (Bochner and Ellis 1996). Yet by choosing not to share a traumatic experience out of feelings of responsibility towards others, the harm to myself may continue unabated and the opportunity to help others could be lost (Adams 1992). My portrayal of the lives of my characters 'is inevitably a violation' for my words can never adequately encompass the whole person (Josselson 1996: 62). Therefore, if I were to assume that everyone in my story would read it (Ellis 2007), the application of Sikes' (forthcoming) family and friends 'litmus test' would ensure that all participants in my research are being ethically treated. Lastly, if I cannot guarantee anonymity for my 'others' despite fictionalization and characterization then seeking informed consent might be viewed (by some) as an option. I do not seek to criticize this ethical mandate in general, but I must emphasize how a seemingly neutral practice would seriously affect the construction and sharing of this narrative (Adams 2008). If qualitative research is restricted to only those who had given explicit consent, then enquiries whose aim is to produce accounts of social phenomena would likely decrease (Hammersley and Atkinson 1995).

As a retrospective exercize, it would open a 'can of worms'. Seeking informed consent in these specific circumstances would guarantee that the sharing of my story be subjected to psychic and ethical violence. It would influence what can and cannot be shared and who can and cannot explicitly be included. Most importantly of all, it would make me extremely vulnerable by putting myself right back in harm's way (Tolich 2010). The only possible outcome would be self-censorship, 'the most dangerous of all possible types of censorship' (Anderson 2006: 13), for I have no doubt that the bully would refuse permission. This would effectively silence my voice, making it impossible to 'heal and get on with life' (Ellis 2007: 24). It is important to consider here whether the well-being of the researcher is always less important than the well-being of the other, even others who have behaved badly? Ellis (2007: 25) believes not always. 'Sometimes you may decide not to take your work back to those you write about'.

Instructions, advice, considerations and options have been coming at me from all directions, yet I am still stuck as to the best way forward. I tried to ensure anonymity for both myself and the 'others' in my story from the start: to protect everyone. I endeavoured not to hurt or offend by adopting fictionalization and characterization, or by changing names – even though Davis (1991, cited in Morse 2002) says that this would have a negative impact on the value of the study – and have worked hard to ensure that this will not be the case. As Ellis (2007: 25) says, 'in the best of all worlds, all of those involved in our studies will feel better. But sometimes they won't; you won't.' Despite not feeling good about it, I find it difficult to ignore the fundamental personal characteristics that have played their part in my 'victimhood' from the beginning: characteristics common to the 'bullied person profile' and identified by Field as 'standing up for what is right' and being 'uncompromising' in terms of 'moral standards' (1996: 111).

In the end ...

The intent of this chapter was to contribute to the current debate on autoethnography as a research approach in the context of workplace bullying in UK Higher Education. It has demonstrated the forces driving the prevalence of workplace bullying within the sector whilst portraying the prevalence of some of the current methodological debates around research into this phenomenon. It has also shown the affordances and limitations of autoethnography in this context, focusing in the process on the implications of such research for both the target and the perpetrator of workplace bullying.

My particular aspirations for the research were that it would enable me to achieve greater, and hopefully healing, insights into workplace bullying. And there is no doubt that my understanding of the problem itself, and the context in which I have experienced it, have increased dramatically, for as Hughes (1999: 282, cited in Haynes 2006) has said, reflection on one's experiences can 'enable learning from experience.' He has also said however that reflection can be empowering for the researcher, yet at the end of this research I believe that my voice has lost rather than gained power, for despite my personal intentions as autoethnographer, the fact is that my research has taken place within the shared public experience of HE, and as such has been impacted upon by a variety of 'general and perpetual dialogue[s] about life possibilities' (Bruner 1995, cited in Haynes 2006: 206). The 'life possibilities' that have emerged largely concern ethical consternation regarding what might be regarded as appropriate protection for both the researched and the researcher and how to go about providing that protection.

As the research has progressed and the environment in HE has become ever more challenging, I have become more and more conscious that subjectivity can be unpleasant and potentially dangerous (Ellis and Flaherty 1992). Even when associated with an important topic such as workplace bullying, there is concern as to whether the sometimes extreme emotional, cognitive and physical experiences relating to the phenomenon are too unsettling and possibly risky to reveal given the current cost cutting, career curbing climate that currently exists within HE in the UK. Although the voice of the autoethnographical researcher should be valued for its potential to depict the unpleasant and the dangerous, thought has to be given as to the potential negative impacts of the research occurring as a result of that voice, on the perpetrator, the target and indeed the organization, given the status quo. This is not to be dismissive of the benefits of autoethnography that have been demonstrated earlier in the chapter, both in organizational research in general and HE in particular, for it is becoming increasingly popular (Doloriert and Sambrook 2009). Instead, it is merely suggested that further consideration be given to the impact of potentially controversial autoethnographical data about workplace bullying on institutions experiencing the unrelenting turbulent working environment that presently comprises HE within the UK and the staff within them.

Ultimately it has been 'further consideration' of these challenges, relating particularly to protecting those involved in this research, that has led me to believe that, despite the perpetrator not being named, revealing my identity as author of this research is akin to revealing her/his identity. As a result, a serious dilemma has emerged regarding the ethics of placing this research in the public domain having not sought permission (for the reasons identified earlier) for her/his involvement. On publication, both the bully and the institution will be labelled in the same way that I have been labelled as a victim, and I have concerns that my career may suffer from my writing. Therefore, after much consideration and some sadness due to the constraining effect this course of action may have on my 'voice', I have chosen to protect the identities of all participants through 'going to press' using a pseudonym.

References

Adams, A. (1992) *Bullying at Work: How to Confront and Overcome it*, London: Virago.

Adams, T. E. (2008) A review of narrative ethics, *Qualitative Inquiry*, 14: 175–94.

Anderson, G. (2006), Carving out time and space in the managerial university, *Journal of Organisational Change*, 19 (5): 578–92.

Atkinson, P.A. (2006) Rescuing autoethnography, *Journal of Contemporary Ethnography*, 35 (4): 400–4.

Becker, H. S. (1967) Whose Side Are We On?, *Social Problems*, 14 (3), Winter, 1967: 239–47.

Behar, R., (1996) *The Vulnerable Observer: Anthropology that Breaks your Heart*, Boston: Beacon Press.

Bochner, A. P. and Ellis, C. (1996), 'Talking over Ethnography', in C. Ellis and A. P. Bochner (eds) *Composing Ethnography*: 13–45. Walnut Creek, CA: AltaMira.

British Educational Research Association. Available at www.bera.ac.uk/

Brody, H. (2002) *Stories of Sickness*, (2nd edn), Oxford: Oxford University Press.

Brooks, M. (2006), Man-to-man: A body talk between male friends, *Qualitative Inquiry*, 12: 185–207.

Chatham-Carpenter, A. (2010) Do Thyself No Harm: Protecting Ourselves as Autoethnographers, *Journal of Research Practice*, 6 (1).

Clandinin, D. J., and Connelly, F. M. (2000) *Narrative Enquiry: Experience and Story in Qualitative Research*, San Francisco: Jossey-Bass.

Clough, P. (2002) *Narratives and Fictions in Educational Research*, Buckingham: Open University Press.

Colclasure, D. (2010) The Ethics of Cultural Studies: Review of Joanna Zylinska, The Ethics of Cultural Studies, *Other Voices*, 4 (1), March 2010. Available at www.othervoices.org/4.1/dcolclasure/index.php, accessed 3 April 2012.

Cowan, R. L. (2012) It's Complicated: Defining Workplace Bullying from the Human Resource Professional's Perspective, *Management Communication Quarterly*. Available at mcq.sagepub.com/content/early/2012/02/0893318912439474, accessed 04 April 2012.

Delamont, S. (2007) Arguments against Auto-Ethnography, *Qualitative Researcher*, 4: 2–4.

Denzin, N. (1989) *Interpretive Interactionism: Applied social research methods series, Vol. 16*, Newbury Park CA: Sage Publications.

—. (2003) *Performance ethnography: Critical pedagogy and the politics of culture*, Thousand Oaks, CA: Sage Publications.

De Vita, G., and Case, P. (2003) Rethinking the Internationalisation Agenda in UK Higher Education, *Journal of Further and Higher Education*, 27 (4).

Doloriert, C., and Sambrook, S, (2009) Ethical confessions of the "I" of autoethnography: the student's dilemma, *Qualitative Research in Organizations and Management: An International Journal*, 4, (1): 27–45.

Drucker, P. E. (1992) The new society of organisations, *Harvard Business Review*, September–October 1992.

Einarsen, S. (1999) The nature and causes of bullying at work, *International Journal of Manpower*, 20 (1/2): 16–27.

Einarsen, S., Hoel, H., Zapf, D. and C. L. Cooper (eds) (2003) *Bullying and Emotional Abuse in the Workplace: International Perspectives in Research and Practice*, Taylor and Francis: London.

Ellis, C. (2004) *The Ethnographic I: A Methodological Novel about Autoethnography*, Walnut Creek, CA: AltaMira.

—(2007) Telling Secrets, Revealing Lives Relational Ethics in Research With Intimate Others, *Qualitative Inquiry*, 13 (1): 3–29.

Ellis, C., Adams, T. E., and Bochner, A. P. (2011) Autoethnography: An Overview, *Forum: Qualitative Social Research*, 12 (1), Art. 10 – January 2011.

Ellis, C., and Flaherty, M. G. (1992) (eds) *Investigating Subjectivity: Research on lived experience*, London: Sage Publications.

Field, T. (1996) *Bully in Sight: How to Predict, Resist, Challenge and Combat Workplace Bullying*, Didcot, Oxfordshire: Success Unlimited.

Flemmons, D., and Green, S. (2002) 'Stories that conform/stories that transform: a conversation in four parts', in A. Bochner. and C. Ellis (eds) *Ethnographically Speaking: Autoethnography Literature, and Aesthetics*, New York: AltaMira Press: pp. 87–94.

Fournier, S. (1998) Consumers and their brands: Developing relationship theory in consumer research, *Journal of Consumer Research*, 20: 343–74.

Freadman, R. (2004) 'Decent and indecent: Writing my father's life', in J. P. Eakin (ed.) *The ethics of life writing*, Ithaca, NY: Cornell University Press, pp. 121–46.

Further and Higher Education Act (1992). Available at: www.legislation.gov.uk/ukpga/1992/13/contents, accessed 22 May 2012.

Hammersley, M., and Atkinson, P. (1995) *Ethnography: Principles in Practice*, (2nd edn), London: Routledge: 263–87.

Hannabus, S. (2000) Being there: Ethnographic research and autobiography, *Library Management*, 21 (2): 99–107.

Haynes, K. (2006) INSIDER ACCOUNT. A therapeutic journey? Reflections on the effects of research on researcher and participants, *Qualitative Research in Organizations and Management: An International Journal*, 1 (3): 204–21.

Hoel, H., and Stalin, D. (2003) 'Organisational antecedents of workplace bullying', in S. Einarsen, H. Hoel, D. Zapf and C.L. Cooper (eds) Bullying and Emotional Abuse in the Workplace: International Perspectives in Research and Practice, London: Taylor and Francis, pp. 203–18.

Humphreys, M., and Watson, T. J. (2009) 'Ethnographic practices: from "writing-up ethnographic research" to "writing ethnography"', in S. Ybema, D. Yanow, H. Wels, and F. Kamsteeg (eds), *Organizational Ehnography: Studying the Complexities of Everyday Organizational Life*, London: Sage Publications, pp. 40–55.

Jenkins, M., Winefield, H., and Sarris, A. (2011) Consequences of being accused of workplace bullying: an exploratory study, *International Journal of Workplace Health Management*, 4 (1): 33–47.

Johnson, T. S. (2008) Qualitative Research in Question: A narrative of disciplinary power with/in the IRB, *Qualitative Inquiry*, 14: 212–32.

Josselsson, R. (1996) 'On writing other people's lives: Self-analytical reflections of a narrative researcher', in R. Josselsson (ed.) *Ethics and Process in the Narrative Study of Lives*, Thousand Oaks, CA: Sage, pp. 60–77.

Kinchin, D. (2005) *Post Traumatic Stress Disorder: The Invisible Injury*, Didcot, Oxfordshire: Success Unlimited.

King, T. (2003) The truth about stories, in D. J. Clandinin (2006) 'Narrative inquiry: a methodology for studying lived experience', *Research Studies in Music Education*, 27 (44): 44.

Lewis, D. (2004) Bullying at work: the impact of shame among university and college lecturers, *British Journal of Guidance and Counselling*, 32 (3): 281–99.

Lincoln, Y. (1995) Emerging criteria for quality in qualitative and interpretive research, *Qualitative Inquiry*, 1: 275–89.

Luft, Luzio-Lockett, A. (1995) Enhancing relationships within organisations: an examination of a proactive approach to 'bullying at work', *Employee Counselling Today*, 7: 12–22.

Maguire, M. H. (2006) Autoethnography: Answerability/Responsibility in Authoring Self and Others in the Social Sciences/Humanities, *Forum: Qualitative Social Research*, 7 (2), Art. 16 – March 2006.

Medford, K. (2006) Caught with a Fake ID: Ethical Questions About Slippage in Autoethnography, *Qualitative Inquiry*, 12 (5): 853–64.

Morse, J. (2002) Writing My Own Experience, *Qualitative Health Research*, 12, (9): 1159–60.

Orwell, G. (2004) *Why I Write*, London: Penguin.

Polkinghorne, D. E. (1987) *Methodology for the Human Sciences: Systems of Inquiry*, New York: State University of New York Press.

Plummer, K. (1995) *Telling Sexual Stories: Power, Change and Social Worlds*, London: Routledge.

Rappert, B. (2010) Revealing and concealing secrets in research: the potential for the absent, *Qualitative Research*, 10 (5): 571–87.

Rayner, C., Sheehan, M., and Barker, M. (1999) Theoretical approaches to the study of bullying at work, *International Journal of Manpower*, 20 (1/2): 11–6.

Rushton, J. (2001) 'Managing Transformation', in D. Warner and D. Palfreyman (eds) (2001) *The State of UK Higher Education: Managing Change and Diversity*, Buckingham: Open University Press, pp. 169–77.

Seigne, E., Coyne, I., Randal, P., and Parker, J. (2007) Personality traits of bullies as a contributory factor in workplace bullying: An exploratory study, *International Journal of Organization Theory and Behavior*, 10: 118–32.

Shank, R. C. (1990) *Tell Me a Story: A New Look at Real and Artificial Memory*, Cambridge: Cambridge University Press.

Sikes, P. (forthcoming) 'Truth, truths and treating people properly: ethical considerations for researchers who use narrative and auto/biographical approaches', in I. Goodson, A. M. Loveless and D. Stephens (eds) *Explorations in Narrative Research*. Rotterdam: Sense Publishers.

Silverman, D. (1999) *Doing Qualitative Research: A Practical Handbook*, London: Sage Publications.

Slattery, P. and Rapp, D. (2003) *Ethics and the Foundations of Education: Teaching Convictions in a Postmodern World*, Boston: Allyn & Bacon.

Smith, B. (1999) The abyss: Exploring depression through a narrative of the self, *Qualitative Inquiry*, 5: 264–79.

Sparkes, A. C. (2000) Autoethnography and narratives of self: Reflections on criteria in action, *Sociology of Sport Journal*, 17: 21–43.

—(2002) *Telling Tales in Sport and Physical Activity: A Qualitative Journey*, Exeter: Human Kinetics.

Stronach, I., and Maclure, M. (1997) *Educational Research Undone: the postmodern embrace*, Buckingham: Open University Press.

Tal, K. (1996) *Worlds of Hurt: Reading the Literatures of Trauma*, Cambridge: Cambridge University Press.

Tehrani, N. (2004) Bullying: a source of chronic post-traumatic stress, *British Journal of Guidance and Counselling*, 32 (3), August 2004.

Thomas, H. and Cornuel, E. (2011) Business school futures: evaluation and perspectives, *Journal of Management Development*, 30 (5): 444–50.

Thomas, M. (2005) Bullying among support staff in a higher education institution, *Health Education*, 105 (4): 273–88.

Tolich, M., (2010) A Critique of Current Practice: Ten Foundational Guidelines for Autoethnographers, *Qualitative Health Research*, 20 (12): 1599–610.

Trahar, S. (2008) It starts with once upon a time, *Compare: A Journal of Comparative and International Education*, 38 (3): 259–66.

—(2009), Beyond the Story Itself: Narrative Inquiry and Autoethnography in Intercultural Research in Higher Education, *Forum: Qualitative Social Research*, 10 (1), Art. 30 – January 2009.

Vickers, M. H. (2002) Researchers as Storytellers: Writing on the Edge-And Without a Safety Net, *Qualitative Inquiry*, 8 (5): 608–21.

—(2008) Researchers as Storytellers: Writing on the Edge-And Without a Safety Net, *Qualitative Inquiry*, 18 (5): 608–21.

Watson, T. J. (2000) Ethnographic fiction science: making sense of managerial work and organisational research processes with Caroline and Terry, *Organization*, 7 (3): 31–8.

Chapter 5

'The teeth and the tongue'

A narrative inquiry journey in Ghana

Janetta Sika Akoto

Introduction

This chapter shares a methodological journey. In my research into the perceptions and experiences of nine senior women administrators in four Ghanaian public universities, the focus was on their interactions with their academic colleagues in order to determine their perceptions and experiences of this working relationship. Narrative inquiry was the methodological choice for exploring these perceptions and experiences because of the possibilities it offered in researching the small group of participants.

I begin with a brief explanation of the title of this chapter. This is followed by sharing some thoughts on narrative inquiry. Next I share the methodological dilemma encountered in the research journey, focusing on some conflicts in the application of the methodological choices in the study. In sharing with the reader 'the teeth grinding against the tongue' of my engagement with narrative inquiry, I shall illustrate how I blended my indigenous ways of knowing with a methodological approach I was at first strongly attracted to and subsequently subjected to critical reflection to ensure that it was in tune with the sensitivities of my own culture. The role that autoethnography played here is explained. Finally, I highlight the spaces it opened for the application of creativity in the research, rendering it more widely accessible.

The title

The title of this chapter is developed from the proverbial Akan Adinkra[1] symbol 'ɛse ne tɛkrɛma' [translation: The teeth and the tongue]. 'The teeth and the tongue', according to this symbol, play interdependent roles in the mouth. They may come into conflict, but they work together for the common good. The complex nature of this symbol, which signifies friendship and interdependence in the Ghanaian Akan society, and the need to find a mid-point or consensus informed and guided the selection of my methodological approach as I embarked on this journey. Through engaging in narrative inquiry and reconnecting with my indigenous ways of knowing, I became compelled to create a fusion of knowledge amicably dependent on both the Ghanaian and 'Western' contexts. There was a need for me to blend the 'new methodology' and knowledge as perceived in my cultural context as the way forward to researching in it. This painstaking process of finding the mid-point, being responsive to the philosophical assumptions of my methodology and my indigenous knowledge was like the teeth grinding against the tongue.

The Akan Adinkra symbol 'ɛse ne tɛkrɛma'. (Illustration by Kwadwo Ohene-Akoto)

First thoughts about narrative inquiry

Selecting an appropriate methodology is fundamental to any research undertaken as this forms the foundation on which it is developed and built upon. In knowing, understanding and journeying along a chosen methodological path, researchers are able to advance the aims that guide their research endeavour. Being seduced by the potential of narrative inquiry to interpret the meaning of the experiences of the nine senior women administrators in their work relationships with their academic counterparts in four of Ghana's public universities, I began to familiarize myself with the more complex debates about the methodology. The use of narrative inquiry is assuming a higher profile within social science research, and involves assembling stories, whether written, verbal, oral or visual, with a focus on capturing the meanings that people (with both their personal and social stories) attribute to their lived experiences (Clandinin and Connelly 2000; Gubrium and Holstein 2009; Riessman 2008; Josselson 1996; Webster and Mertova 2007). Narrative inquiry can include a range of approaches and methods such as autobiography, informal conversation and life stories, and seeks to analyze the narratives collected as stories about social phenomena (Lieblich et al. 1998).

Trahar (2006) indicates that narrative inquiry may be interpretivist, yet it also draws on postmodernism and post-structuralism. Riessman and Speedy (2007: 428) point out that narrative in human science 'has "realist", "post-modern", and "constructionist" strands'. I positioned myself within a broadly interpretive perspective, bearing in mind Usher's (1996: 18) assertion that 'in social research, knowledge is concerned not with generalisation, prediction and control but with interpretation, meaning, illumination'. My aim was to make meaning out of the stories my participants considered significant to their work lives. Indeed I share the view held by Pinnegar and Daynes (2007: 4), that what 'narrative researchers hold in common is the study of stories or narratives or descriptions of a series of events', and that researchers use narrative inquiry as both a method and phenomenon of study. Narratives are the primary devices by which human existence is rendered significant and for, 'linking individual human actions and events into interrelated aspects of an understandable composite' (Polkinghorne 1988: 13). The human centredness of narrative inquiry, according to some scholars, occurs in context, and is spoken or written through the lens of both the narrator and the researcher. Trahar (2008: 261), for example, writes that 'Another significant difference between narrative inquiry and many other qualitative methodological approaches is the extent to which the researcher's story becomes intrinsic to the study'. From familiarizing myself with the debates around narrative inquiry, my own view was that it was going to offer a wide range of possibilities not only to make known the stories of my participants, but also forms of knowledge in my context. For me, narrative inquiry was going to serve the dual purpose of immersing myself in knowledge from my context and advancing it using a methodological approach that I had subjected to intensive scrutiny in order to ensure its congruence with that context.

'The teeth grinding against the tongue'

Internal conflicts and dilemmas preceded my methodological journey when I settled on the choice of narrative inquiry. In 2008, when undergoing my research methodology training for my PhD, I discovered that research could be approached using narrative inquiry. My background in theatre studies and this methodological approach instantly became intertwined, and I made a firm decision to explore it further. Immediately, I thought that such an approach could be revolutionary for teaching, learning and research in my home context, although I had doubts about its acceptance as a serious research method, given that quantitative research and the more 'traditional' qualitative approaches are the ones that continue to be given credibility in Ghana. The internal conflicts and dilemmas were also about my own ability to negotiate this approach, which was new to me. Narrative inquiry, in my view, was steeped in a philosophy foreign to my culture and it therefore demanded a greater responsibility in its application in my context. Embarking on this journey, the most important factors that kept leading me to methodological crossroads were how to negotiate the process so that I would find a balance between my responsibility to what I perceived as the demands of the UK academic context and my own responsibility towards the sensitivities of my cultural background. The challenge, in my estimation, was how the differences in the ways of knowing in the two contexts could co-exist in harmony perhaps to enrich and highlight the diversity in knowledge in both. I wanted to shine a torch on my indigenous knowledge often overlooked as 'legitimate knowledge' in mainstream academic discourses. Dovetailing the ways of knowing and education in the UK with my Ghanaian background was my own response to finding a fit for a methodological journey that had begun in a context that I perceived to be informed by 'Western' thought and assumptions. I did not want my application of narrative inquiry in the Ghanaian context to be perceived as another form of academic colonialism. In particular, I was influenced by Oyèwùmí's (1997) concern that many scholars in the West:

> Have assumed the Western constructions as universal … In African Studies, historically and currently, the creation, constitution, and production of knowledge have remained the privilege of the West …Western conceptual schemes and theories have become so widespread that all scholarship, even by Africans, utilizes them unquestionably.
>
> (Oyèwùmí: x)

Transferring narrative inquiry into my context was obviously going to have many implications including the concern raized by Oyèwùmí. I needed to be careful about carrying out narrative inquiry in a manner that was in tune with the sensitivities of my context and was apprehensive about falling into the vicious circle, where many African scholars have been accused of furthering academic neo-colonialism as they produced academic writings that are not grounded in their own philosophical perspectives.

Bearing in mind that many African scholars, including Oyěwùmí (1997) and Manuh (2007) have critiqued how academics in the West also tend to generalize their peculiar experiences on many issues in academic discourse when it comes to Africa's experience, resulting in dislocating cultures, I did not want to appear to be working without reference to these concerns. Manuh's (2007: 141) words kept ringing in my ears:

> Many scholars see their work as subordinate to that of Northern scholars, who rarely refer to the work of African scholars, while they have to refer to work of Northern scholars to show their awareness and familiarity with debates elsewhere and to stand the chance of getting their work published in international journals.

These complexities of negotiating alternative ways of knowing and representation were apparent in my research. The challenge I began to encounter was how to negotiate this transposition of narrative inquiry along with all its embedded theoretical assumptions (that I perceived to be typically Western) to reflect the unique experience of my participants and my context. Was I also advancing the dominance of the West's knowledge and implications of its privileged position as a reference point for studies about my context by my choice of methodology? Was I going to apply Western paradigms to my work to achieve something uniquely Ghanaian or, by doing so, would I be producing a distortion of my story? Bearing in mind the concerns expressed earlier by the two esteemed African academics, I recognized the need to fuse many pieces of the puzzle in my story with this new methodology to project uncharted knowledge in my context as a new way of learning about that context and to generate debates on new ways of doing research in it. But how was I going to do this when my educational background was still tied to the apron strings of its colonial past?

Breaking free from the colonial past and unlearning positivism

I became quite reflective about the mode of education in my context that leans heavily on its colonial past and began to question the impact of that foundation of education on me and the role played by Europeans and colonialism in changing my orientation about what constituted legitimate knowledge. As a people, the Akans of Ghana (a tribe where I take my lineage) have relied on oral tradition as a way of preserving their history but, contrary to perceptions in other cultures that ours is entirely an oral tradition, there have also been alternative ways of knowing, such as the use of symbolism and drawings which still exist in modern Akan society today. These alternatives had not been clear to me until this recent self-awakening was spurred on by Pinnegar and Daynes (2007: 5) who maintain that narrative inquiry employs a number of approaches, methods and strategies, including metaphors, 'to analyze and make general sense of experience' which abound in my cultural context. That my context had unique forms of documenting its history and knowledge, not only oral, opened up avenues for exploration in my study. I discovered that I had an advantage of living the experience of oral tradition, which had been part of my upbringing both at home and in the extended socio-cultural environment. I knew that I could also rely on my knowledge of symbolism (and symbols) and proverbs in my context to enrich my study.

The possibilities this methodology offered also clashed with my own previous research experience, which leaned heavily towards positivism, and, though I was inclined towards narrative inquiry, positivism continued to beckon. I encountered internal struggles in unlearning positivism as, in my estimation, this was one way of engaging and immersing myself in my chosen methodology. I encountered many positivists when I decided what to study, too. Indeed the issue that kept coming up from personal friends who were experienced academics centred on how to go about researching my topic. Some people suggested that I undertake a comparative study between Ghana and the UK in order to achieve rigour. Others suggested I needed to work with larger populations than my proposal outlined because the small number of people that I proposed to work with was more suitable for a pilot study. These suggestions were perhaps well intended, but it also highlighted the slow acceptance (perhaps non-acceptance) of narrative inquiry in Ghanaian academia and particularly in my context. It brought home forcefully my belief that this form of research may not be viewed as serious academic work where I come from. The resultant effect of my interactions with experienced academics back home in Ghana was the self-doubt, which reared its ugly head, coupled with my own insecurities as a novice narrative inquirer on an uncharted course. I wanted to explore in depth and not in quantity (or at least not in huge numbers), and I perceived narrative inquiry could better serve my purpose. Yet there was the question of the expectations of the academic community in my home country that are perhaps still quite set in their preference for quantitative and traditional qualitative methodologies. Pryor et al.'s (2009) publication entitled *Exploring the Fault Lines of Cross-cultural Collaborative Research* highlights the newness of qualitative research methodology in the Ghanaian context when some of the contributors also alluded to their deficiencies in that research methodology. Perhaps this too is an indication of their continued association with a research culture still steeped in quantitative methodologies.

Looking for ways to document human experiences remained my primary interest, something that paid attention to subjectivities and of interest to those being researched. But was I veering too far off the charted course? If the way that qualitative research was carried out was still in its formative stage and quite a challenge to some researchers, as highlighted by Pryor et al. (2009) then how was narrative inquiry going to fare both in my hands and in my context? I was interested in finding out how my participants constructed the world around them through their own interpretations of the multiple perspectives it embodied (Glesne 2006). And yet the internal conflict experienced over the choice of narrative inquiry as a methodology for my research that I have highlighted was a source of constant challenge in the journey.

'The unprepared researcher'

The newness of narrative inquiry in my context was also reflected in the challenges I encountered during my interactions with some of my participants during the interview process. There were challenges, for example, in negotiating narrative interviewing. Following advice about narrative interviewing that I read in the literature on narrative inquiry may not have worked for me as expected in the field. I chose to share my own stories of my work experiences during the interview session to encourage reciprocal gestures from my participants. But sharing my stories in the course of the interviews did not unlock the pouring out of stories but rather shifted the power uncomfortably in my encounter with some of my participants. I became the poor inchworm crawling along in my misery and woes of working in higher education; I felt judged at times. I felt like I was responsible for my peculiar experiences, and some of my participants unknowingly contributed to this feeling. I came out of some interview sessions feeling rather little and helpless, regretting sharing my 'victim stories'. This feeling was also aggravated because I did not have a set of questions to ask. It became obvious that some of my participants would have loved to have questions (more specifically, questionnaires) sent to them beforehand. One of my participants remarked that the encounter would have been more fruitful if I had done this. Personally, I considered our meeting very fruitful, but perhaps she did not because she thought she was not well prepared for our encounter. As mentioned earlier, perhaps the long association with quantitative and more traditional methods of qualitative research had some role to play. My mastery over the methodology adopted for the study was in doubt. In so many ways I also got the impression that I appeared quite unprepared in their eyes. When I explained that the method I was employing views having a definite set of questions for an interview session somewhat limiting, I got the impression that they were very sceptical. I, as a narrative inquirer, had also struggled with not having definite questions for the same reasons, therefore my own personal disposition, steeped in my earlier academic training, and my current journey into narrative inquiry began to clash. The affordances of narrative were to allow the stories to emerge through following trails of our conversations, and yet the unspoken demand of my context was a direct opposite. A consequence of this was to portray me as an inexperienced and unprepared researcher in the eyes of some of my participants.

The value of autoethnography

Autoethnography was also a tool adopted to help me to infuse myself into the study. A key area for reflection is that of the researcher's status within the research arena. Holiday (2002), acknowledging the subjective role of qualitative researchers, notes how imperative it is for them to make transparent their perspectives, as they are pivotal to the written study. Research involving insiders, such as I was, carries with it the assumptions that backgrounds, insights and sensitivities will be understood and appreciated in a way not open to an outsider researcher. I agree with Hockey's (1993: 119) assertion that if the insider researcher shares the social world of the research participants there is less likelihood of experiencing the 'culture shock of disorientation'. However, prior acquaintance, underlying personal bias and preconceived ideas can adversely affect a research journey. Moch (2000) expresses this apparent conflict, as a constant source of inner struggle prone to ethical concerns, but also as a rich source of great reflection. This conflict was evident to me and was exacerbated by my shared background with my participants. Researching the professional lives of colleagues from the insider perspective exposed my own expectations that my participants would respond to the research in a particular way. However, the advantages in my choice of approach were very effective in gaining access and building trust. The intrinsic value brought to my study by being a member of the group under scrutiny was, in my experience, priceless.

Autoethnography has multiple perspectives and the debates about categorizing and defining it as a method of research have generated varied scholarly opinions. Reed-Danahay (1997: 9) has attempted to synthesize these views by grouping them into those scholars who tie autoethnography to 'ethnographic autobiography or to native autobiography'. Autoethnography as a genre of writing and research connects the personal to the cultural, placing the self within a social context (Reed-Danahay 1997). It combines autobiography, the story of one's own life, with ethnography and the study of a particular social group. In autoethnography, the researcher also becomes the primary participant through the research in the process of writing personal stories and ethnographic narratives. Though my aim was not to be the primary participant, my focus was how to interweave my own experiences where they clearly resonated with those of my participants. In so doing, I began studying a social group while sharing my own experiences where applicable. Chang (2008) notes that autoethnography offers a research method friendly to researchers and readers because autoethnographic texts are engaging and enable researchers to gain a cultural insight of self in relation to others, on which cross-cultural partnerships can be built. 'Autoethnography is not about focusing on self alone, but about searching for understanding of others (culture/society) through the self' (Chang 2008: 48–9). Holt (2003: 2) also argues that 'autoethnography is usually written in the first person and features dialogue, emotion and self-consciousness'. As I explored autoethnography, I was particularly drawn to it as a genre of writing because it 'entails the incorporation of elements of one's own life experience when writing about others' ((Reed-Danahay 1997: 7). Writing about myself as part of my research was, however, new to me.

In writing about the self, my readings on narrative inquiry urged me to write using pronouns that reflected the first person, but how was I going to use 'I' and 'me' to reflect a cultural context that did not promote individualism but communality? Writing and expressing issues to reflect the personal was particularly difficult. I began to relate to Riessman's (2008) observation that a Western narrative convention for writing about personal experiences privileges the individual over family or the community. How was I going to use autoethnography so that it embraced the inherent communal spirit of my context and was also responsive to my imagined conventions of the contexts within which the methodological approach had developed? As a strategy, in talking about the self, I also shared a history of a group of people. I used personal stories that reflected the larger society and also satisfied the autoethnographic experience I set out to share. The adoption of autoethnography helped me to tap into the oral tradition and the art of storytelling from my context. This made it necessary for me to write outside the 'box'.

Writing outside the 'box'

The fusion of my cultural context with that of my context of study required that I work outside the 'box'. Therefore my writing wove together personal stories and histories of my people. This part enabled me to share insights and perspectives from my people that had been handed down to me orally. I used emails as a conduit to relay these stories, which had direct bearing on the narratives, shared by my participants. The imaginary email exchanges between my parents and me served a useful purpose of inserting other knowledge from the context of the research. The information supplied in the emails incorporated my personal stories and some legends of the Akan people of Ghana that have added depth and a rich dimension to the narrative inquiry journey. Writing outside the 'box' was very liberating because it emboldened me to express opinions on issues emanating from the narrative of my participants through other voices. Choices about which oral information to incorporate in the emails were determined by the experiences shared in the narratives of my participants.

Each email was strategically sandwiched as a form of prologue to a subsequent chapter or as an epilogue to a preceding one. The narratives in the emails gave snippets of my journey, touching on the challenges encountered as I navigated this rather unknown terrain as well as sharing accounts that rendered significant my cultural background. Trahar (2011: 125) writes that 'the fictional construction of experiences is considered to be a legitimate and persuasive form of research reporting', and this is what the incorporation of the emails sought to achieve. The email exchanges never actually took place but are versions of true accounts from those involved. Initially they were based on conversations with my late father, who was fascinated with my choices of methodologies and showed great interest in how this journey would proceed. He sadly passed on before my ideas crystallized, and thereafter I resorted to writing to my mother, recalling some family histories she had shared with me as I was growing up. The stories were about the strength of the women in my family and histories about colonialism in Ghana that could perhaps not necessarily be found in the history books. Her rendition of her realities on the gendered perspective of the Akan society helped in painting for me a more balanced picture that has long eluded Akan women, often seen as helpless, passive recipients of patriarchy.

Another dimension is the practical way the stories in the emails were represented without citing a documented source. This way I was able to infuse legitimate knowledge from my context in my study without constraints, and thus to subvert the academic writing convention, that necessitated citing documented sources to substantiate claims. The need to quote other authors to substantiate claims had been made clear to me throughout my academic training, through reminders from academics, books and articles consulted. Drawing attention to these personal stories and histories employed in the study, which did not necessarily have documented sources to quote, to support arguments proffered had become a crucial concern for me as researcher. I spent a lot of time in reflection over how to make those stories count in my study and the email conduits offered a way forward.

My background in performance arts also came in useful. Dramaturgy as a way of representing aspects of my own history and culture was infused so that parallels could be drawn from the narratives of my participants. Drama was particularly helpful in the application of dialogic/performance analysis (Riessman 2008) to the narratives of my participants. The individual narratives were transformed into scenarios that were situated in meaning emerging between my participants in a social and historical context marked by the multi-voiced chorus in making meaning out of their particular experiences. The drama opened up a space to represent participants' emotions about the hidden internal politics and nuanced experiences in their personal work life narratives. In piecing together the individual narratives into a complete play, meaning emerged between people amidst the personal narratives shared, and in so doing readers and audience were engaged to make their own interpretations of the narratives shared by my participants. Here, too, I was able to insert my opinions thorough a character I created. My character in the play said very little but was very forward in sharing frustrations with the system I was researching. Riessman (2008: 111) notes that in adapting dialogic/performative methods, one should be prepared to acknowledge that audiences will read the narratives in all sorts of ways as 'readers are inherently part of the interpretive process, bringing their positioned identities and cultural filters to interpretation'. One advantage of adopting drama was the ability to disguise the identities of my participants, which was of great importance to some of them.

More spaces open up for exploration...

As I began to mature in my understanding of narrative inquiry, so also did my awareness of the depth and breadth of the flexibility of the methodology. It opened spaces up for exploration. One significant move was the manner in which I managed to blend traditional Akan art through the use of symbols, which also had accompanying proverbs that carried messages about everyday life among the Akan people. (One of the symbols 'ɛse ne tɛkrɛma' was adopted as the title for this chapter).

The critical role symbolism and proverbs played in my methodological journey enabled me to say so much with very few words. Interspersing my recommendations with these proverbs helped in uniquely positioning me to immerse myself in the knowledge of my culture in my concluding words. I employed seven Adinkra symbols of the Akan people of Ghana, namely **'Afuntunmreku Dɛmkyemreku'**[2], **'Nkɔnsɔnkɔnsɔn', 'ɛse ne tɛkrɛma' 'Fihankra', 'obi nka obi', 'boa me na me mmoa wo' and 'nea onnim no sua a, ohu'.** These symbols are significant for the wisdom and the insightful messages they carry about life. Four of the symbols were incorporated into a designed Kente[3] cloth. This piece of art deliberately carried diverse messages of significance to the study in how it offered recommendations and alternative ways of negotiating the work relationships between academics and senior administrators in Ghana's public universities. With the use of these symbols to demonstrate the depth of my indigenous knowledge, particularly in how so much is said with as few words as possible to achieve the desired results, I positioned myself within mainstream knowledge from my context.

(A piece of Kente cloth incorporated with four Adinkra symbols. Designed by Kwadwo Ohene-Akoto)

Finally ... narrative inquiry in Ghana

I agree with Stephens' assertion (2011: 1) that 'we live at a time in which narrative or story is taking a "turn" in the development of qualitative research methodology', and that this calls for a 'fundamentally different ... and more meaningful representation of reality ... more about the constructing of our cultures and identities'.

The significance of this narrative turn for research in Ghana cannot be overemphasized, in view of the context's continued association with more positivist methodologies. The important role stories play in constructing meaning for the way of life of Ghanaian people is reflective and evaluative of experiences and feelings about their world (ibid). The ability of narrative inquiry to follow trails, subjectivities and to achieve resonance opens up new ways of engaging with research in the academic community, for researchers to be more responsive to their audiences and to be clearly in tune with the trend towards a more human-centred research and probing of subjectivities. By engaging with narratives, researchers are more likely to have avenues for communicating research findings to Ghanaian society that are approachable, simplified and responsive to the sensitivities of the larger non-literate population, in a manner that will engender societal (attitudinal) change. What I mean by this is that, in societies where there are a large number of non-literate people, adopting methodologies that are relatable, rather than riddled with complex statistics, will better serve efforts to rally people, to achieve national goals. I also agree with Sikes (2006a) that creative styles of writing, such as the aspects of autoethnography, employed in conjunction with narrative inquiry, are a good way to render academic work more accessible, allowing particular points to be made in a more forceful manner, because they enable a representation of the people being written about in a more humanistic way.

Riessman (2008: 8) indicates that narratives serve many purposes as tools to 'remember, argue, justify, persuade, engage, entertain, and even mislead'. Narrative inquiry enabled me to centre and document aspects of my own culture that hitherto had remained somewhat fragmented and 'informal', and consequently were perhaps not considered legitimate knowledge in academia in either Ghana or the UK. There was a clear sense of direction in my methodological journey that ignited a greater responsibility in me to immerse myself in the knowledge of my people to demonstrate the existence of other forms of knowledge. This reality, as I meandered through the maze and required, like the proverbial Akan Adinkra symbol 'ɛse ne tɛkrɛma', that I had to find the right balance in employing narrative inquiry as the conduit. And through engaging in narrative inquiry and reconnecting with my indigenous ways of knowing, I created a fusion of knowledge amicably dependent on both contexts.

In choosing to work with narrative inquiry, I embarked on a journey of self-awakening. My reflections on the appropriateness of the application of the methodology indicate the flexibility inherent in narrative inquiry as it opened vast avenues for the conduct of my research. Ideas and philosophies from different contexts at times jarred when juxtaposed and yet inspired that self-awakening that I discuss in this chapter. Using narrative inquiry, I delved deeply to share histories and knowledge, centring them on an academic platform. My perception of narrative inquiry as inherently steeped in 'Western' philosophies thus fades. The open spaces it creates continue to challenge me to interrogate and reflect on other ways in which research can be made more accessible in my context.

The challenges juxtaposed against the triumphs in the application of narrative inquiry in the Ghanaian context tell the tale of the proverbial 'ɛse ne tɛkrɛma'. In hindsight, this methodological choice was my journey of self-discovery. I started with a staggering step of self-doubt, coupled with anxiety about the acceptability of narrative inquiry as a serious methodology in my context. A journey of discovery leads to self-awakening. A methodology embedded in philosophical assumptions not necessarily mine became the conduit for sharing narratives from my cultural background. Different philosophical assumptions meet and are juxtaposed. I walked a tight rope that required a careful balancing act. The tongue grinds against the tongue, yet both find that interdependence works for the common good – as I discovered.

References

Akoto, J. S. (2011) *The unsung professionals of higher education: A narrative inquiry into perceptions and experiences of some senior women in administration in universities of Ghana*, unpublished dissertation, University of Bristol.

Berge, L. B. (2007) *Quantitative Research Methods for the Social Sciences*, 6th edn, London: Pearson Education Inc.
Bruce Willis, W. (1998) *The Adinkra dictionary. A visual primer on the language of Adinkra*, Washington, DC: The Pyramid Complex.
Chang, H. (2008) *Autoethnography as Method*, Walnut Creek, CA: Left Coast Press.
Clandinin, J. D. (ed.) (2007) *Handbook of Narrative Inquiry Mapping a Methodology*, Thousand Oaks, CA: Sage Publications.
Clandinin, J. D., and Connelly, F. M. (2000) *Narrative Inquiry Experience and Story in Qualitative Research*, San Francisco, CA: Jossey-Bass.
Clough, P., and Nutbrown, C. (2002) *A Student's Guide to Methodology: Justifying enquiry*, Thousand Oaks, CA: Sage Publications, Inc.
Denzin, N. (1989) *Interpretive Biography*, Newbury Park, CA: Sage Publications.
Glesne, C. (2006) *Becoming Qualitative Researchers: An Introduction*, Boston, MA: Person.
Gubrium, J. F., and Holstein, J. A. (2009) *Analyzing Narrative Reality*, London: Sage Publications.
Hockey, J. (1993) Research methods: Researching peers and familiar settings, *Research Papers in Education*, 8 (2): 199–225.
Holiday, A. (2002) *Doing and Writing Qualitative Research*, London: Sage Publications.
Josselson, R. (2007) 'The ethical attitude in narrative research', in J. D. Clandinin (ed.) *Handbook of Narrative Inquiry Mapping a Methodology*, Thousand Oaks, CA: Sage Publications, Inc, pp. 537–66.
—(ed.) (1996) *Ethics and Process in the Narrative Study of Lives*, London: Sage Publications.
Josselson, R., and Lieblich, A. (eds) (1993) *The Narrative Study of Lives*, Newbury Park, CA: Sage Publications, Inc.
Lieblich, A., Tuval-Mashiach, R., and Zilber, T. (1998) *Narrative Research: Reading, Analysis and Interpretation*, London: Sage Publications.
Manuh, T., Sulley, G., and Budu, J. (2007) *Change and Transformation in Ghana's Publicly Funded Universities: A Study of Experiences, Lessons & Opportunities*, Accra: Woeli Publishing Services in association with Higher Education in Africa and James Currey: Oxford.
Mishler, E. G. (1986) *Research Interviewing: Context and narrative*, Cambridge, MA: Harvard University Press.
—(1999) *Storylines: Craftartists' Narratives of Identity*, Cambridge, MA: Harvard University Press.
Moch, S. D. (2000) *The Researcher Experience in Qualitative Research*, London: Sage Publications.
Oyěwùmí, O. (1997) *The Invention of Women. Making an African sense of Western Gender Discourses*, Minneapolis: University of Minnesota Press.
—(ed.) (2005) *African Gender Studies A Reader*, New York: Houndsmills; Basingstoke: Palgrave Macmillan.
Pinnegar, S., and Daynes, G. J. (2007) 'Locating narrative inquiry historically: Thematics in the turn to narrative', in J. D. Clandinin (ed.) *Handbook of Narrative Inquiry Mapping a Methodology*, Thousand Oaks, CA: Sage Publications, Inc, pp. 3–34.
Polkinghorne, D. E. (1988) *Narrative Knowing and the Human Sciences*, Albany: State University of New York Press.

Pryor, J., Kuupole, A., Kutor, N., Dunne, M., and Adu-Yeboah, C. (2009) Exploring the fault lines of cross-cultural collaborative research, *Compare: A Journal of Comparative and International Education*, 39 (6): 769–82.

Reed-Danahay, D. (1997) 'Introduction', in D. Reed-Danahay (ed.) *Auto/Ethnography*, New York: Berg, pp. 1–17.

Riessman, C. K. (1990) Strategic uses of narrative in presentation of self illness: A research note, *Social Science and Medicine*, 30 (11): 1195–200.

—(1993) *Narrative Analysis*, Newbury Park, CA: Sage Publications Inc.

—(2008) *Narrative Methods for the Human Sciences.* Thousand Oaks, CA: Sage Publications Inc.

Riessman, C. K., and Speedy, J. (2007) 'Narrative inquiry in the psychotherapy profession', in D. J. Clandinin (ed) *Handbook of Narrative Inquiry Mapping a Methodology*, Thousand Oaks, CA: Sage Publications, Inc., pp. 426–56.

Sikes, P. (2006a) Decolonizing research and methodologies: Indigenous peoples and cross-cultural contexts, *Culture & Society*, 14 (3): 349–58.

—(2006b) On dodgy ground? Problematics and ethics in educational research, *International Journal of Research & Method in Education*, 29 (1): 105–17.

Sikes, P. and Gale, K. (2006) 'Narrative approaches to educational research'. Available at http://www.edu.plymouth.ac.uk/resined/, accessed 15 June 2012.

Smorti, A., McKeough, A., Ciucci, E., Pyryt, M., Wilson, N., Sanderson, A., and Fung, T. (2007) What shapes narrative thought? Effects of story type and culture, *Narrative Inquiry*, 17 (2), 329–47.

Speedy, J. (2008) *Narrative Inquiry & Psychotherapy*, New York: Houndmills; Basingstoke: Palgrave Macmillan.

Stephens, D. (2011) Review essay: Narrative and biographical methods in education and social sciences research, *International Journal of Educational Development*: 1–2.

Trahar, S. (2006) 'Introduction. The contribution of narrative research to comparative and international education: An editor's story', in S. Trahar (ed.) *Narrative Research on Learning: Comparative and International Perspectives*, Oxford: Symposium Books, pp. 13–23.

—(2006) 'A part of the landscape: The practitioner researcher as narrative inquirer in an international higher education community', in S. Trahar (ed.) *Narrative Research on Learning: Comparative and International Perspectives*, Oxford: Symposium, pp. 201–19.

—(2008) Narrative methodological approaches: Their contribution to comparative and international education, *Compare*, 38 (3): 259–66.

—(2009) Beyond the story itself: Narrative inquiry and autoethnography, *Intercultural Research in Higher Education*, 10 (1): 30.

—(2011) *Developing Cultural Capability in International Higher Education. A Narrative Inquiry*, Abingdon: Routledge.

Trahar, S., and Hyland, F. (2011) Experiences and perceptions of internationalisation in higher education in the UK, *Higher Education Research & Development*, 30 (5): 623–33.

Webster, L., and Mertova, P. (2007) *Using Narrative Inquiry as a Research Method: An Introduction to Using Critical Event Narrative Analysis in Research on Learning and Teaching*, London: Routledge.

Notes

1 Adinkra symbols have been used as proverbial tools for the examination of the meanings of what the Akans make of life, people and things over time.

2 The Akan Adinkra symbols used were Afuntumireku and Dɛnkyimireku FIG 5.3 [Translation: A Siamese twin (crocodile), who have conjoined stomachs but each struggles for larger portions of food at meal times because they each want to satisfy their taste buds] this symbol cautions against greed, 'Nkɔnsɔnkɔnsɔn', FIG 5.4 [translation: Chain], the promotion of the ideal that in unity and excellent human relations lies strength, 'ɛse ne tɛkrɛma' [translation: The teeth and the tongue] signifies friendship and interdependence. The teeth and the tongue play interdependent roles in the mouth. They may come into conflict, but they need to work together for the common good. 'Fihankra', FIG 5.5 meaning house or compound represents closeness of family and unity. It is also a symbol of security and safety and is used in my study to stress the need for interdependence in the workforce in Ghanaian higher education), 'Boa me na me mmoa wo' FIG 5.6 (Literally meaning 'Help me and let me help you'. The urge is for cooperation and interdependence), 'Obi nka obi', FIG 5.7 ('Bite not one another'. A symbol of peace and harmony) and 'Nea onnim no sua a, ohu', FIG 5.8 ('He who does not know can know from learning'. A symbol of knowledge, life-long learning and continued quest for knowledge).

3 Kente is a hand-woven ceremonial cloth of the people of the Asante kingdom. It is often woven in strips measuring about four inches wide, and sewn together into larger pieces of cloths. (In recent time some artists have also used broad looms to weave the Kente cloth). It comes in various designs, colours and sizes and is worn during very important social and religious occasions. The Kente cloth through its visual representation shares the history, philosophy, ethics, oral literature, moral values and social code of conduct, religious beliefs, political thought and aesthetic principles and culture of the people. The variation used in this chapter is an artistic design from Mr. Kwadwo Ohene-Akoto.

Chapter 6

Seeing with new eyes

Becoming a narrative inquirer in higher education practice

Narina A. Samah

Introduction: Embarking on an inquisitive journey

The American educationalist John Dewey (1938: 38) said 'Every experience is a moving force. Its value can be judged only on the ground of what it moves toward and into'. Dewey's words resonated throughout my doctoral journey in England, a journey that heightened my awareness of the impact of a meaningful learning experience on my personal and professional selves. What I experienced, I believe, illustrated what Mezirow (2003) terms transformative learning, 'learning that transforms problematic frames of reference – sets of fixed assumptions and expectations (habit of mind, meaning perspectives, mindsets) – to make them more inclusive, discriminating, open, reflective, and emotionally able to change' (p. 58). To me, there was some 'truth' in this notion. If a learning process was meaningful, then it could change a person's conception, perception or assumption about certain matters.

This chapter presents my story as a practitioner-researcher experiencing narrative inquiry for the first time. I had always been sceptical about qualitative research, but as soon as I was introduced to narrative inquiry, I was convinced that this approach would guide me to embrace my dual roles as a practitioner-researcher. Metaphorically, my research journey was a maiden voyage, which started out uncharted. It was like preparing a vessel for sailing towards a vast, open sea of qualitative inquiry. The idea of presenting my research as a metaphor of a traveller on an ancient sea voyage was inspired by Trahar's (2006b) nomadic journey of narrative inquiry, and also by Whelan's (1999) story of self-study, exemplified through their experiences as university lecturer and schoolteacher respectively. Despite the ambiguity and the unforeseen challenges, I was brave enough to set out towards my destination and gradually I found my own routes. The initial directions were gathered from reading and listening to stories by other researchers with whom I shared the same research interest, such as Doecke (2004), Freese (2006), Helsing (2007) and Kitchen (2005a, 2005b), experienced voyagers who had taken a similar journey to the one that I travelled.

My inquisitive journey begins: Embracing narrative inquiry

I graduated with degrees in psychology and am a teacher educator in a Malaysian public university. My academic research experience was confined to the quantitative positivist/empiricist traditions. Thus, being introduced to different 'alternative inquiry paradigms' (Guba and Lincoln 1999: 109) in social science research, together with their underlying philosophical and methodological issues was indeed intellectually stimulating.

The discovery of narrative inquiry as a research methodology opened the way to studies similar to mine but with variations in area, scope, foci, setting and context. Kitchen's (2005a, 2005b) narratives of his journey of professional knowledge and growth affected me considerably. They provoked my own critical reflection on my responsibility as a university teacher/lecturer and made me scrutinize the effectiveness of my past teaching practice. My awareness was later reinforced by other practitioner research within the setting of teacher education such as the work of Doecke (2004), Freese (2006) and Helsing (2007).

From the accumulated knowledge gained throughout these different learning experiences, I eventually formulated my research puzzle (Clandinin and Connelly 2000). It was one that was grounded in the view that knowledge was constructed from learning experience (Boud, Cohen and Walker 1993; Prosser and Trigwell 1999), and through critical reflection (Brookfield 1995, 2000; Kreber and Cranton 2000; Schon 1991a, 1991b). Specifically, I framed mine as a narrative inquirer's research into her practice, one that offered the means of making transparent an inquisitive journey towards reframing personal and practical knowledge in teaching (Clandinin and Connelly 2000; Connelly and Clandinin 1988).

I also found that narrative inquiry as a way of conducting practitioner research (Conle 2001; Zeichner 1999; Zeichner and Noffke 2001) is compatible with self-study in teacher education. Self-study is the way of examining 'teaching and researching into practice in order to better understand: oneself, teaching, learning; and the development of knowledge about these' (Loughran 2004: 9). Learning from experience through self-study allows a teacher educator like me to 'capture, unpack and portray the complexity of teaching and learning about teaching in ways that lead to deeper understandings of practice' (Loughran 2005: 13). The concept of self-study also served as the research orientation because it is 'a formalisation of reframing' (Hamilton and Pinnegar 1998: 1). Reframing is the process used by Schon (1991b) to demonstrate reflection-in-action during which teachers hear differently or see differently (as discussed in Russell and Munby 1991).

Embedded in the story of my research journey were my personal experiences as an international student studying in a British university, together with being a Malay Muslim lecturer teaching in a multicultural Malaysian public university. The cultural aspect of the research emerged when I conducted my preliminary study. Insights from my awareness on this aspect of learning made me rethink whether I had taken for granted the element of culture while trying to re-examine my teaching practice. When I became aware of the importance of culture and values in my research, I could not deny that I was then including the 'auto' or self and the 'ethno' or culture in my research (Ellis 2004: 31). Therefore I welcomed autoethnography – 'the writing about the personal and its relationship to culture' (Ellis 2004: 37) – as another approach for my study. In my attempt to relate my current learning experience to my past teaching practice, as an effort to reframe it, I became aware that I had actually 'zoom(ed) backward and forward, inward and outward ... (until the) distinctions between the personal and cultural become blurred' (Ellis 1999: 673).

Hence, while narrative inquiry was my main methodology, i.e. the vehicle, which carried me through the journey of making meaning out of my personal learning experiences, both self-study and autoethnography served as the mechanisms which geared my navigations within 'the metaphorical three-dimensional narrative space' and 'the four directions of inquiry' (Clandinin and Connelly 2000: 50). The story of my journey of reframing my personal practical knowledge unfolded from 'narrative (a look at a story of self), autoethnography (a look at self within a larger context), and self-study (a look at self in action, usually within an educational context)' (Hamilton Smith and Worthington 2008: 17). The combined approaches were significant as they 'privilege self in the research design, recognising that addressing the self can contribute to our understanding of teaching and teacher education' (ibid.). The integration of these approaches made it possible for my research to be presented as a story of practitioner research; one that offered the means for making transparent a journey towards 'personal professional knowledge' (Kitchen 2005b: 207).

Encountering postmodernism: Islamic reflections

The critique of culture in the phenomenological paradigm together with hermeneutic interpretivism led me to postmodernism, as I understood this philosophical perspective to be one strand informing narrative inquiry. My readings on postmodernism posed another challenge for me because different authors offered various interpretations of it. 'To define postmodernism is hardly possible' (Alvesson 2002: 18), maybe because postmodernism 'is the most slippery of terms' (Crotty 1998: 183). Despite the early challenges, what I learned was that postmodernism requires one to understand the historical, cultural and socio-political change and development within Western civilization. To me, postmodernism suggests the relativism of knowledge, which propagates the idea that there is no straightforward way of establishing truth; 'reality is blurred' (Lyon 1999: 9). Further reading on postmodernism was slightly discouraging for me, in particular when realizing its sceptical attitude towards metanarratives, which were viewed, traditionally, to 'give cultural practices some form of legitimation or authority' (Butler 2002: 13). Postmodernists reject the holistic nature of these grand narratives and are against the 'claims of any kind of overall, totalising explanation' (ibid: 15). Postmodernism holds that authority and totality have significant political implications: they allow one party to remain in power while subordinating and marginalizing those who are not. Therefore, most postmodernists are liberating agents, championing those individuals or groups who fail to conform to the values imposed by the grand narratives.

According to Butler (ibid) 'postmodernists tend not to be well informed about current practices in science and religion'. Objectivist reality, absolute forms of knowledge and universal truth are impossible. Thus, most postmodernists consider themselves cultural relativists. For a Malay Muslim researcher whose ontological and epistemological perspectives on reality and knowledge are firmly embedded in the absolute truth of the divine revelation, it was disheartening to learn about these contradicting notions at first, particularly as I knew that most Muslim scholars 'reject epistemological relativism' (Wan Mohd Nor 1989: 9). As a Muslim, I firmly uphold the essentials of the Islamic world view that 'Everything that exists originates from God, including knowledge' (Wan Mohd Nor 1989: 36).

I was torn between my belief system, one that is firmly embedded in the absolute truth of the Islamic world view, and my newly discovered ideas about postmodernism. At one point, I even questioned whether it was possible for a Muslim researcher to work within postmodernism. While I was attempting to position my research, philosophically, memories of my previous academic background surfaced. The learning approach based on the philosophy of Islamization of knowledge that had been dominant in the university where I had studied as an undergraduate had taught me an important lesson. I was fortunate that the book on the general principles of Islamization of knowledge by AbuSulayman (1989) was still with me. Two paragraphs reminded me of its essentials:

> The "Islamization of knowledge" is scientific knowledge that originates from Divine norms and ideals. It is rational in its outlook, its approach, its search, its critical examination of the problems of life, and its treatment of individual society, nature and the laws that govern its workings.
>
> Through the "Islamization of knowledge", the Ummah is cognizant of the need and importance of the scientific and cultural achievements that the human race has inherited and achieved. However, these must be thoroughly examined and critically checked in the light of Islam, its comprehensive norms, its guidance and its ideals. (p. 85)

The second paragraph guided me to rethink my position as a Muslim researcher who grounded her narrative inquiry within the interpretivist/phenomenological paradigm and was drawn to a postmodernist world view. As a Muslim learner, rather than denying Western-oriented knowledge and philosophy, I needed to evaluate their compatibility with the Islamic framework.

I remembered reading Ahmed (1992: 6) on postmodernism and Islam, 'while Muslims appreciate the spirit of tolerance, optimism and the drive for self-knowledge in postmodernism, they also recognize the threat it poses them with its cynicism and irony'. This explained clearly the nature of my intellectual conflict at that moment. Although I was discouraged by the philosophical assumptions of postmodernism, his subsequent words persuaded me that I should not be. What I needed to consider was its positive aspect, especially when what it 'offers us by its very definition is the potential, the possibility, the vision of harmony through understanding' (Ahmed 1992: 61).

I believe that 'into the predicament that postmodernism plunges us there is also promise' (Ahmed 1992: 265). Instead of focusing on the contradictory ideas that postmodernism posed to my own philosophical outlook, I could consider those that would expand my horizon of thinking. I learned to appreciate the postmodernist dimension that values local stories, situated within cultural contexts (Etherington 2006; Trahar 2006a, 2007). This was particularly important in making sense of the underlying issue, which was the foundation of my research puzzle, as well as my chosen strategy of inquiry:

> The concept of postmodernity is worth pursuing because it alerts us to a series of highly important questions. It raises our sensitivity and helps us see certain issues as problems to be explained. It obliges us to lift our eyes above narrowly technical and discrete issues …
>
> (Lyon 1999: 7)

This concept supported my quest to re-examine my teaching practice. I found such concepts to be parallel to my ideas because I was becoming more conscious of the importance of acknowledging the cultural elements in my research. In fact, the ideas that suggest acknowledgement, consideration and respect toward other cultures remind me of a particular verse in the Holy Qur'an that says:

> O mankind! We created you from a single (pair) of a male and a female, and made you into nations and tribes, that ye may know each other (not that ye may despise each other). Verily the most honoured of you in the sight of Allah is (he who is) the most righteous of you. And Allah has full knowledge and is well acquainted (with all things).
>
> (*al- Hujuraat* 49:13, translated by Ali 1991: 1342–3)

Such were the affirmations that I sought and received and that gave me the confidence to embark on my journey, and to be sure it was heading in the right direction.

A self-critical inquiry: Confronting my puzzle of practice

> *As I made my way to the classroom, I glanced at my watch to check the time. It was almost five past eight and I was running late. Definitely not a good first impression to the students, I thought. It was the first Thursday of the month, and*

the first meeting took place in the early hour of the morning. I should have left my room earlier, I thought again, but I could not seem to compose myself since waking up that morning. I was wondering, why was I being so nervous? What was I anxious about? At this point I hated the idea of being dramatic. As an attempt to ease the uptight emotion, I tried to rationalize why I was behaving so absurdly. This was not my first time ever teaching the philosophy of education course. It was three years ago when I last conducted the course, right before my study leave. Logically, the familiarity of handling the same course for almost every semester should have reinforced my proficiency in the subject matter. Every time a new academic semester begun, it was always delightful to meet and greet the first year students. Still, I could not shake off the emotion, as I knew that I could not lie to myself nor could I ignore the feelings, however irrational they were.

(10 July 2008; personal insight in teaching journal)

That was the first week of July 2008 and illustrated vividly here are my inner thoughts recorded in my teaching journal. My research had brought me back to my familiar educational landscape. From July to October 2008, I was back in the university for my research fieldwork. Once again I took up my roles and responsibility as a teacher/lecturer. During this four-month period I taught an educational foundation course to undergraduate students. My research fieldwork kept me 'in the midst' – I was 'located somewhere along the dimension of time, place, the personal, and the social' (Clandinin and Connelly 2000: 63). With my newly discovered knowledge, I was ready to engage in the process of reflection-in-action, in 'hearing and seeing differently' (Russell and Munby 1991: 164). In addition, unpacking my teaching to reframe my practice was encouraging me to challenge my 'sets of fixed assumptions and expectations (habits of mind, meaning perspectives, mindsets)' (Mezirow 2003: 58).

During the fieldwork, I challenged these habits of mind by embracing the role of a critically reflective teacher/lecturer (Brookfield 1995), to transform them into ones that were 'more inclusive, discriminating, open, reflective, and emotionally able to change' (Mezirow 2003: 58). Brookfield proposes four distinctive lenses to re-examine teaching practice; three of which I adopted. By including my personal philosophy, learning experiences and past teaching practice, I utilized the first lens, my autobiography as a learner and a teacher. By studying the stories of other researchers who had taken similar research journeys to mine, I employed the 'theoretical literature' as the second lens (Brookfield 1995: 30). Most importantly, I included my students' feedback on my teaching as the third lens through which I scrutinized my professional self.

Getting my bearings: Being a Malay Muslim university teacher

I believe that my uncertainties and dilemmas about teaching were deeply rooted in the way I viewed my practice. The way I saw my professional self was defined by three dimensions of autobiography: as a student who was a product of the

Malaysian educational system; as one who had been brought up in a Malay Muslim culture; and as an academic in a faculty of education without any professional teacher training. Having two degrees in psychology had a great impact on my career decision. Teaching allowed me to apply my knowledge in psychology in order to help others achieve positive developments. I view teaching as facilitating student learning and as a way to equip students with knowledge to help them in developing a well-balanced personality. In other words, educating students is my attempt to promote a balanced development between intellect, emotion, self and soul – the four elements that support the dual nature of an individual learner self: physical and spiritual.

Such a viewpoint is embedded in my belief as a Muslim. Islam lays great emphasis on the acquisition of knowledge through education by both men and women, and imparting it to others (Rizavi 1986: viii). As a Muslim teacher/lecturer, I strive to uphold these essentials of the Islamic world view by manifesting them through my practice. The creed of a Muslim is derived from the Holy Qur'an, the words of God and the teachings of the last prophet, Muhammad, peace be upon him (Wan Mohd Nor 2010b).

In Islam, 'education is designed to produce a God fearing (*taqwa*) servant of Allah who is aware of his (sic) individual vertical relations with Allah (*hablum minaLlah)* and his (sic) social horizontal relations with his fellow man (sic) (*hablum minan Nas)*' (Hashim 1999: 34). This is pertinent to the concept of Islam as a religion that emphasizes the importance of a community or *ummah* (Nasr 2004). Apart from the revealed knowledge, the other sources of knowledge in Islam are the *hadith* (the sayings and doings exemplified by the Prophet of Islam, Muhammad, peace be upon him), the natural phenomena, human psychology and history (Wan Mohd Nor 1989). The knowledge I have acquired as a student, especially my knowledge in psychology, becomes 'the *amana* or trust' (Wan Mohd Nor 1989: 16) that I have willingly accepted. In fact, as a Muslim teacher, I am also regarded as a *mu'allim*, a learned one, who is the bearer of responsibility towards acquiring knowledge (Ab. Halim 2007). For this particular reason, a Muslim teacher like me has been given the trust and accountability for the acquisition and promulgation of knowledge. Thus, I truly believe that it is my responsibility to apply such notions in my teaching.

Moreover, this core Islamic concept regarding knowledge is compatible with the Malay culture within which I have been brought up. Deeply embedded in the socio-cultural values is the idea that stresses the accountability and integrity of a teacher as a respected professional. A teacher is regarded as the most vital factor in the educational system in Islam, therefore he or she has a very important responsibility (Rizavi 1986). In Islam, a Muslim teacher is not only a *mu'allim*, but also a *murabbi* (a trainer of souls and personalities) (Ab. Halim 2007). With such status, teachers are given respect and authority to guide students by setting themselves as examples to their students.

In the Malay culture, the emphasis is not only on the importance of knowledge, but also on the benefit of possessing knowledge. Knowledgeable persons are those whom society consults, thus positioning them highly. This status is granted to those who are considered not only knowledgeable, but also who possess good character. In other words, the process of acquiring knowledge is perceived as a process of character building. With knowledge, individuals are indirectly equipped with *budi*, defined as 'wisdom, understanding or intellect' (Lim 2003a: 31). The concept of *budi* has become part of the Malay mind as it encompasses every aspect of Malay life. Most importantly, it determines the Malays in 'their thinking (judgement), their moral attitudes, their goodness, and how argument should be presented' (Lim 2003a: 31). This is supported by the verses of a classic Malay *syair* or poem called *Syair Alif Ba Ta*, penned by an unknown writer in 1893 (Noriah 2003: 125):

Adalah Melayu empunya bahasa,	And the Malays it is their culture,
Bukan memandang ribu dan laksa,	Thousands and billions are not the measure,
Hanya memandang budi dan bahasa,	Only good deeds and manners they treasure,
Hati terlambat badan binasa.	When the heart is won nothing's left for sure.
Ada orang sempurna budi,	All those good characters,
Sebarang pekerjaan boleh menjadi,	Successful they'll be whatever they're after,
Akalnya baik tiada keji,	With a sound mind they will not falter,
Barang kemana mendapat puji.	Only praises for their endeavour.

Looking back at my practice, I realize that my passion for teaching lies in my personal belief that I am accountable in providing students with the knowledge related to education and humanities in order to prepare themselves as teachers. Facilitating students in gaining insights into their roles and responsibilities as future teachers and assisting them in making the link between the educational concepts and their own personal experiences is my personal mission in developing their professionalism. To meet the expectations of being 'a good teacher' to my students, I have always taken my teaching practice seriously, especially in relation to my pedagogical knowledge and skill.

Navigating uncertainties: Re-examining teaching practice

Nonetheless, as soon as I started teaching back at the university, I reverted to my traditional teacher self. During the early part of the semester, my teaching strategy was based totally on lecturing. I was teaching educational philosophy and was aware from the responses from my previous students that the course was too abstract for most of them. I assumed that lecturing was the best method for me to convey the topics. I realized that this was not the case after reading some of the students' journal entries:

> Today we learned about the meaning of philosophy. The lecturer asked about our own personal philosophy. Well, my philosophy is "I may not be the first or the best, but I don't want to be neither the last nor the worst". Actually I don't really perceive philosophy as a hard course to learn. But I got problem to connect it to our life. Because I haven't yet seen how actually philosophy related to our daily life and how do we have to apply it in our teaching in future. Hopefully she could elaborate briefly on this later on.
>
> (E-mail from student 1, 20 July 2008)

> I felt bored ....Why not for the next class, you do differently? We could have group activity? It's great if we could have some games ... can beat sleepiness ... moreover our class is in the morning isn't? I bet there are others who are sleepy too ... so, if you could plan some games, it would be interesting won't it? This is just some suggestions.
>
> (E-mail from student 2, 28 July 2008)

At first, it was disheartening to read such feedback because it implied that my lecture failed to assist students' understanding. Nevertheless, I learned that for me to be a critically reflective teacher and a reflexive researcher, I needed to be open to any criticisms or negative responses offered by my students. I decided that throughout my fieldwork, I would not allow myself to be trapped in a 'vicious circle of innocence and blame' (Brookfield 1995: 1). I had been consistently reminded that as critically reflective academics/practitioners we needed to 'see our practice in new ways by standing outside ourselves and viewing what we do through four distinct lenses' (Brookfield 1995: 8). In my attempt to improve my teaching approach, I then planned and implemented a number of active learning activities. Incorporated into my teaching strategy was the characteristic of cooperative learning which I adapted from the work originally developed by Robert E. Slavin (O'Donnell, Reeve and Smith 2007). The active learning activities were specifically designed as an attempt to transform my traditional teaching strategy into a student-centred approach. Most of the activities required students to be engaged in active reading, group discussions and group presentations. From my students' journal entries, I found such approaches to be effective for teaching an abstract course like educational philosophy:

> It was fun and interesting as there was discussion among the students. Some of the students also voiced out their own opinions and questions about philosophy and the questions were explained by the presentation group members. This can train the students' confidence in presentation. Besides that, we can see that the students can explain, answer and solve the problems which have been asked very well. During the lectures, Ms. Narina explained

> different philosophies hold by one person if one is a teacher, a lecturer and a facilitator. Now I realize this fact and this help me a lot in my life if I have become a teacher in the future.
>
> (E-mail from student 3, 22 August 2008)

> ... I feel that 2day activites is very good. We work in group to discuss the question about why do i need to study the philosophy. I work in personally, I sure dun now how to answer the question. In group, I can heard to more opinion. I feel that is a way to improve. and also we will no so boring if work in group. We will feel sleepy if just listening to what miss narina talking about.
>
> (E-mail from student 4, 31 July 2008)

These entries made me realize that I would not have reached this stage without my students' participation. During the implementation of the classroom activities, I gained information about students' learning through their weekly journals. By sharing with me their reflections on their learning experiences, my students had become my fellow travellers (Trahar 2006; 2011) on my research journey. We were in the same boat, on our way to making meaning of what we had learned so far.

Stories of the fellow travellers: Listening to students' personal learning experiences

Towards the end of the fieldwork, I was still receiving mixed comments from several students. Once again, I was left in doubt about what I had achieved. I was willing to share the learning responsibility with my students; nevertheless, the journal entries were informing me that some of them were not ready for such responsibility. From the later entries, and supported by my classroom observations, I realized that my students could be broadly categorized into two groups of learners. One group consisted of those who were mature students, with the ability to gain in-depth understanding of the course content and relate to relevant educational issues. By possessing such maturity and potential, these students were facilitative towards their classmates while actively participating in group activities. The other group of students were those who were reluctant to give their views and to participate in classroom activities. This was a small group, always attentive to their classmates, but who made no attempt to participate in discussions.

Based on my observation and the entries received from these two groups of students, I was drawn to explore their personal learning experiences. Prosser and Trigwell's (1999) and Ramsden's (2003) suggestions that university teachers should understand students' prior learning experiences in order to understand their current ones supported the endeavour. Most importantly, I wanted to find out whether they were willing to accept the responsibility from me and then share it with their classmates. Between early September 2008 and late October 2008, I spoke to a number of students who were willing to share with me their insights into their personal learning experiences. I focused on two whose personal stories I found to be fascinating, inspiring and intriguing (Atkinson 1998). Listening to them connected with parts of my personal and professional lives thus their stories were significant in how I see my personal practical knowledge of teaching. Talking to these two students made me realize that in re-examining my personal practical knowledge, I needed to extend it beyond pedagogy.

Ramsden (2003: 6) wrote 'We can improve our teaching by studying our students' learning – by listening to and learning from our students'. Now that I look back and reflect on these episodes from my research journey, I realize how true these words are to me. By listening to the stories of my two fellow travellers, Nur and Aswad (pseudonyms) I was actually listening to each person's 'narrative identity' (McAdams, Josselson and Lieblich 2006: 4). In these two stories of personal learning experiences, I identified that Nur and Aswad constructed their identities as learners as they positioned themselves in various contexts throughout their childhood, adolescence and young adulthood. During these life stages, each one related their personal self to significant others in order to define themselves as individual learners. The central features that could be traced from both storylines were how these students related their personal learning experiences while in school to their family values, socio-economic background and process of socialization. These constructed experiences then seemed to shape their perceptions towards their tertiary learning process. Listening to their stories resonated with my own personal learning experiences and inevitably evoked the conscience of both my personal and professional selves. In between the lines of their stories, and mine, were the inscribed cultural elements on which we grounded our conceptualization of learning, education and knowledge as a whole.

These were enlightening episodes, reminding me that in my effort to transform my practice I needed to reconsider the cultural aspect of learning. This does not mean that I had been ignorant about the concept in the past. Throughout my experience of teaching in a multicultural Malaysian public university, I had observed that students' cultural background was one of the factors that influenced their views on their learning process and on education. Nevertheless, it had always been my conviction that although Malaysians differed in terms of ethnic groups – the Malays, Chinese, Indian and other ethnic minorities – in general we shared more or less the same Eastern culture, norms and values. Although this might appear to be a naïve generalization, as a Malay living in Malaysia, it was a premise that I had held to. It had always been one of my 'taken-for-granted frames of reference' (Mezirow 2003: 59).

The information gathered from Nur's and Aswad's stories challenged my assumptions about the first year students' learning. Nur's life story highlighted that her learning experiences at different stages throughout the formal education system were not the only important elements that shaped her identity as an independent learner. From her life story, I learned how family values instilled in her from childhood had become the root of her self-consciousness and her sense of responsibility as a learner. The way Nur strongly related herself to her family expectations by showing her respect for her parents and obligation to repay their good deeds were examples of the traditional values that encompass family centredness in Malay culture. On the other hand, I found Aswad's story complemented the words of Boud, Cohen and Walker (1993: 13), who suggested 'learning does not occur in isolation from social and cultural norms and values'. His learning and working experiences as part of the process of socialization illustrated that relationship and group orientation were contributing factors that moulded his self-esteem.

This episode was a cautionary tale in my enthusiasm to implement cooperative or collaborative classroom activities, which can be regarded as 'Western-influenced approaches to learning' (Tweed and Lehman 2002: 93). These approaches value the 'Socratic-oriented learning (that) involves overt and private questioning, expression of personal hypotheses and the desire for self-directed tasks' (Tweed and Lehman 2002, 93.). My classroom activities based on the concept of cooperative learning, developed by Slavin (1980; 1987) might empower some students like Nur to become independent and self-directed learners. These students could then extend their positive attitudes to learning by becoming peer tutors who facilitated their colleagues' process of learning. The same activities might, however, create unnecessarily adverse effects on the self-esteem of those students such as Aswad. For them, this kind of learning approach might create the danger of transforming their sense of *rendah diri* (humbleness) into *hina diri* (self-denigration), which should be avoided (Lim 2003b: 206). I realized that without sensitivity to this cultural aspect of learning, 'teachers may unknowingly contribute to the decline of motivation' among students, and 'stimulate a sense of alienation from the rest of the class or from the course itself' (Wlodkowski 1991: 9).

Hearing the voices of Nur and Aswad caused me to rethink and reconsider a number of cultural and psychological issues regarding students' learning. My assumption based on the notion 'that Western ideas must be right for every context' (Littlewood 2000: 31) was challenged. This particular episode also reminded me to avoid any 'dumbing-down' (Haggis 2006: 523) of concepts, theories or models of student learning which were developed in the Western context. These were not the only lessons learned from my conversations with these two fellow travellers. Meeting Nur and Aswad and listening to their personal learning experiences was, in fact, one of the most perceptive episodes from my research journey. I realized that as a lecturer, I should explore students' prior learning experiences to understand their perceptions towards their current learning environment. These perceptions, developed from their accumulated learning experiences, became the basis of their evaluation of my classroom teaching and their expectations of how the course should be conducted. Nur's and Aswad's stories also shed light on the cultural aspects of learning, helping me to understand that I needed to be careful in adapting and implementing particular learning concepts and approaches, especially those developed in a different socio-cultural and educational context. I should have heeded Trahar (2007: 12) when she cautions about the danger of 'slipping into a West is Best philosophy'.

Looking back, moving forward: Insights so far

My intellectual journey as a practitioner researcher was an insightful one. It was one that had allowed me to see what was happening around me with a pair of new eyes. Implementing narrative inquiry offered an alternative method for 'experiencing the experience' (Clandinin and Connelly 1994: 414) of my teaching. Narrative inquiry also provided me with a conceptual framework, or 'the commonplaces' as Connelly and Clandinin (2006, cited in Clandinin, Pushor and Orr 2007: 22) termed it. I found that these commonplaces permitted simultaneous explorations of my personal experiences 'within the dimensions of an inquiry space' (Clandinin, Pushor and Orr 2007: 23) – temporality, sociality and place. These were newly discovered research concepts for me. I am now convinced that narrative inquiry accommodated my research as it served as the foundation from which I made sense of my own learning and teaching experiences, as well as those of my students.

Narrative inquiry was indeed the means for me to be a critically reflective teacher/lecturer from 'the three dimensional narrative inquiry space' (Clandinin 2006: 46). This inquiry space covered the personal and social dimension (interaction), the past, present and future dimension (continuity) and the place (situation). I can now understand the applicability of these fundamentals of narrative inquiry, as they were relevant to the intention, scope and context of my research puzzle. In my study, the dimensional space of situation was experienced when I returned to my educational landscape where I taught. Revisiting my teaching by conducting an educational foundation course with undergraduate students provided the opportunity for me to re-experience my teaching. The teaching and learning experiences made me re-examine my past teaching strategy and approach so as to find ways to improve. Therefore by having done this, the dimensional space of continuity was explored. Throughout the experience of unpacking my teaching, I attended to the dimensional space of interaction when I acknowledged the socio-cultural influences on personal learning experiences – students' and mine.

While making sense of the experiences during my research journey, I was also interacting in the 'four directions of inquiry: inward and outward, backward and forward' (Clandinin and Connelly 2000: 50). As a postgraduate research student and a teacher/lecturer during my fieldwork, I confronted my own personal dilemma and taken-for-granted assumptions regarding my teaching practice. As a methodology, narrative inquiry has taught me to research into my own learning and teaching experiences by experiencing them simultaneously and questioning the issues that emerged critically during the journey within these four directions. Scrutinizing my personal and professional selves from these directions, I learned to challenge 'sets of fixed assumptions and expectations (habits of mind, meaning perspectives, mindsets)' and made them 'more inclusive, discriminating, open, reflective, and emotionally able to change' (Mezirow 2003: 58).

Becoming a critical and reflexive researcher taught me to be ethical and respectful, and also humble in foregrounding the voices of my students as the research participants. This brought me closer to the traditional concept of self *muhasabah*, i.e. the continuous practice of critical reflection and introspection on selves. In the Malay Muslim culture, exercising *muhasabah diri* is the platform for an individual 'to review what has been done, to learn what was wrong and what was good for society, to make corrections, and to improve ourselves for the following day' (Rogers 2001: 433). The concept of *muhasabah* is regarded as 'a second order virtue' in Islamic ethics (Carney 1983: 171). It is consistent with what Fatimah (2010: 224) highlighted, the self-introspection approach 'is the very nature of virtue ethics … known as the science of the soul (it) deals with self-knowledge, the inner dimension of the human being for the purpose of moulding human personality or character'. I believe that as a teacher/lecturer and a researcher, these Islamic concepts serve as my guidance. This is because practising self introspection is considered to be 'having a good character' (Zaroug 1999: 61).

In a way, this offered the 'deconstructive power and possibilities' (Manathunga 2007: 25) for me to rediscover my identity as a Malay Muslim university teacher/lecturer. I realized that I needed to be transparent in the way I negotiated my self as a Malay Muslim researcher who worked within a Western approach to research. The Western traditions of philosophy, anthropology and sociology embedded in qualitative methodological approaches to research have been criticized as linked to European imperialism and colonialism (Denzin and Lincoln 2007; Smith 1999). I now believe that my research can be regarded as an example of dewesternization of a Western epistemic framework consistent with Wan Mohd Nor's (2010b) Islamization of the present-day knowledge project (IPDK). According to the author, although most Muslim scholars reject epistemological relativism, IPDK however is:

> … (N)either religious fundamentalism, nor a narrow form of ethnocentrism or indigenisation, nor a matter of identity politics. On contrary, it is arguably an offer of a more comprehensive option within the current discourse and practice on alternatives to Eurocentrism….. It is also an attempt that should be taken seriously in enriching the discourse on decolonisation, postcoloniality, and coloniality, which could offer a non-hegemonic, non-ethnocentric, non-gender, and non-fundamentalist claim to epistemic universality. (p. 8)

I believe the process of research that I experienced through narrative inquiry was consistent with the concept of 'dynamic stabilism' (Wan Mohd Nor 2010:

15) which suggests there is no harm in integrating contemporary thought into the existing traditional belief system, provided that one has a comprehensive understanding of the fundamentals of such a system. My research exemplified such a process, through which I learned that although it was important to have an idealistic view about my practice, I needed to be critically reflective and not to be overly occupied by idealistic thoughts. These were the elements from the philosophical foundation of my practice that I could challenge, transform and reinterpret. Learning to negotiate the shift in my professional identity, from a traditional Malay teacher to a democratic tutor/facilitator, was an attempt to discard my perfectionist thoughts about my practice. This attempt made me aware that I could always be transformative by learning how to reinterpret the meanings that underlie my philosophical ideas so as to rationalize my notions and my actions in my practice. Narrative inquiry served as a vital guide in this process of attaining personal growth and will continue to enable my professional development in the future.

References

Ab. Halim Tamuri (2007) Islamic education teachers' perceptions of the teaching of akhlaq in Malaysian secondary schools, *Journal of Moral Education,* 36 (3): 371–86.

AbuSulayman, AbdulHamid (1989) *Islamization of Knowledge: General Principles and Work Plan*, Virginia: The International Institue of Islamic Thought.

Abdul Omar Shuriye 'Islamic ethics on professional values', paper presented at the International Seminar on Islamic Thoughts, Bangi, Selangor, Malaysia, December 2004.

Ahmed, Akhbar S. (1992) *Postmodernism and Islam*, London: Routledge.

Ali, Abdullah Yusuf (1991) *The Meaning of The Holy Qur'an*, Brentwood, MD: Amana Corporation.

Alvesson, M. (2002) *Postmodernism and Social Research*, Buckingham: Open University Press.

Atkinson, R. (1998) *The Life Story Interview*, Thousand Oaks, CA: Sage Publications.

Bassey, M. (1996) 'Three paradigms in educational research', in A. Pollard (ed.) *Readings for Reflective Teaching in Primary Schools*, London: Cassell, pp. 43–45.

Barone, T. N. (2004) Moral dimensions of teacher-student interactions in Malaysian secondary schools, *Journal of Moral Education,* 33 (2): 179–96.

Berry, A., and Loughran, J. (2002) 'Developing an understanding of learning to teach in teacher education', in J. Loughran & T. Russell (eds) *Improving Teacher Education Practices Through Self Study*, London: RoutledgeFalmer, pp. 13–25.

Biggs, J. (1999) What the student does: teaching for enhanced learning, *Higher Education Research & Development,* 18 (1): 57–75.

Boud, D., Cohen, R., and Walker, D. (1993) 'Introduction: Understanding learning from experience', in D. Boud, R. Cohen & D. Walker (eds) *Using Experience for Learning,* Buckingham: The Society for Research into Higher Education & Open University Press, pp. 1–17.

Brookfield, S. D. (1995) *Becoming a Critically Reflective Teacher*, San Francisco: John Wiley & Sons.

—(2000) 'Transformative learning as ideology critique', in J. Mezirow & Associates (eds.) *Learning As Transformation: Critical Perspectives On A Theory In Progress*, San Francisco: Jossey-Bass, pp. 125–48.

Butler, C. (2002) *Postmodernism: A Very Short Introduction*, New York: Oxford University Press Inc.

Carney, F. S. (1983) Some aspects of Islamic ethics, *The Journal of Religion*, 63 (2): 159–74.

Clandinin, D. J. (2006) Narrative inquiry: a methodology for studying lived experience, *Research Studies in Music Education*, 27 (44): 44–54.

Clandinin, D. J. and Connelly, F. M. (1994) 'Personal experience method', in N. K. Denzin & Y. S. Lincoln (eds) *The Handbook of Qualitative Research*, Thousand Oaks, CA: Sage Publications Inc., pp. 413–427.

—(2000) *Narrative Inquiry: Experience and Story in Qualitative Method*, San Francisco, CA: Jossey-Bass.

Clandinin, D. J., Pushor, D., and Orr, A. M. (2007) Navigating sites for narrative inquiry, *Journal of Teacher Education*, 58 (21): 21–35.

Conle, C. (2001) The rationality of narrative inquiry in research and professional development, *European Journal of Teacher Education*, 24 (1): 21–33.

Connelly, F. M. and Clandinin, D. J. (1988) *Teachers as curriculum planners: Narratives of experience*, New York: Teachers College, University of Columbia.

Creswell, J. W. (2007) *Qualitative Inquiry & Research Design: Choosing Among Five Approaches*, 2nd edn, Thousand Oaks, CA: Sage Publications Inc.

Crotty, M. (2003) *The Foundation of Social Research: Meaning and Perspective in the Research Process*, London: Sage Publications.

Denzin, N. K. and Lincoln, Y. S. (eds) (1994) *Handbook of Qualitative Research*, Thousand Oaks; London; New Delhi: Sage Publications.

—(eds.) (2005) *The SAGE Handbook of Qualitative Research*, 3rd edn, Thousand Oaks, CA: Sage Publications Inc.

Dewey, J. (1938) *Experience & Education*, 1997 edn, New York, NY: Touchstone.

Doecke, B. (2004) Professional identity and educational reform: confronting my habitual practices as a teacher educator, *Teaching and Teacher Education*, 20 (2): 203–15.

Ellis, C. (1999) Heartful autoethnography, *Qualitative Health Research*, 9 (5): 669–83.

—(2004) *The Ethnographic I: A Methodological Novel About Autoethnography*, Walnut Creek, CA: AltaMira.

Etherington, K. (2004) *Becoming a Reflexive Researcher: Using Our Selves in Research*, London: Jessica Kingsley Publishers.

—(2006) 'Reflexivity: using our 'selves' in narrative research', in S. Trahar (ed.) *Narrative Research on Learning: Comparative and International Perspectives*, Oxford: Symposium Books, pp. 77–92.

Fatimah Abdullah (2012) 'Teaching Islamic ethics and ethical training: benefiting from emotional and spiritual intelligence', *International Journal of Humanities and Social Science*, 2 (3): 224–32.

Freese, A. R. (2006) Reframing one's teaching: discovering our teacher selves through reflection and inquiry, *Teaching and Teacher Education*, 22: 100–19.

Guba, E. G. and Lincoln, Y. S. (1994) 'Competing paradigms in qualitative research', in N. K. Denzin and Y. S. Lincoln (eds) *The Handbook of Qualitative Research*, Thousand Oaks, CA: Sage, pp. 105–17.

Haggis, T. (2006) Pedagogies for diversity: retaining critical challenge amidst fears of 'dumbing down', *Studies in Higher Education* 31 (5): 521–35.

Hashim, R. (1999) Islamization of the curriculum, *The American Journal of Islamic Social Sciences*, 16 (2): 27–42.

Hamilton, M. L., and Pinnegar, S. (1998) 'Introduction: reconceptualizing teaching practice', in M. L. Hamilton (ed.) *Reconceptualizing Teaching Practice: Self-study in Teacher Education,* London, New York: Routledge, pp. 1–4.

Hamilton, M. L., Smith, L., and Worthington, K. (2008) Fitting the methodology with the research: An exploration of narrative, self-study and auto-ethnography, *Studying Teacher Education,* 4 (1): 17–28.

Helsing, D. (2007) Regarding uncertainty in teachers and teaching, *Teaching and Teacher Education,* 23: 1317–33.

Hertz, R. (1997) Reflexivity and voice, in R. Hertz (ed.) *Reflexivity and Voice,* Thousand Oaks, CA: Sage Publications Inc., pp. vii–xvii.

Joseph, C. (2006a) It is so unfair here … it is so biased': negotiating the politics of ethnic identification in ways of being Malaysian schoolgirls, *Asian Ethnicity,* 7 (1): 53–73.

—(2006b) Negotiating discourses of gender, ethnicity and schooling: ways of being Malay, Chinese and Indian schoolgirls in Malaysia, *Pedagogy, Culture & Society,* 14 (1): 35–53.

Kitchen, J. (2005a) Looking backward, moving forward: understanding my narrative as a teacher educator, *Studying Teacher Education,* 1 (1): 17–30.

—(2005b) Conveying respect and empathy: becoming a relational teacher educator, *Studying Teacher Education,* 1 (2): 195–207.

Kreber, C. and Cranton, P. A. (2000) Exploring the scholarship of teaching, *The Journal of Higher Education,* 71 (4): 476–95.

Lim, K. H. (2003a) Budi as the Malay mind, *IIAS Newsletter,* 31: 31.

—(2003b) 'Budi as the Malay mind: A philosophical study of Malay ways of reasoning and emotion in peribahasa', unpublished thesis, University of Hamburg.

Lindblom-Ylanne, S., Trigwell, K., Nevgi, A. and Ashwin, P. (2006) How approaches to teaching are affected by discipline and teaching context, *Studies in Higher Education,* 31 (3): 285–98.

Littlewood, W. (2000) Do Asian students really want to listen and obey?, *ELT Journal,* 54 (1): 31–6.

Loughran, J. (2005) Researching teaching about teaching: self-study of teacher education practices, *Studying Teacher Education,* 1 (1): 5–16.

Loughran, J., and Russell, T. (eds) (2002) *Improving Teacher Education Practice Through Self-study.* London: RoutledgeFalmer.

Loughran, J. J. (2004) 'A history and context of self-study of teaching and teacher education practices', in J. J. Loughran, M. L. Hamilton, V. K. LaBoskey and T. L. Russell (eds.) *International Handbook of Self-Study of Teaching and Teacher Education Practices,* Dordrecht: Kluwer Academic Publishers, vol. 1, pp. 7–39.

Lyon, D. (1999) *Postmodernity,* 2nd edn, Buckingham: Open University Press.

McAdams, D. P., Josselson, R. and Lieblich, A. (2006) 'Introduction', in D. P. McAdams, R. Josselson and A. Lieblich (eds) *Identity and Story: Creating Self in Narrative,* Washington: American Psychological Association, pp. 1–11.

Manathunga, C. (2007) 'Unhomely' academic developer identities: more post-colonial explorations, *International Journal of Academic Development,* 12 (1): 25–34.

Maykut, P. and Morehouse, R. (1994) *Beginning Qualitative Research: A Philosophic and Practical Guide*, London: The Falmer Press.

Mezirow, J. (1997) Transformative learning: theory to practice, *New Directions for Adult and Continuing Education,* 74: 5–12.

—(2000) 'Learning to think like an adult: core concepts of transformation theory', in J.Mezirow & Associates (eds) *Learning As Transformation: Critical Perspectives On A Theory In Progress*, San Francisco: Jossey-Bass, pp. 3–33.

—(2003) Transformative learning as discourse, *Journal of Transformative Education,* 1 (58): 58–63.

Nasr, Seyyed Hossein (2004) *The Heart of Islam: Enduring the Values of Humanity*, New York: Harper One.

Noriah Mohamad (2003) Syair Alif Ba Ta: The poet and his mission, *Sari,* 21: 109–27.

O'Donnell, A. M., Reeve, J. and Smith, J. K. (2007) *Educational Psychology: Reflection for Action*, Danvers, MA: John Wiley & Sons.

Phillion, J. (2002a) Narrative multiculturalism, *Journal of Curriculum Studies,* 34 (3): 265–79.

—(2002b) Classroom stories of multicultural teaching and learning, *Journal of Curriculum Studies,* 34 (3): 281–300.

—(2002c) Becoming a narrative inquirer in a multicultural landscape, *Journal of Curriculum Studies,* 34 (5): 535–56.

Prosser, M., Martin, E., Trigwell, K., Ramsden, P., and Middleton, H. (2008) University academics' experience of research and its relationship to their experience of teaching, *Instructional Science,* 36: 3–16.

Prosser, M. and Trigwell, K. (1999) *Understanding Learning and Teaching: The Experience in Higher Education*, Buckingham: Society for Research into Higher Education & Open University Press.

Ramsden, P. (2003) *Learning to Teach in Higher Education,* 2nd edn, London: RoutledgeFalmer.

Ramsden, P., Prosser, M., Trigwell, K., and Martin, E. (2007) University teachers' experiences of academic leadership and their approaches to teaching, *Learning and Instruction,* 17: 140–55.

Rizavi, S. S. (1986) *Islamic Philosophy of Education*, Lahore: Institute of Islamic Culture.

Rogers, P. J. (2001) The whole world is evaluating half-full glasses, *American Journal of Evaluation*, 22 (3): 431–5.

Russell, T. and Munby, H. (1991) 'Reframing: the role of experience in developing teachers' professional knowledge', in D. A. Schon (ed.) *The Reflective Turn: Case Studies In and On Educational Practice*, New York: Teachers College: Columbia University, pp. 164–87.

Schon, D. A. (1991a) 'Introduction', in D. A. Schon (ed.) *The Reflective Turn: Case Studies In and On Educational Practice*, New York, NY: Teachers College Press, pp. 1–12.

—(1991b) *The Reflective Practitioner: How Professionals Think In Action*, England: Ashgate Publishing Limited.

Slavin, R. E. (1980) Cooperative learning, *Review of Educational Research,* 50 (2): 315–42.

—(1987) Cooperative learning: Where behavioral and humanistic approaches to classroom motivation meet, *The Elementary School Journal,* 88 (1): 29–37.

Smith, L. T. (1999) *Decolonizing Methodologies: Research and Indegeneous Peoples*, London: Zed Books Ltd.

Trahar, S. (2006a). 'A part of the landscape: the practitioner researcher as narrative inquirer in an international higher education community', in S. Trahar (ed.) *Narrative Research on Learning: Comparative and International Perspectives*, Oxford: Symposium Books, pp. 201–19.

Trahar, S. M. (2006b) 'Roads less travelled: Stories of learning and teaching in a multicultural higher education environment', unpublished thesis, University of Bristol.

Trahar, S. (2007) *Teaching and Learning: The International Higher Education Landscape – Some Theories and Working Practices.* Bristol: Higher Education Academy Education Subject Centre (EsCalate).

—(2009) *Beyond the Story Itself: Narrative Inquiry and Autoethnography in Intercultural Research in Higher Education*, Forum Qualitative Sozialforschung / Forum: Qualitative Social Research, 10 (1). Available athttp://www.qualitative-research.net/index.php/fqs/article/view/1218/2654, accessed 20 February 2009).

—(2011) *Developing Cultural Capability in International Higher Education: A Narrative Inquiry*, Oxon: Routledge.

Tweed, R. G., and Lehman, D. R. (2002) Learning considered within cultural context: Confucian and Socratic approaches, *American Psychologist*, 57(2): 89–99.

Wan Mohd Nor Wan Daud (1989). *The Concept of Knowledge in Islam and Its Implications For Education in A Developing Country*, New York: Mansell Publishing Limited.

—(2010a) 'Al-Attas: A Real Reformer and Thinker', in Wan Mohd Nor Wan Daud and Muhammad Zainiy Uthman (eds.), *Knowledge, Language, Thought and the Civilization of Islam: Essays in Honor of Syed Muhammad Naquib al-Attas*), Skudai: Penerbit UTM Press, pp. 13–57.

—(2010b) 'Dewesternisation and Islamisation: Their Epistemic Framework and Final Purpose', in N. Omar, W. C. Dan, J. S. Ganesan and R. Talif (eds) *Critical Perspectives on Literature and Culture in the New World Order*, Newcastle upon Tyne: Cambridge Scholars Publishing, pp. 2–25.

Whelan, K. (1999) 'Traveler on a journey', in F. M. Connelly & D. J. Clandinin (eds.), *Shaping A Professional Identity: Stories of Educational Practice*, New York, NY: Teachers College, Columbia University, pp. 20–31.

Wlodkowski, R. J. (1999) Motivation and diversity: A framework for teaching, *New Directions for Adult and Continuing Education*, 78: 7–16.

Zaroug, A. H. (1999) Ethics from an Islamic perspective: Basic issues, *The American Journal of Islamic Social Sciences*, 16 (3): 45–63.

Zeichner, K. (1999) The new scholarship in teacher education *Educational Researcher*, 28 (9): 4–15.

Zeichner, K., and Nofke, S. (2001) 'Practitioner research', in V. Richardson (ed.) *Handbook of research on teaching*, Washington, DC: AERA, pp. 289–332.

Chapter 7

Narrative inquiry in a divided island

Dealing with sensitive and complex methodological issues in Cyprus

Evgenia Partasi

Introduction

The story told in this chapter derives from my experience of carrying out research on the divided island of Cyprus. I set out to explore the way the experiences of students and teachers are shaped by the diversity of their classrooms. Conducting research within my own cultural context, especially when this is characterized by political and social turbulences, I was often confronted with beliefs and views that I criticized, but at the same time shared, as a member of the particular group.

I was raized within the myth of a monocultural Greek Cypriot society, based on Greek Christian Orthodox traditions. Nourished by nationalistic and ethnocentric doctrines, this myth established and protected the domination of the Greek Cypriot community on the island. This appeared as a necessity that would guarantee the survival of the community that was threatened by the island's division. Public opinion for a long time has refused to realize the recent changes in the island composition, raising problems of racism and xenophobia. Although schools are becoming more diverse, teachers and the educational system remain unprepared and unequipped to deal with these complexities. Intrigued by this complexity, I set out on a journey to explore the way all these factors and elements interact in a diverse school context.

The research on which this chapter draws took place in the divided city of Nicosia and specifically in three classrooms in two primary schools with multicultural student populations – 40 per cent of the students were considered as non-Cypriots[1]. It is important to note that one of the schools was just a few hundred meters from the buffer zone. The data collection included observations, interviews with teachers and students, texts produced by the children in various activities and a reflexive diary kept during the inquiry. At this point, it is essential to mention that this study set out as traditional qualitative research and not narrative inquiry. Prior to this study I was unfamiliar with narrative methodology.

I discovered it along the way, as it provided me with the means to solve many of the methodological and ethical issues that arose during the inquiry. I was able to provide insights into how my positioning, experiences and beliefs influenced and shaped my research. This chapter tells my story of the inquiry, moving backward and forward in time, inward towards my internal aspirations and beliefs, and outward towards the research environment.

Setting the context

Cyprus, an island in the Mediterranean Sea, presents as an interesting case for the study of multiculturalism because of a unique three-dimensional characteristic. It has always been multicultural due to a long history with numerous conquerors that has resulted in the creation of a diverse population comprised of Greek Cypriots, Turkish Cypriots and the Armenian, Maronite and Latin minorities.

Due to its wealth and strategic position, Cyprus experienced conquest by numerous powers that invaded and raided the island, leaving their marks on history and culture (Eurydice 2009). Many of the dominant powers of each era passed through the island. Egyptians, Mycenaean Greeks, Romans, Ottomans and the British among others made Cyprus part of their empires. Cyprus emerged as an independent state in 1960, after a five-year anti-colonial struggle against the British, with Greece, Turkey and Great Britain as guarantor powers. Independence did not satisfy the desires of the Cypriot people: Greek Cypriots craved for unification with Greece, while Turkish Cypriots demanded partition. Therefore, both Turkish and Greek Cypriots considered independence as a painful compromise, which resulted in inter-ethnic conflicts between 1963 and 1974. In 1974 the Greek Junta organized a coup against the Cypriot Government, aiming for union. As a response, Turkey seized the opportunity to invade the island and divide it, fulfilling the goal of partition. Despite the swift collapse of the coup and restoration of the legitimate government of Cyprus, Turkey undertook a second wave of invasion in August, in violation of UN ceasefire agreements, and expanded its occupation to 36.2 per cent of the Republic's sovereign territory.

Since then, the island has been divided into two supposedly homogeneous parts: Turkish in the north and Greek in the south. The Republic of Cyprus became a member of the European Union on 1 May 2004, but the effect on the occupied territory is restricted until the solution of the Cyprus Problem. The United Nations have led the basis for negotiations between the two communities for many decades now. This is the second dimension of the unique case of Cyprus: the division of the island and the people.

The third dimension has been a result of globalization. During the last few decades, Cyprus has been receiving a significant number of immigrants from Asia and the former eastern bloc. According to the last census conducted in 2011, the percentage of non-Cypriots residing on the island has increased to 21.4 from 9.4 per cent in 2001. Cypriot society influenced by nationalism and ethnocentrism has long cultivated a myth of homogeneity and monoculturalism (Bryant 2004), thus perceiving multiculturalism as a new phenomenon resulting from migration and globalization. Problems of racism, xenophobia, intolerance and discrimination are increasing (ECRI 2001).

As far as education is concerned, research has demonstrated that the education system remains ethnocentric and nationalistic (CER 2004; Christou 2006; Papadakis 2008) and that very little has been done in order to accommodate the increasing diversity of the student population (Demetriou and Trimikliniotis 2007; Panayiotopoulos and Nicolaidou 2008). In many cases, non-Cypriot students are experiencing marginalization and discrimination (Angelides et al. 2003, 2004), while teachers are unprepared and ill-equipped to teach in multicultural and multilingual environments (Panayiotopoulos and Nicolaidou 2007; Partasi 2009). Although some studies have reported both positive and negative attitudes towards diversity and multiculturalism (Hadjitheodoulou-Loizidou and Symeou 2007; Nicolaou, et al. 2007; Partasi 2010, 2011), much more needs to be done.

All three dimensions coexist in space and time, influencing and nourishing each other in many complex ways. The argument I will attempt to establish in this chapter lies in the way narrative inquiry can be a valuable tool in conducting research in such complex and dynamic settings, especially in the study of sensitive issues, such as racism, integration and multiculturalism.

The use of narrative inquiry in the study of multiculturalism (e.g. Phillion 2002; Phillion et al. 2005) has been foregrounded in the literature, therefore I am not going to advocate further for this. However, personally I was totally unfamiliar with 'narrative' methodologies prior to this research. This was partly because 'narrative inquiry' had never been used in Cyprus. This is also evident by the fact that the term 'narrative' has not been translated into Greek yet. Although education has been a thoroughly researched area, the majority of these inquiries have been quantitative. There is a great concern over reliability and objectiveness, together with scepticism about relational forms of inquiry, such as narrative.

Influenced by these beliefs – which I also endorsed mainly during my undergraduate studies on the island – I was extremely sceptical towards this methodological approach. My concern to produce something that would be perceived as a reliable result led me into designing my project as a 'conventional' qualitative inquiry by collecting data through interviews and observations. I had no intention of making myself part of the inquiry. However, I kept finding my way back in. No matter what I did, my voice was loud and clear in the texts I produced. All my interpretations and conclusions were shaped by my personal experiences and beliefs. I realized that it was my personal involvement in this inquiry that made it so unique. I learned that narrative afforded me with the insight to deal with the complexities that arose during the inquiry. It provided me with the means to face my own assumptions, fears and prejudices, as well as the necessary space to discuss and even challenge my participants' discriminatory behaviours.

Space for interaction and reflection

Relational forms of inquiry, such as narrative, provide space for interaction between the research itself and the researched, by allowing or even requiring reflection on behalf of the researcher on all stages and aspects of the research. According to Etherington (2004), reflexivity can contribute to solving the power gap created between the researcher and the researched. Reflexivity is a moral and methodological concern in narrative inquiry (Etherington 2004, 2006; Josselson 1996). By being reflexive, the researcher attempts to acknowledge the way in which his/her own experiences and pre-understandings shape the inquiry and the results. By giving ourselves – and other people as well – a voice and the right to bring our experiences into the research, we are creating a sense of power and authority in the text. 'Reflexivity creates a dynamic process of interaction within and between ourselves and our participants, and the data that informs decisions, actions and interpretations at all stages of research' (Etherington 2004: 81).

Based on the premise that the researcher's role is central in narrative inquiry, it is obvious that 'the researcher does not find narratives but instead participates in their creation' (Neander and Skott 2006: 297). For this reason, Clandinin and Connelly (2000) advocate extra caution on behalf of researchers in order not to become too involved in the research project and influence the research. The researcher's pre-understandings lead narrative research. Presumptions are the starting point of the analysis, which is also shaped by the new experiences gained through the inquiry (Widdershoven and Smits 1996). By acknowledging that the narrative inquiry has been inevitably influenced by the researcher's values and beliefs, both the research process and the outcomes are made transparent (Etherington 2006). Hence, throughout the analysis, I attempted to acknowledge and reflect on the way that my personal beliefs, opinions and expectations as an individual, a Greek Cypriot woman, a researcher and a teacher have influenced the research process and the interpretation of the data.

What is more, Clandinin and Connelly (2000) draw on Dewey's notion of interaction (1938) and call researchers to move in four dimensions; inward and outward, backward and forward. Backward and forward refer to temporality: past, present and future. By inward, they mean toward internal conditions, feelings, hopes, aesthetic reactions and moral dispositions. And by outward, they mean the environment. All these four dimensions define temporality.

One of the ways I employed in trying to make this process as transparent as possible was by incorporating 'snapshots', some of which are included in this chapter. These snapshots are pieces of writing, trying to illustrate specific moments, events and thoughts and providing readers with a 'thick description' (Geertz 1973) of the surrounding context, and the events that occurred, together with my personal thoughts and reactions at these specific moments. 'Snapshots' are presented in text boxes and with a different font style from the rest of the text. They serve a dual purpose: mainly to act like videos or photographs capturing specific moments, but also to provide me – as a writer – with the space I need to express some beliefs and thoughts on the issues discussed in the chapter, creating a more engaging text. This feature is in accordance with the methodological approach of narrative inquiry which calls for reflexivity and acknowledgement of the ways in which researchers influence the research itself. In other words, my own story as a researcher becomes part of the research. Also, these 'snapshots' help to establish reflexivity and transparency in the text.

When expectations confront reality

I started this inquiry full of the excitement of fulfilling a dream; I was starting an innovative research project in an extremely interesting and under-researched area and context. The potential seemed endless. However, this excitement was accompanied by a palpable concern for the outcome. Would it turn out to be as I expected? But what exactly was I expecting to find? My starting point was confused, as from the beginning I was aware that the situation I was about to describe would be anything but ideal. Among the reasons that drove me into choosing this topic was the awareness of poor practice and the desire to contribute to the improvement of current practices. My readings about multiculturalism in Cypriot classrooms painted a discouraging image. Based on that and my personal experience of teaching or talking to other teachers about their experience, I was expecting to find an 'ugly' picture, with inappropriate teaching approaches and negative experiences for the children. I was prepared for the worst. Regarding teachers, I had created a 'deficient' role model in my mind, and in a sense I was measuring the teachers against that.

At the beginning I was unaware of acting this way. It only became clear to me when reading Phillion's (2002) work, where she described exactly the opposite situation. She narrates how in the initial stages of her inquiry she was searching for 'Ms. Multicultural'; a (semi) fictional character, an amalgam of the literature, her ideology, beliefs and desires. She started her inquiry looking for the perfect teacher. I was doing exactly the opposite. Phillion's description was the reverse reflection of my expectations. I had also, like Phillion, and probably like every other inquirer, set out in search of a specific model. But mine was not perfect, and this complicated things a lot.

My initial negative aspirations were quickly replaced by overexcitement that the reality was not as bad as I anticipated, leading me to sublimate what I was observing. Going into the field and collecting the data, especially in the first school, my initial impression and interpretation were that things were not as bad as I expected. I was overwhelmed by finding out that the teaching practices and climate in school were not as bad as I thought they would be. Especially with regard to the children's socialization and integration in the school's community, I was amazed by how good things were. From what I had known up until then, I had created a negative image in my mind concerning the experiences of pupils in multicultural schools. I was surprised to see that teachers with no training in teaching multicultural classrooms were drawing on their general teaching knowledge and experience, driven by their good intentions and love for their work and the children. So I started presenting an over-optimistic, idealized picture of what I was observing. I thought that the teacher-participants were doing an excellent job, and that they could act as role models for other teachers as well.

Even though I was not fully convinced of this ideal situation I was describing, and part of me was questioning these results, for a long time I was in denial. I can now identify a number of reasons that contributed to that. Firstly, there was the excitement of being proved wrong, as described earlier, which carried me away. Moreover, deep inside me I was hoping for a positive outcome. I was aware that it takes a long time for things to change in Cyprus and usually this does not happen before it is too late. The policy would remain deficient for many years to come, while diversity and multiculturalism in schools would increase tremendously. Therefore, my desire was to find out that there was still hope; that there could be examples of good practice upon which we could draw in order to improve things without requiring many changes in the system (like policy initiatives, resources and training). I was looking for role models in the existing situation; someone who could give the right answers to how things could be improved with minimal effort. And for a great part of the inquiry, I was seeking these in the teachers and students' practices and behaviour. Inevitably, this may have led me to overlook many other significant things; that is why it is important to acknowledge that this has been my purpose for a long time and the influence this had on the inquiry. Nevertheless, I now consider this as a great asset of this work.

Revisiting the literature and reading more on how things should be ideally, I realized that, even though the reality I was describing was not as bad as I had anticipated at the beginning, and could be perceived as 'acceptable' under the circumstances (lack of policy and support), it could also be much better. Therefore, I tried to adjust my viewpoint and also focus on what could be improved. I tried to emphasize the good elements that I observed, attempting to understand the reasons why they were so good, and draw on these to suggest how the deficiencies could be improved.

I have struggled to try to find a balance between the reality and my personal expectation, both positive and negative. Even I myself am not able to distinguish the borderlines that differentiate the two. This is where narrative has been a catalyst; it perceives the research as a mixture of the reality the researcher experiences during the inquiry, blended with her ideology and desires leading it throughout its course.

Roles: Responsibilities and aspirations

One of my struggles throughout the inquiry was a concern over the contribution I wished to make by carrying out this research. Apart from getting me a degree, I was concerned about what it would offer to the participants who would dedicate so much of their time and energy to it. And at the end, what good would it do to the research community in general and my country specifically? These concerns were related to my personal hopes and beliefs and were expressed in the way I positioned myself and the roles I chose to perform on the various occasions related to the inquiry; being in the field as a researcher, a teacher, a friend and even analyzing the data and sharing the outcomes with others. Moreover, people had different expectations from me, each of which I had a different desire to adopt on different occasions.

On many occasions I saw myself as a colleague of my teacher-participants; I wanted to help during classes, express my opinion and comment on their teaching approach, and even suggest how they could improve their teaching. Kyriakos – one of my teacher-participants – for example, encouraged me to move around and interact with pupils when they worked independently or in small groups. However, as many of them asked for my help, I usually got carried away and helped them with their work. And because I saw that Kyriakos was finding this useful, because in a sense I was sharing his workload and in this way more children would get help in less time, I kept doing it, treating it as a way of returning the favour of allowing me to research his class.

However, being on the research site as a researcher usually conflicted with the roles others were expecting me to perform. On many occasions the teacher, and especially the headteacher, would ask me to do things or assign responsibilities that were not appropriate.

We need you to substitute for Kyriakos tomorrow

School B during the second week of the inquiry.

3 teachers would be absent the following day, creating a lot of problems in the school, because of the lack of personnel to cover for them.

'We need you to substitute for Kyriakos tomorrow', the headteacher told me.

I felt that I was asked to do things I didn't want, but each decision I made would influence the outcome of my work. Refusing would upset the headteacher, making my work there more difficult or even compromising my access to the research field. Accepting would probably change the relationship I had developed with the children. I was there for a different reason. Moreover, I was not 'covered' to substitute for anyone. That would be illegal and could jeopardize my current and future research. So I decided to share this last concern with him.

'But Mr. Charis, I am not authorized to be alone with the children. If something happens you would get into trouble.'

'Don't worry about that. Nobody cares about these things.' he replied while leaving the room with an apathetic look on his face.

It was obvious that he found my comment and my concerns unreasonable. He asked me to do something and I could not get out of it without causing trouble.

I should do it then. It wouldn't do any harm, would it?

The headteacher's reaction gave me the impression that he thought I was being stupid for even thinking that this was not appropriate and that he was not willing to negotiate this with me. He had done me a favour by assisting me with my research, I owed him and this was a way to start paying him back. As Lieblich (1996) puts it, I was in debt for asking the teachers to cooperate. What I want to emphasize here are the complexities of the roles we are required to perform during the inquiry. Some of them are related to the research, while others may distract from the purpose and focus. Finding the golden mean between them is the greatest challenge narrative inquirers face. On many occasions the researcher may have to negotiate their obligations to others involved in the research (Laine 2000). Due to the narrative nature of my study, I was able to reflect on the ethical dilemmas I faced, reflect on my positioning, explain and even defend my actions.

Being a teacher myself influenced the inquiry to a great degree. Having a knowledge of the literature and some experience of teaching, I often got into the process of putting myself in the position of the teacher, thinking how I would react in specific circumstances and treat the 'problems' and issues that arose. This process inevitably involved judging the practices and behaviour I was observing, something that influenced the analysis. However, I constantly tried to remind myself that what I was observing was an isolated utterance and I could never be able to fully understand and explore all the events that had led to and influenced the behaviour of individuals at any given moment. Moreover, I tried to tackle this issue by prompting discussions with the participants – informally during recess or in the interviews I had with them. By doing this I was trying to explore the reasons that made them react in a specific way. Each person has his/her personal theory that informs his/her decisions and actions.

As the main purpose of my presence in the school was to carry out this inquiry, my main role was to be a researcher. What was appropriate behaviour for a researcher? And where does someone stop being a friend of the participants or a teacher and become just a researcher? In narrative inquiry, personal relationships simultaneously enrich the data and complicate them, as it is not easy to distinguish the information participants share in privacy from that which they wish to include in the data (Webb 2006; Andrews 2007). And even when these issues are resolved in some way, the researcher faces more difficulties in their interpretation. A researcher should be accurate in representing what he/she observes and transfer an authentic interpretation of the reality to the academic world. In order to achieve that, some would say that the researcher should withdraw from the research site and the inquiry and analyse the data with fresh eyes – be as distant from them as possible. But I felt that I could not do that, mainly because I started forming my interpretations and conclusions during the data collection. All the expectations and desires, as described in the previous section, had penetrated the research texts and the data. I could not differentiate between them.

Moreover, my relationships with my participants kept me trapped in my desire to present the nicest picture I could. Especially in the case of the teachers with whom I had developed a closer relationship, and felt that they had opened up their hearts to me when explaining their personal beliefs and the values underpinning their work. I could spot good intentions and a lot of love in their motives. So how could I talk about what they did wrong? How could I blame them?

Dealing with difficult issues, facing my own prejudices

I consider that the greatest challenge I had to face during the inquiry was deciding how to treat difficult issues that came up, like discrimination and racism. Conducting research in one's own culture can be extremely complicated. The values nourishing us during our upbringing in a specific context and country usually include being proud of it and wanting to present it in the best way possible. It is not easy, therefore, to criticize and attribute negative characteristics to one's own people. The methodological approach of this research has allowed me to deal with these issues and bring them forward. This process illuminates all these tensions, which become part of the research itself, which is enriched by them.

One of the main concerns was the issue of racism. I was keen to observe the presence or absence of racist attitudes and actions among children and teachers, as well as the way teachers dealt with this issue. Teachers placed a great emphasis on the issue of racism and classroom discourse was usually related to it. One of the main concerns of all teachers was the use of discriminatory words by the pupils. And number one on their list was the word 'black'. Throughout the inquiry and on different occasions, more than four individual teachers criticized the use of this word. Moreover, some of them were even reluctant to use it in conversations with me or between them.

Why does he hesitate to say 'black'?

An informal conversation with Marios before the start of the inquiry

'One of the girls in my classroom is . . . coloured ... But I look beyond her colour. For me they are all the same.'

He hesitated, trying to think of the right word to use. It was obvious that the first one that came into his mind was 'black'.

Why did he hesitate so much to use it? Is it so bad to say that someone is black?

Why say that somebody is tall and skinny is acceptable, but saying that he is black is not?

Could a single word be so important?

This specific word is considered very offensive in the context of Cyprus. With reference to a person, it is perceived as an insult, even though in other contexts, like the UK, it is absolutely acceptable. And still I can feel the shock I experienced when I first saw a publication at the University of Washington entitled *Induction for Black Students*. What is considered to be a privilege gained through long struggles and fights in a certain context, would be perceived as extremely discriminatory and racist in another. So how should I deal with this? How should I characterize these attitudes? Where do cultural conventions finish and where does racism start?

On many occasions I was surprized to realize that I shared many of the beliefs and stereotypes expressed by the participants. Hearing them talking about Pontians[2] or Turkish Cypriots in a way that I would consider as being racist, I was shocked to catch myself agreeing with them. As a member of the same culture and context, I shared many of the beliefs and stereotypes that constitute part of the grand narratives of our culture. This inquiry helped me realize many of my personal stereotypes and prejudices by seeing them reflected in my participants. It got me into the process of exploring my own opinions and attitudes and starting to evaluate them. And even more important, searching for their origins; trying to understand the way they have been imposed on me and the reasons that contributed to their creation. Prior to the start of this inquiry, I did not think of myself or the Cypriot people as being racist, but my findings suggest that there is a growing underlying tendency in that direction. And acknowledging that something is wrong is the first step towards dealing with it, even though admitting one's own weaknesses is rarely easy.

Nonetheless, it was extremely interesting to realize that the participants shared these concerns. Children presented an ambiguity, as they were strictly against racism, but at the same time they appeared reluctant to characterize someone as racist. Knowing that something is wrong does not imply that you will not do it. These issues are extremely serious and complex and can only be treated through appropriate training.

Sharing the outcomes

Interpretation and analysis of the data is a continuous process that is not restricted to the time the researcher looks at the data and writes up a report. It is a process that begins even before he/she enters the research site, shaped by his/her expectations, continues mentally throughout the inquiry and even after the data collection has finished. It also occurs while the researcher shares the outcomes with others. Even in informal conversations when you are asked about your work, the way you choose to talk about it informs your interpretation. For me, the way I talked about my work and shared the outcomes with others has had a great influence on the way I formed my results. Each time someone asked me about my work, I would choose a different story to tell.

At the beginning, I found it very difficult to respond to the question *'So, what did you find?'* I did not know what to say. *What should I say?* What did they *want* to hear; the truth, my truth or their truth? Especially when talking to people outside the world of education and academia, the situation easily became complicated. At the beginning, I would try to explain my findings in detail, which on many occasions would end up in an extensive discussion about whether multiculturalism is a good or a bad thing. But through time and experience, I got better at giving targeted answers. I would try to share information and narratives, which they would be interested to hear. Depending on the person I was talking to, I would choose specific elements of my study to disclose. I would share a different narrative with one of my participants, others to a colleague of mine, something else to a teacher or a friend who was curious to learn about my work. I would choose different meanings and messages that I felt would 'fit' better with what they wanted to know. The way people responded to the outcomes and narratives I was sharing with them and the reflection they gave me informed my interpretations. And a great part of this 'sharing' occurred while presenting pieces of my work in conferences.

We just gather together and talk badly of our country

Belfast, June 2010, 'Living Together in Divided Societies' conference

I was presenting some of the outcomes of my doctoral research. In the same session, four papers on Cyprus were presented, all dealing with similar issues, all ending with a discouraging message; 'things are no good and there is no indication they will get better.'

This became even clearer with a comment by a lady from the audience:

'I have been sitting here listening to you and I cannot help but think that the same thing you are saying today about Pontians is identical to what we were saying about repatriates 10 years ago. It's just the names and the target groups that change, the rest remains the same. Nothing else seems to be changing.'

'Is that what we actually want? To gather together and talk badly of our country?'

As I mentioned earlier in this chapter, the outcome of the study has been one of my main preoccupations for a very long time. And getting disapproving reactions made it very difficult for me to handle the 'discouraging' findings. The way the education system currently works is discriminatory and assimilationist and people from the dominant group are not comfortable with hearing it. However, my research reports some positive elements as well. Therefore, I have chosen to tell a story with a 'hopeful' ending. I tried to be as 'realistic' as possible, but also emphasize the good elements I experienced in schools. Because I feel that this is what I have to share, this is the story I choose to tell.

The most difficult moment for me was sharing my interpretations with the participants and getting their opinion about them. After completing the analysis, I arranged individual meetings with each of them. My main concern was not to offend them in any way. I felt they had given me so much by taking part in my research and I did not feel comfortable in criticizing their work. But at the same time I wanted to provide my readers with a complete description of what I witnessed. Therefore, I tried to solve this issue by focusing on the motives and beliefs that the teacher's approach revealed, rather than emphasizing their actions as such. In the discussions I had with them after the inquiry, I went through the events and issues I decided to include in the accounts of the research and explained to the participants my interpretation of these events. I was surprised by how well they perceived my comments and opinions and the way they used these as starting points upon which they offered their own alternative interpretations, hearing these stories several months later. This process has proven to be valuable for me, as it provided me with the opportunity to collect multiple interpretations of certain events and re-examine the way I analysed and interpreted my results.

To sum up...

In this chapter, I have focused on my experience as a researcher in a complex environment and how the narrative methodology I chose to adopt assisted me in dealing with sensitive issues that arose during its course. It allowed me to narrate my personal story while engaging with this research and, hopefully, open a window on to the way my personal beliefs, expectations and desires have influenced the way it evolved over time. By acknowledging that the inquiry itself is a blend of reality and personal experience, my personal involvement and subjectivity in the process was not only legitimized, but even valued as an important factor.

Conducting research in one's own culture is never easy, especially when this context is as complex as a divided island. Creative writing techniques, like 'snapshots', can provide solutions of 'voice', by exculpating the writer from criticizing his/her own particular group. Difficult issues, such as racism, are made more accessible. Through the relations developed, I was confronted with stereotypes and prejudices that I shared with many of the participants. Narrative provided me with the space, not only to discuss these realizations and concerns, internally and externally, but also make these discussions a valuable part of my work.

The roles I chose or was asked to perform during the inquiry, and the aspirations and responsibilities accompanying each one of them, also played an important part. I was able to discuss the ethical dilemmas I faced, justify the choices I made and acknowledge the influence of these decisions on the course of the inquiry. Through narrative, I could manoeuvre between roles and responsibilities.

Moreover, a great part of the research story I chose to narrate in my thesis was shaped by all the attempts I made to share it with others. As I contrast the field texts with the outcomes I reported, I realize the multiple ways in which the narrative account of this inquiry could be created. I acknowledge that there could be endless stories that could be told about this research. Nevertheless, that is the story I chose to tell in that specific instance and narrative provided me the space for presenting and explaining the background that informed the choices I made.

References

Andrews, M. (2007) 'Exploring Cross-Cultural Boundaries', in D. J. Clandinin (ed.), *Handbook of Narrative Inquiry: Mapping a Methodology*, Thousand Oaks, CA: Sage Publications Inc., pp. 489–511.

Angelides, P., Stygian, T., and Leigh, J. (2003) Forging a Multicultural Education Ethos in Cyprus: reflections on policy and practice, *Intercultural Education,* 14 (1): 57–66.

—(2004) Multicultural Education in Cyprus: a pot of multicultural assimilation?, *Intercultural Education,* 15 (3): 307–15.

Bryant, R. (2004) *Imagining the Modern: The Culture of Nationalism in Cyprus*, London: LB Tauris.

CER (Commission for Education Reform) (2004) *Democratic and Humanistic Education in the Eurocypriot Polity*, Nicosia: Ministry of Education and Culture.

Christou, M. (2006) A Double Imagination: Memory and Education in Cyprus, *Journal of Modern Greek Studies*, 24: 285–306.

Clandinin, D. J., and Connelly, F. M. (2000) *Narrative Inquiry: Experience and Story in Qualitative Research*, San Francisco, CA: Jossey-Bass.

Demetriou, C., and Trimikliniotis, N. (2007) 'The Cypriot Roma / Gypsies and the Failure of Education: Anti-Discrimination and Multiculturalism as a Post-accession Challenge', paper presented at the The Minorities of Cyprus: Past, Present and Future conference, Nicosia, November 2007.

Dewey, J. (1938) *Experience and Education*, New York: Collier Books.

ECRI (European Commission against Racism and Intolerance) (2001) *Second Report on Cyprus*, Strasburg: Council of Europe.

Etherington, K. (2004) *Becoming a Reflexive Researcher: Using Our Selves in Research*, London: Jessica Kingsley.

—(2006) 'Reflexivity: using our "selves" in narrative research', in S. Trahar (ed.), *Narrative Research on Learning: comparative and international perspectives*, Oxford: Symposium Books, pp. 77–92.

Eurydice (2009) *Organisation of the education system in Cyprus*, Brussels: EACEA Eurydice Unit, European Commission.

Geertz, C. (1973) *The Interpretation of Cultures*, New York: Basic Books.

Hadjitheodoulou-Loizidou, P. and Symeou, L. (2007) Promoting closer ties and cooperation between the school, the family and the community in the framework of intercultural education, *International Journal about Parents in Education,* 1: 63–72.

Josselson, R. (ed.) (1996) *Ethics and Process in the Narrative Study of Lives*, Thousand Oaks, CA: Sage.

Laine, M. D. (2000) *Fieldwork, Participation and Practice: Ethics and Dilemmas in Qualitative Research*, London: Sage Publications.

Lieblich, A. (1996) 'Some Unforeseen Outcomes of Conducting Narrative Research

With People of One's Own Culture', in R. Josselson (ed.), *Ethics and Process in the Narrative Study of Lives*, Thousand Oaks: Sage, pp. 172–86.

Lieblich, A., Tuval-Mashiach, R., & Zilber, T. (1998) *Narrative Research: Reading, Analysis, and Interpretation*, Thousand Oaks, CA: Sage Publications Inc.

Neander, K., and Skott, C. (2006) Important Meetings with Important Persons: Narratives from Families Facing Adversity and their Key Features, *Qualitative Social Work*, 5: 295–311.

Nicolaou, A., Nitsiou, C., and Charalambous, S. (2007) Cypriot High Schools as Cultural Mosaics: Students' Perspectives and Experiences, *The International Journal of Diversity in Organizations, Communities and Nations*, 7 (5): 343–51.

Panayiotopoulos, C., and Nicolaidou, M. (2007) At crossroads of civilizations: multicultural educational provision in Cyprus through the lens of a case study, *Intercultural Education*, 18 (1): 65–79.

Papadakis, Y. (2008) *History Education in Divided Cyprus: A Comparison of Greek Cypriot and Turkish Cypriot Schoolbooks on the 'History of Cyprus' (PRIO Report 2/2008)*, Oslo: International Peace Research Institute (PRIO).

Partasi, E. (2009) Identity and Belonging in a Culturally Diverse Classroom in Cyprus, *International Journal of Diversity in Organizations, Communities and Nations*, 9 (4): 146–56.

—(2011) Experiencing Multiculturalism in Greek-Cypriot Primary Schools, *Compare*, 41 (3): 371–86.

Phillion, J. (2002) *Narrative Inquiry in a Multicultural Landscape – Multicultural Teaching and Learning*,. Westport, Connecticut: Ablex.

Phillion, J., He, M. F., and Connelly, F. M. (eds) (2005) *Narrative & Experience in Multicultural Education*, Thousand Oaks, CA: Sage Publications Inc.

Trahar, S. (2006) *Narrative Research on Learning: Comparative and International perspectives*, Oxford: Symposium Books.

Webb, S. (2006) 'Learning from Elsewhere: ethical issues in a planned piece of narrative research in New Zealand', in S. Trahar (ed.) *Narrative Research on Learning: comparative and international perspectives*, Oxford: Symposium Books, pp. 221–38.

Widdershoven, G. A. M., and Smits, M. J. (1996) 'Ethics and Narratives', in R. Josselson (ed.), *Ethics and Process in the Narrative Study of Lives*, Thousand Oaks, CA: Sage Publications Inc., pp. 275–87.

Notes

1 The term 'non-Cypriots' refers to students whose parents do not have a Cypriot background and were either born in Cyprus or abroad.

2 The Pontian Greeks are a Greek ethnic group originating from the shores of the Black Sea and Pontus. At the beginning of the twentieth century, they migrated to other countries. More recently, there has been migration from Russia, Kafkasus and Georgia to Greece, and at a later stage to Cyprus. Different terms have been used for this category of migrants; 'Greek of Pontos', 'Greek Pontians', 'Rossopontioi', 'Pontioi', each of which bears different political assumptions.

Chapter 8

A conversation with Ah Leung

Christina Yip Pui Lin

> We achieve our identities and self-concept through the use of the narrative configuration, and make our existence into a whole by understanding it as an experience of a single unfolding and developing story.
>
> (Polkinghorne 1988: 150)

Introduction

As an experienced teacher, I agree that teachers' professional development would best be promoted if they were given the autonomy in deciding the content of their work and teaching pedagogy (Hargreaves 2000). However, the impact of educational reforms, influenced by a range of contextual and political factors (Morris and Scott 2003), as in the case of Hong Kong, has moved the teaching community towards a new management culture, which has led to teachers being increasingly controlled and monitored. Faced with unfamiliar responsibilities upheld in an array of educational reforms, there is a need to understand how teachers negotiate their professional identities in the present climate and how they perceive their 'selves' in different working environments. Seeking to strike a chord with a group of experienced teachers I met on a professional development course, I attempted to gain an understanding of teachers' professional identity negotiations through attending to teachers' own voices, which develop as we interpret and reinterpret our experiences through the process of narrative inquiry. I also examine how my 'self' and the participants' 'selves' construct and reconstruct our professional identities in a context wherein the pendulum of government policies has swung against teachers. In doing so, I have to delve into my personal practical knowledge (Connelly and Clandinin 1985) and the role of human experiences in acquiring conceptual knowledge throughout my learning and teaching process. While I was reliving my experiences and researching this puzzle, I was also conducting narrative inquiry with four other English teachers, lending an ear to their voices or 'whispers' as I tinkered with similar puzzles in their lives, a process fraught with uncertainties and problems. This chapter thus aims to give voice to the disturbing experiences that have developed within me while embarking on the narrative journey in the context of Hong Kong.

Reflection on narrative tensions

Based on the underlying premise that narrative inquiry is 'the belief that individuals make sense of their world (most) effectively by telling stories' (Bailey and Tilley 2002: 575; Bruner 1990: 13), the methodology –sharing one's experiences with others – seems to lend itself beautifully to relating teachers' difficulties and recording their experiences, even though there are many other challenges to it as a methodological approach in my local context of Hong Kong.

Like many other teacher-researchers in Hong Kong, our previous research orientation has created sets of criteria used for judging a piece of 'qualified academic work' (Yu 2005: 32). Other reasons for the scepticism towards narrative inquiry in Hong Kong, according to Yu and Lau (2011), include the small number of tertiary institutions, thus posing challenges for researchers to attempt alternate and unconventional methodologies. In addition, the relatively complicated language contexts in Hong Kong, as compared to Mainland China and Taiwan, where the written form of Chinese is different from its spoken form, compound the resistance to narrative. This chapter further portrays tensions I encountered while searching for identities of a group of secondary teachers in Hong Kong. To this end, I share how I grapple with these tensions at the beginning of the research process, showing the impact of the intellectual context where I was brought up – Hong Kong, a British colony from 1842 to 1997.

Reflection on the educational reform in the local context

Towards the end of the twentieth century, some government officials were committed to the need for substantial changes to the education sector, especially after the 1997 handover to Chinese sovereignty. However, the government still faced what Morris and Scott (2003) describe as 'an inherited culture of inertia and cynicism towards reform' (p. 17). This observation is probably based on the premise that most educational reforms promoted prior to the shift of sovereignty in 1997 served a symbolic purpose (Morris and Scott 2003).

> The superior man is modest in his speech, but exceeds in his actions.
> (Confucius, Analects, Verse 29, Chapter 14)

> 子曰:『君子恥其言而過其行。』
> 《孔子》、《論語》《憲問第十四章、第二十九句》

It is well known that Chinese society harbours a strong Confucian moral overtone, making it arduous for teachers to unleash their emotions publicly about educational polices, not to mention the upcoming and seemingly ongoing reforms in the educational landscape. It is also believed that another significant implication of teachers' reticence is the strong Confucian orientation towards education, which accentuates the role of teachers as a model of learning and to promote academic performance in examinations, thus rendering it problematic for teachers to share their difficulties in the face of educational reforms

Tapping the sounds of the silenced with stories

> The world's earliest archives or libraries, were the memories of women.
> (Trinh 1989: 121)

Experiences are formed and defined with time. Through telling and reflecting on my own experiences, my life is made transparent and I reach a better understanding of the difficulties I had during the research process. The symbolic meaning these experiences carry explains how and why I chose to use narrative inquiry to investigate the ways in which educational reforms in Hong Kong are shaping the lives and identities of teachers. Using the Chinese tradition of massage as a metaphor affords me the opportunity to reflect on my research journey, to run the gamut of my research puzzle and to refine the meanings of my experiences. While enjoying the therapeutic powers of this Chinese tradition, I also explain how my narrative journey, punctuated with moments of revelations, was fraught with scepticism from my colleagues and from Ah Leung, my masseur, which led to my own self-doubt about the use of narrative inquiry in a traditional Chinese context. The imagery employed and the fictitious conversation with my masseur demonstrate, in a powerful way, the value of narrative inquiry and its academic significance as a methodological approach for inquiry into teacher identities. In what follows, I am going to recall some critical episodes to better represent my reflections on the resistance I have encountered while embarking on the narrative journey.

Navigating my route of inquiry

I was reading Moen (2006) on the use of narrative when my daughter approached me.

> 'Mom, do you know how to chart a scattered diagram for statistics?'

My daughter was working on her own research methodology assignment. She had gathered some statistical information on her topic, which was about the Internet participation of young people in Hong Kong. My impulse was to say,

> 'Sorry, I've never worked on such a method and please don't confuse me with your figures.'

If I trawled my experience, I would only come up with using one type of qualitative research, content analysis, which I had used for a previous dissertation on language studies; and a quantitative approach, for other course work.

Realizing that I was being a bit inconsiderate, I turned to her Excel file and tried my best to explain it to her. Seeing my problem, my daughter gazed at my computer and asked sympathetically,

> 'How's your thesis?'
>
> 'Well, perhaps I am too focused on my reading, so that I can't see the wood for the trees at the moment. But it's coming fine.'
>
> 'Let me have a look at your writing!'

She grabbed my paper and sat down to give it a good read. She cleared her throat pretending that she was going to read aloud a speech.

> '... *I was only 17 years old when I finished Form Five. When I received a letter from the college of education asking me to come for an interview, I rummaged through all my closets, looking for a decent dress to wear ...* '

She was reading one of my personal reflections to be included in Mei's story, one of my participants, as a response to the narrative about her early teaching experiences.

> 'What is this, Mom? Why are there so many 'I's in your paper, I mean in an academic paper. You certainly are writing something much more serious than what I am doing.' She stopped her reading and spoke in a serious tone.
>
> 'Well, I think you are talking about the acceptability of this particular methodology in the academic world. The suggested reading given to me by my supervisor said that this is absolutely legitimate. Let me find that for you.'
>
> 'No, thanks. I'm just asking for interest. My understanding is that there should be a rigid format in academic writing, not that kind of ... thing that I have just read.'

She was clearly uneasy as she discovered that her critique was directed to her mom. After a brief pause, she continued.

> 'Shouldn't there be some voices of experts, I mean scholars, educators, well whatever, but certainly not yours.'

My daughter pointed out some edgy questions that were pressing me at that moment. My concerns grew as I realized the difficulty in convincing myself of the legitimacy of using narrative inquiry as a methodology especially when more traditional approaches predominate in this academic landscape and perpetual skeptical remarks were heard. I gained my focus and began to defend my choice.

> 'Well, I think this structure helps make me more transparent. By including MY own voice in my research process, I can include more possibilities in revealing my experiences.'

My daughter decided to drop the topic as she considered it to be beyond her intellectual level. This is one of the episodes where I experienced my initial uncertainties created not by my daughter, but more by my own perceptions. My research deals with teacher identity, but how was I going to plan for it?

According to Moen (2006), using a narrative is one of the best ways to structure people's experiences and dialogic interactions with others and the world. Teachers, like most other storytellers, create narrative descriptions about their experiences and attempt to make sense of the behaviour of others (Zellermayer 1997). Recognizing the significance of smaller local narratives, Lyotard (1984) also concludes that knowledge should be locally determined. Thus, my use of teachers' narratives has an added benefit. The stories and voices of this marginalized sector can now be made public. In using the multiplicity of voices, beliefs and approaches to analyse their realities, I have to include what my participants say and do not say and what they do. The 'multivoicedness' of the narratives also helps organize our experiences of the world while we construct and reconstruct our identities (Moen 2006).

Defining the concept of 'truth' and 'memories'

While still figuring out what constituted the legitimacy of my work, I remembered the comments of Michael,[1] one of my colleagues. Since he had demonstrated an interest in my research, I had shown him the prologue, which I had written long before I started my analysis. After reading a few lines, he unleashed his merciless criticism.

> 'Is this a thesis that you are writing?' he asked, incredulously.

> 'Well, I'm using what is called narrative inquiry. It allows the researcher's voice to be included … '

He interrupted me, saying,

> 'I'll never use this kind of style in writing an academic paper. Maybe I'm out of fashion or you're too postmodern. I'm not being offensive, but see, I don't like the use of conversations in academic studies. It pretty much looks like a story, I mean, fiction. Or is it a biography? You have a lot of descriptions of your own feelings and … '

He said it sternly, like a teacher, moving his index finger along the lines of his student's assignment. For a brief moment, I was numb with anger.

> 'OK, Mr. Michael, it is the reconstruction of meaning, rather than the "truth" that you expect. There is no singular truth of a situation. For each participant, what we know as the "truth" is contextual and these "truths" will resonate for others who have similar experiences.'

His criticism seemed to hinge on the questions of legitimacy connected to the issues of truth and rationality (Conle 2001: 22). I tried hard to keep my cool. Seeing my agitation, Michael relented and said more gently,

> 'I'm just wondering why you have to choose autoethnography, or what you call narrative inquiry. What's the point? Have you ever considered your defence in the committee? I admire your energy and perseverance, but why do you have to dig into your memories to look for resonance?'

I was keen on defending my decision and explained impatiently:

> 'I think you have to agree with me that memories may be culturally determined, as we construct our memories within a particular context. By using the narrative methodology, participant teachers are provided with an avenue to recount their experiences in the form of stories. I want to re-present what they have experienced in a readable format. Or perhaps, I just want to get my thesis done and earn my doctoral degree. End of story, Michael.'
>
> 'Calm down, Christina. I think I understand what you mean. You try to dig deeply into somebody's life experiences and then you write down his or her story.'
>
> 'What I am doing is more complicated than that. It's like combining the typical question-and-answer interviews with my sharing of personal experiences with the participants. During this process, we also reflect on the process of our communication as I respond to the participants' revelation of their personal details. Of course, I also aim to understand these stories, as you say. I'm sure this will do me good as well ... '
>
> 'Of course, if you pass your viva. That's VERY good!'
>
> 'That's one thing. The other thing is that I am also telling my own story while I re-present their stories. This will provide an avenue for doing something meaningful for yourself and the world.'

Unknowingly, I was quoting what Ellis (2004: xviii) said about autoethnography. I was rather shocked by my persistence in defending the method, which was spurred on by the criticisms from the people around me. Michael is not a local teacher; he is a Native-speaking English Teacher (NET) from the United States, who was employed under the NET Scheme to teach English in Hong Kong. My impression is that these teachers are more familiar with the academic world, so I felt frustrated after hearing his comments. Exhausted by all these tensions, I logged off my computer and decided to go to old Mr Leung for a massage.

The revelations of a 'masseur'

Mr Leung is a partially blind but experienced masseur. His regular patrons call him Ah Leung, which pleases him, as he considers it a sign of friendship. I visit him from time to time, especially when I am exhausted, when I need to lay my head snugly in the massage bed, close my eyes and immerse myself in contemplation. Many unresolved issues float up in my mind as a kind of 'continual unfolding in which the narrative insights of today' appear chronologically as events of tomorrow (Clandinin and Connelly 2000: 166). The physical comfort I derive from the 'therapeutic' massage shares equal billing with the mental reflection it affords me. It is a process through which I seek to construct or reconstruct my other 'self'. Such a 'movement' 'in direct experience is an alteration in the qualities of objects and space and' enables me to gain 'an aspect of this qualitative change' (Dewey 1934, 1958: 207).

Since I was diffident about my work, I aspired for another evolution or 'change' at old Ah Leung's parlour. As I stepped into the room, I was titillated by the scent of flowers that permeated the whole place. I greeted him as usual and rolled on to the bed. I was longing for a spell of rest and tranquility. I felt his fingers begin to knead my back.

> 'Ah!' I heard myself say, as the massage intensified. I felt myself drifting off.

> 'How's your thesis going?' Ah Leung asked. 'Your neck is very stiff.'

I gave him a soft sigh, half asleep.

> 'Are you busy with your interviews?'

I felt my neck tighten. I get so irritated when people bombard me with questions about my thesis.

> 'I have not yet sorted out everything ... '

> 'So, you need your microphone and recorder, right? I think all I need to get my job done is my hands,' Ah Leung interrupted me. 'They are the only tools I have.'

'I do, but not all the time. Sometimes, we just talk about our daily lives. It is the "phenomenon" that I am more interested in. I treat every meeting we have as a period of storytelling, as we humans are storytellers. We "lead storied lives" (Clandinin and Connelly 2000: 2) and, therefore, the study of their narratives, I mean their stories, is to analyze how humans experience the world.'

'I am curious about how this is done. Do you write a memoir of encounters with your research participants?'

'Right. How am I going to do this? I really don't know for sure. But I do know that we collaborate to construct and re-construct our stories in which we play roles both as storytellers and characters in our stories. Through "stories lived and told" by us, we make sense of our experience (Clandinin and Connelly 2000: 2). I also develop a good relationship with my research participants.'

My voice was muffled, as I was speaking through the face hole in the bed. I took a deep breath and tried my best to speak clearly.

'While reflecting on our stories, I am also seeking to find the impact their stories had on me as a teacher.'

(Trahar 2002:195)

'So, you have no plan about what you are writing? That's what I do sometimes. I rely on my instincts.'

'I thought you said that it is your fingers that guide you through the process?'

I was glad to have initiated this sudden dialogue.

'I do rely on my fingers, but I rely more on my experience in getting my job done. I was taught to start with a patient's neck and shoulders. But I don't really follow all the steps in the prescribed sequence. My patients tell me their problems, and I then figure out the best way to help them relax within the given time. I bet yours is different. You are writing serious stuff and you definitely need a PLAN.'

Ah Leung dissected the issue with surgical precision. A shudder swept over my body as I felt the chill in my backbone. I was trying hard to remember some of the materials I had read last night. Yes, I had to admit it was a real struggle for me to move away from the linear approach and come up with some kind of 'messiness' in writing. Moreover, the protean nature and attitude required in narrative inquirers (Connelly 2003) perplexed me. However, as the research process went on, I found that the process of explaining my research participants' stories progressed thematically. I raised my head a bit to defend myself but quickly decided to duck back into the hole to compose my explanation.

> 'There is a way to do it. I've learned to take "field notes". Field notes can be descriptive and reflective. Descriptive field notes record the objective part of the data – the stories or the factual verbatim accounts of my friends. Reflective field notes, on the other hand, record my thoughts and perceptions on what I have collected. These subjective notes describe what I think, what my friends mean, and what they likely refer to. These field notes come before the draft of the story and before the plotline is devised.'
>
> (Ellis 2004: 117)

I was in the middle of clarifying things when another query landed on me.

> 'You record teachers' stories, right? So why don't you just write a book about yours or the teachers' memoirs on teaching? Why go through all this trouble? What makes them different?'

Ah Leung would not be dissuaded from asking about my methodology – my weakest link at this moment. I felt pain all over my body and my legs. I rallied my last bit of conviction after the 'sharp blow' had hit me.

> 'Good questions. But my friend, when I'm writing about my friends' stories, I am also in the 'field' at some point. I mean, I don't just tell the stories; I have to interpret them, too. I also have to understand and hybridize them – like integrating the newly constructed stories of the teachers into stories of myself.'

My enthusiasm for the topic gathered momentum as I continued. I was, in fact, moving to the 'how' of my research (Heidegger 1927: 72).

> 'The aim of my study is to gain a deeper understanding of the meaning of daily experiences to the teachers by asking about the experience before they have tried to categorize it. In doing so, I am trying to construct rich interpretive descriptions of the experiences of my participants' lived time, lived space, lived human relationships and lived body. So, in my study, I will ask my participants to relate their past experiences when they were learners, their lived experiences as teachers and their plans for the future. This will allow the teachers to "narratively" understand their experiences in response to changes in the educational context.'
>
> (van Manen, 1990)

I felt the tension ease up as I 'lectured' Ah Leung. I felt his hand on my sore legs. As my mind began to drift, I heard a distant voice commend my 'hard' work.

> 'Yes, this is exactly what we think about narrative inquiry. It is the best way of representing and understanding experience. Experience happens narratively. Narrative inquiry is a form of narrative experience. Therefore, educational experience should be studied narratively'. It was the rationale of Clandinin and Connelly. (2000: 18–9)

I had been reading their work these past few days. I opened my eyes and saw Ah Leung patting my left leg gently.

> 'Wake up, ma'am. Time's up. Are you alright?'
>
> 'Yeah. I'm sorry, I must have been dreaming just now,' I said, embarrassed.
>
> 'Indeed you were. You slept like a log.'

Ah Leung went out of the room. Alone now, I sat up, trying to recall what I had gone through in the last hour. I turned from side to side and moved my head backward and forward. My animated discussion with Ah Leung had been a dream. Was my 'problem' solved? I drank some water and left Ah Leung's parlour. The sunlight was blinding but I did not mind. I was feeling quite relaxed and uplifted. I heard my inner voice pipe up as I headed for the university library.

> 'Yes, I am a social scientist who will write to research and, at the same time, do research while I write. I think I will acquire the initial information from my participants and inform them of my research framework. Before the interview commences, I will encourage them to select pseudonyms for themselves, though we have mutually agreed upon the flower labels assigned to them. Of course, I will have my participants' stories and I will also interpret or re-interpret these stories, according to the themes that emerge from the narratives collected.'

This episode illustrates how I have been challenged to interrogate my attempt to use a less linear approach in writing a research text. It also showcases how I wrestle with theories so as to gain a foothold in my research journey.

Demystifying dialogic analysis

I took the bus, as it was before rush hour and I could probably get a seat on the upper deck. There were very few people on the bus and I chose a seat near the window – a rare stroke of luck. I looked down, watching people hurry across streets, chase after buses and speak as though in pantomime because I could not hear them.

I suddenly recalled what I once read in Clandinin, and Connelly's book (2000). Every person needed to be understood, but they were like the pedestrians on the street: I could not understand them as individuals. Why were they in a hurry? What were the couples talking about? These people should all be understood in relationship and in a social context. If anything striking happened or if I were inspired by anything I saw, I would tell my daughter and my students; I might even write it down in my diary. In doing so, I might have interpreted what I had seen and translated it to my audience. These newly created stories do not simply comprise verbally expressed dialogues, but also emotionally charged meanings subordinated to my interpretation.

I began to see myself talking to my participants in a café. Our encounter, in the form of interviews, would lead to an interactive process, representing a newly established relationship that is constituted dialogically. Riessman (2008) presumes that when we speak, we are like performers; thus, the narratives involved can be analyzed as scenes, positioning them within the greater context of the story. To understand and analyze my participants' stories, I considered the context and the concept of time – both the past and the present. Hence, as a researcher using narrative inquiry, I should not merely record the indigenous view of our shared life-world, but also present the interviewer and the interviewee's interactive assessment and response to stories told.

Who is tending to (y)our experiences?

As a storyteller and researcher, I found that the most rewarding moments were those in which my participants and I shared our experiences. I continued, however, to wrestle with discomfort. One such occasion was, as I described earlier, when Michael, my colleague, criticized my style of writing. Another was when I dreamt that Ah Leung, the masseur, had grilled me about my hypothesis, proof, methodology and so on. The study was a long and arduous journey until I came to Hart (2002), who contends that, as a narrative researcher, I am like a storyteller 'seeking meanings that may help us to cope with our circumstances' (p. 155). In order to attend to our experiences, we have to make new meanings out of these espoused experiences. Our historical experience influences the present 'self' and projects the new 'self' into possibilities in the future.

Being the writer of 'narratives' and 'stories' for my participants

The terms 'narrative' and 'story' have been used interchangeably in literature. A story may be seen as the closest a person can come to an experience, as he, she or others tell it (Clandinin and Connelly 1994). Stories are also considered a person's identity derived from his or her culture. The story allows us to construe who we are in terms of 'self' and gives us a sense of unity with common beliefs in terms of culture (Gudmundsdottir 1991). In my research, the participants recounted experiences as learners and teachers. They told me their stories, and I, the researcher, described and interpreted these through the writing of their narratives and use of narrative inquiry.

Inspired by Richardson's (1994) critique, I came to realize as I began writing my field notes that throughout the research process, analysis and interpretation were intertwined. In hindsight, I also realized that from the very first time I assigned the flower label[2] to represent my participants, my writing had taken shape. While I was tracing and categorizing the data I collected, I was also engaged in reflection, which led me to the use of song images and other metaphors throughout the retelling of the accounts. All these revealed the way I thought and interpreted my participants' narratives. This reflective process also sparked more insightful interpretations and representations, which drove me to delve further into my experiences. To acknowledge some of the shared narrative themes identified in my ongoing conversations with my participants, I incorporated discussions of pertinent theoretical insights throughout. For the same reason, my comments and discussions were interwoven throughout the text. In doing so, I deviated from a more conventional way of writing, which is focused, problem-centred, linear and straightforward (Richardson 1994).

Though I had concerns about my claim to authority and queried who would take my work seriously, writing from an involved position seems more natural to me now. Richardson's (2000) discussion of the postmodernist view of authoritative knowledge took me one step further. I am more confident with my choice as no methodology 'has a privileged status' (2000: 928), and taking a postmodernist position 'does allow us to know something without claiming to know everything' (2000: 928). Richardson also reassured her readers that having 'a partial, local, historical knowledge is still knowing' (ibid).

I am grateful to Richardson for this advice. Yes, I understand that my knowledge is 'partial', but it involves over 30 years of teaching and professional development; it is 'local' and 'historical', because it is indigenous and unique when it comes to teaching in the context of Hong Kong, especially to somebody like me, who has been involved in this community as a learner and as a teacher for several decades. More importantly, while exploring my personal experiences and the experiences of others, I am able to critically examine our 'selves' in order to grow and maybe to interest others on our way. It is also during this process that we come to 'confirm, resist, and eventually maintain or transform the accepted norm' (Richardson 2001: 37) of what our identities are.

I was also influenced by Richardson's notion of using sociological analytic writing – 'the collective story' – which 'gives voice to those who are silenced or marginalized' (Richardson 1997: 22). According to her, the collective story not only speaks of the storytellers' past, but is also about their future and social change.

> By emotionally binding people together who have had the same experience ... the collective story overcomes some of the isolation and alienation of contemporary life. It provides a sociological community, the linking of separate individuals into a shared consciousness. Once linked, the possibility for social action on behalf of the collective is present, and therewith, the possibility of societal transformation.
>
> (Richardson 1997: 33)

As I was gathering field notes, my participants and I were drawn closer to each other by our stories – the lived experiences. The process of sharing our lived stories triggered the unconscious experiences and the multiple selves inside. This tended and refined the tangled and unspeakable experiences.

The narrative inquiry approach and research process

> One way of describing narrative inquiry can be described as a methodology based upon collecting, analyzing, and re-presenting people's stories as told by them.
>
> (Etherington 2004: 75)

Narrative inquiry is a systemic approach that seeks to understand subjective experiences by focusing on the stories that recall these experiences. As a methodology, it is nested within the interpretive research paradigm, which honours subjectivity and reflexivity. While I was revealing and re-presenting personal experiences, I was also giving others the opportunity to understand how the events were experienced. With this approach, I was able to explore a particular time and focus on finding meaning about a specific issue – the education reform context in Hong Kong. I was also able to produce rich accounts that reveal my participant teachers' experiences and extend our understanding of the issue discussed.

More issues to be considered

> ... traditional notions of reliability simply do not apply to narrative studies, and validity must be radically reconceptualized.
>
> (Riessman 1993: 65)

Validity

Interviews are a narrative inquiry's main source of data, and they help elicit stories. However, according to Mishler (1986), 'Treating responses as stories opens up many complex analytic problems, and, of course, it represents only one of a number of approaches to issues of meaning' (Mishler 1986: 67). In narrative work, the interview process itself calls on participants to make sense and create meaning from their experiences. Mishler (ibid) sees interviewing as a 'form of discourse between speakers' and argues that 'ordinary language competence shared by investigators and respondents is a critical but unrecognized precondition for effective research practice' (ibid: 7). In an interview, the 'meanings of questions and responses are contextually grounded and jointly constructed by interviewer and respondent' (ibid: 33–4). The co-construction that occurs during the interview made it crucial that I remained constantly reflective on my role in the construction of the narratives. Even the co-construction of the questions was negotiated once the interview was in process. The ambiguity and complexity of language in a question are not the only things affecting the response. In fact, Mishler asserts that the way in which 'interviewers and respondents attempt to "fit" their questions and responses to each other and to the developing discourse' helps resolve any ambiguities in the questions, whether they are simple or complex (1986: 47).

The co-constructed nature of interviewing and analysis is a vital aspect of the narrative inquiry process. Narrative inquiry is an exploration for both the researcher and the participants. As the stories are told, the meanings are put together by the interviewer (myself) and the interviewee through the interaction within the interview setting. Further interpretation occurs in the analytical and representation processes. 'Regardless of the type of narrative inquiry undertaken, the current critique calls attention to the researcher's presence and why it must be taken into account from the start' (Alvermann 2000: 8). However, Clandinin and Connelly (1994) warn that 'when we become characters in their stories, we change their stories' (p. 422). So when we, as researchers, are presenting our participants' stories, we must consider 'how our research texts shape their lives' (ibid) in representing their stories.

Language Issues

Another area that had to be tackled was the language employed in the field notes. Initially, I had a little difficulty figuring things out. Qualitative research is different from quantitative research in that it seeks to represent the diverse perspectives of participants' experiences through a variety of approaches and methods (Denzin and Lincoln 1994; Flick 1998). In addition, qualitative research supports a 'research paradigm in which the subject is also co-researcher, being actively and openly involved' bringing along his or her own worldviews, paradigms, or set of beliefs (Reason and Rowan 1981: 20).

Being non-native speakers of English, my research participants and I conversed in Cantonese, the spoken language of Hong Kong. Thus, maintaining accuracy in representing teachers' views and perspectives in English was challenging. The situation was further complicated because the language we speak is not the same as the written form of the Chinese language. In other words, when I was listening to my participants' narratives, I responded in Cantonese, but when I recorded my field notes and wrote my analysis in my journal, I used English. Thus, while reviewing what I had written in my journal, I had to modify phrases and turn to other vocabularies to better represent the narrators' intended meanings. The process of redrafting and revisiting the field notes often started another cycle of member checking – inquiring of my participants if I had represented their meanings accurately. Furthermore, in eliciting meaning from what I recorded, I had to deal with a range of meanings and discourses to come up with precize and valid translations (Jootun, McGhee, and Marland 2009).

Did I change what happened in their stories? Yes, I did change the words, and I might have altered the stories, but I retained what I believed to be the gist of their stories. What may have changed is the way the stories were presented. The conflicting language issue seemed to be problematic, yet it was worth taking the trouble because it helped refine my analysis. Besides, the participating teachers also found the process useful. They tended to listen to the stories they recorded and become more reflective throughout the process. Often, they would remark on what they had said from a new perspective, which they claimed to be very thought-provoking.

Trustworthiness

Unlike quantitative research, qualitative research does not have any charts and numbers to validate itself. Mishler (1990) claims that our 'social worlds are endlessly being remade as norms and practices change, it is clear that judgments of trustworthiness may change with time, even when addressed to the "same" findings' (p. 420). So rather than generalizing findings for all participant teachers or for all educational contexts, I focused on whether my re-presentations made sense to my participants. Lincoln and Guba (1985) suggest that in order to gain credibility for a study, rigorous research methods including prolonged engagement with participants, persistent observation and member checking should be conducted.

Besides credibility, Lincoln and Guba (1985) suggest providing 'the data base that makes transferability judgments possible' (p. 318). As a researcher, my responsibility was to produce sufficient descriptions that allow readers or other researchers to make sense of my interpretations. In this research, for example, it was made possible as co-construction occurs through the researcher and participant teachers' strong interaction throughout the research process. I also gave accounts about the changes in the educational policies in Hong Kong, owing to some of the political changes that Hong Kong was experiencing in order to contextualise our narratives.

Another challenge I encountered in doing this research rests on the participant teachers' willingness in confiding their stories to me. I came to know these teachers in an educational context, where we were participants on a refresher course; we had no idea about one another's qualifications or teaching experiences. Initially, some were quite hesitant in relating their stories, especially when the interviews touched on some sensitive issues about the school in which they were working and their previous experiences. Thus I had to be meticulous when I was conducting the interview, trying to embrace my 'participant values' (Guba and Lincoln 1994: 115) and sharing my own experiences with them.

Concluding reflections

I have attempted to represent my disturbing experiences of undertaking research using narrative inquiry in Hong Kong. Through reading some stories of my journey, you, the reader, may not only make sense of my difficulties in doing narrative, but you may also have gained some insight into my lived experience as a researcher in Hong Kong, a context where, as yet, narrative inquiry continues to be seldom used.

References

Alvermann, D. (2000) 'Narrative approaches', in M. L. Kamil, P. Mosenthal, P. D. Pearson, and R. Barr (eds), *Handbook of Reading Research*, Vol. 3: 123–39.

Bailey P. H. and Tilley S. (2002) Storytelling and interpretation of meaning, *Journal of Advanced Nursing, 38 (6):* 574–83.

Bruner, J. (1990) *Acts of Meaning*, Cambridge, MA: Harvard University Press.

Clandinin, D. J., and Connelly, F. M. (1994) 'Personal experience methods', in N.K. Denzin and Y. S. Lincoln (eds), *Handbook of Qualitative Research*, Thousand Oaks, CA: Sage Publications Inc., p. 413–27.

—(2000) *Narrative Inquiry, Experience and Story in Qualitative Research*, San Francisco: Jossey-Bass.

Conle, C. (2001) The Rationality of Narrative Inquiry in Research and Professional Development, *European Journal of Teacher Education*, 24 (1): 21–33.

Connelly, F. M. (2003) *Thinking Narratively. What Do Narrative Inquirers Do?* AERA WINTER INSTITUTE: Narrative Inquiry in Social Science Inquiry. Toronto.

Connelly, F. M., and Clandinin, D. J. (1985) 'Personal practical knowledge and the modes of knowing: Relevance for teaching and learning', in E. Eisner (ed.) *Learning and Teaching: The Ways of Knowing*, Chicago: National Society for the Study of Education, pp. 174–98.

Denzin, N. K., and Lincoln, Y. S. (eds) (1994) *Handbook of Qualitative Research,* Thousand Oaks, CA: Sage Publications Inc.

Dewey, J. (1934, 1958) *Art as Experience,* New York, NY: Capricorn Books.

Ellis, C. (2004) *The Ethnographic I: A Methodological Novel about Autoethnography,* Walnut Creek, CA: AltaMira.

Etherington, K. (2004) *Becoming a Reflexive Researcher: Using Our Selves in Research,* London: Jessica Kingsley.

Flick, U. (1998) *An Introduction to Qualitative Research*, Fourth Edition, Thousand Oaks, CA: Sage Publications Inc.

Guba, E. G., and Lincoln, Y. S. (1994) 'Competing paradigms in qualitative research', in N. K. Denzin and Y. S. Lincoln (eds), *Handbook of Qualitative Research,* Thousand Oaks, CA: Sage Publications Inc., pp. 105–17.

Gudmundsdottir, S. (1991) Story-maker. Story-teller: Narrative Structures in Curriculum, *Journal of Curriculum Studies*, 23 (4): 207–18.

Hargreaves, A. (2000) Four ages of professionalism and professional learning, *Teachers and Teaching: Theory and Practice*, 6 (2): 151–82.

Hart, P. (2002) Narrative, knowing, and emerging methodologies in environmental education research, *Canadian Journal of Environmental Education*, 7 (2), 140–65.

Heidegger, M. (1927) 'Being and Time', in D. F. Krell (ed.) *Martin Heidegger: Basic Writings from Being and Time* (1927) *to The Task of Thinking* (1964), 2nd edn, New York: Harper San Francisco, pp. 41–87.

Jootun, D., McGhee, G., Marland, G. R. (2009) Reflexivity: Promoting rigor in qualitative research, *Nursing Standard*, 23 (23), 42–6.

Lincoln, Y., and E. Guba (1985) *Establishing Trustworthiness. Naturalist Inquiry.* Newbury Park, CA, Sage.

Lyotard, J.-F. (1984) *The Postmodern Condition. A Report on Knowledge.* Minneapolis: University of Minnesota Press. (First published 1979).

van, Manen, M. (1990) *Researching Lived Experience: Human Science for Action Sensitive Pedagogy*, New York: State University of New York Press.

Mishler, E. G. (1986) *Research Interviewing: Context and Narrative*, Cambridge: Harvard University Press.

—(1990) Validation in inquiry-guided research: The role of exemplars in narrative studies, *Harvard Educational Review*, 60: 415–42.

Moen, T. (2006) Reflections on the narrative research approach, *International Journal of Qualitative Methodology*, 5 (4), Article 5.

Morris, P., and Scott, I. (2003) Education reform and policy in Hong Kong, *Journal of Education Policy*, 18 (1), 71–84.

Polkinghorne, D. E. (1988) *Narrative Knowing and the Human Sciences*, Albany: State University of New York Press.

Reason, P. and Rowan, J. (eds) (1981) *Human Inquiry: a Sourcebook of New Paradigm Research*, Chichester: John Wiley and Sons.

Richardson, L. (1994) 'Writing: A method of inquiry', in N. K. Denzin and Y. S. Lincoln (eds), *Handbook of Qualitative Research*, Thousand Oaks, CA: Sage Publications Inc., pp. 516–29.

—(1997) *Fields of Play: Constructing an Academic Life*, New Brunswick, NJ: Rutgers University Press.

—(2000) 'Writing: A method of inquiry', in N. K. Denzin and Y. S. Lincoln (eds), *Handbook of Qualitative Research*, 2nd edn Thousand Oaks, CA: Sage Publications Inc., pp. 923–48.

—(2001) Getting personal: Writing-stories, *Qualitative Studies in Education*, 14 (1), 33–8.

Riessman, C. K. (1993) *Narrative Analysis*, Newbury Park, CA: Sage Publications.

—(2008) *Narrative Methods for the Human Sciences*, Thousand Oaks, CA: Sage Publications Inc.

Trahar, S. (2002) Researching learning across cultures, *Counselling and Psychotherapy Research*, 2 (3), 195–200.

Trinh T. Minh-ha (1989) *Woman, Native, Other: Writing Postcoloniality and Feminism*, Bloomington: Indiana University Press.

Yu, W. M. (2005) 'An Experiential Study on the Application of Narrative Inquiry in Teacher Development in Hong Kong', unpublished thesis submitted for the degree of Doctor of Education in the Department of Curriculum, Teaching and Learning, Ontario Institute for Studies in Education of the University of Toronto, Canada.

Yu, W. M., and Lau, C. K. (2011) 'Teaching narrative inquiry in the Chinese community: A Hong Kong perspective', in S. Trahar (ed.), *Learning and Teaching Narrative Inquiry, Travelling in the Borderlands:* Amsterdam: Netherlands: John Benjamins Publishing, pp. 71–86.

Zellermayer, M. (1997) When we talk about collaborative curriculum-making, what are we talking about?, *Curriculum Inquiry*, 27 (2), 187–214.

Notes

1 The people who appear in this paper, other than the writer, remain pseudonymous to protect their identity.

2 Participants in the study were named after the Chinese 'Four Gentlemen in Plants', which includes Plum Blossom (Mei), Orchid (Lan), Chrysanthemum (Kuk) and Bamboo (Cheuk). They have all long been featured in ancient paintings and poems to express loftiness, righteousness, modesty and purity.

Chapter 9

Catalan teacher meets Chilean researcher

(De)constructing subjectivities through the interplay of textual narratives

Verónica Larrain

Introduction: Contextualisation. Writing methods that mediate teachers' representation and subjectivity

Over the last ten years, after turning 30 and emigrating from Chile to Spain, I found myself working with teachers in different research projects and writing about them. By autumn 2002, I was launched on the project of narrative inquiry in education in order to explore how teachers' identities were performed. Since then, I have become very interested in the capacity of narratives to reveal how subjects constitute themselves through writing practices that are interwoven with power/knowledge relations, and that destabilize meaning (Tamboukou 2008: 104–6). In education, there are a series of cultural designations that regulate teacher identity, such as the conceptualization of the teacher as a reproducer of knowledge or as the embodiment of rules and authority, or norms linked to different social status categories. Conditions like: ambiguity; dislocation; hyper-flexibility; instability; the uncertainty regarding what their role is; the (self) exploitation of experiences and emotions; extreme mobility; life-long learning; and the lack of skill limits, have become emblems for a new social model of professional and economic success that has affected the educational context.

Facing this complex panorama, which is a reality in many European countries, I am convinced that the teaching profession as an identity category needs to be revised under the new neo-liberal and post-Fordist frameworks, where social imaginaries and dual logic (private vs public) have radically changed, blurring the boundaries between productive work (at school, in the classroom) and reproductive space (home, street, free time).

In this context, narrative inquiry becomes a powerful tool that we can use to 'de-naturalize ourselves' and implicate ourselves in change. I am certain that developing diverse writing strategies that account for other pedagogical and research practices can generate ways to resist or confront, in order to subvert dominant practices in education and investigation (Rifà 2003). In this light, narratives become a political act which question and change as they respond to the question 'who am I?', a topic so frequently institutionalized by the sciences and administration in a liberal democratic society (Haraway 1991).

In this chapter, I will explain how I use narrative inquiry in order to explore the production of local/global teacher and researcher identities through experimentation with written texts.

The writing strategies included here – *Scenes*, songs, anecdotes and fictional dialogues – were produced in the context of my doctoral thesis, 'The good name. A narrative research around the experiences of subjection in the research relationship'. In a more concise way, '*Scenes*' are meticulous descriptions of the events that happen in the classroom and which are significant for their uniqueness; 'songs' are poems set to music, used as a tool for self reflection; 'anecdotes' are humorous incidents written in order to produce theoretical insights (Gallop 2002) and 'fictional dialogues' (Clough 2002) are writing strategies that intentionally allow the authority which the research experience acquires in the text to be subverted.

These narratives emerged from the research relationship between a Catalan primary school teacher called Nuria (pseudonym) and myself, a Chilean researcher, between the years 2004 and 2007. This study explored how the professional and the personal become profoundly interwoven, and feed off each other, when one tries to respond to complex questions about: 'Who are we?' 'How have we become who we are?' 'Why do we continue to behave in a certain way?' and 'Up to what point can we re-invent ourselves and reformulate our assumptions in educational/academic contexts?' All these questions were raised in the research in order to rethink subjectivity, which I conceptualize as a social, cultural, political and gender-based process. This research was not focused on teaching theory or on school practice. Instead, Nuria and I looked at processes of identification related to the discursive account which constituted us and within which we developed embedded ways of thinking and acting. Thus, this study did not pretend to represent a truth. Instead, it follows a politics of truth, as evidenced by the conditions of its production (Steyerl 2004: 24–5).

Using narratives that came out of the research relationship had important implications in terms of how these narratives constituted us as a specific kind of teacher and researcher. Accompanying Nuria for a period of her life allowed me to see to what extent it was possible to disrupt and/or deconstruct the creative force of identity categories like 'public servant', 'primary school teacher', 'good teacher', 'narrative researcher', altering the language of education and educational research.

Disrupting discourses

During the fieldwork, Nuria worked in two public primary schools. Both institutions were exposed to the powerful narratives that circulate around public schools in Spain. These narratives seek to extend an autonomous model of society characterized by neo-liberalism constituted as a form of governmentality (Popkewitz 1998). In recent years, they have become authorized knowledge regarding the world, children's selves and what it means to be a teacher, together with the responsibilities this implies. Thus, they are a good example of how narratives can be seen, in a Foucauldian sense, as productive, 'narratives do things, they constitute realities, shaping the social rather than being determined by it' (Squire, Andrews and Tamboukou 2008: 15). When I began the study, the network of Spanish public schools was already beginning to experience an important dismantling process, especially in urban areas. On the one hand, there were public, and clearly marginalized, centres with a high percentage of immigrants (such as was the case with Nuria's first school), where teachers typically felt completely overwhelmed. On the other hand, there were widely recognized schools that were in very high demand, by both the teachers and families, even those who did not live close to them (as in the case of the second school).

The way Nuria positions herself mirrors these changes. She has tried to give new meaning to the old understanding of being a teacher, the one that is handed down from the past. For her, being a teacher means embodying a different life, an option which is based on asking questions about her own teaching practice, influenced by her own career experience. It also involves being conscious of having a social, and not only an educational, mission. In this sense, education is a commitment; without commitment no change is possible.

From this position, Nuria has tried to respond to questions regarding *who we are, how we have become who we are*... thus revealing the complex way in which the personal and professional are woven together, especially today. Therefore, an important aspect of this questioning was responding to the inquiries while keeping in mind the regulatory organization of labour under post-Fordism, so that the answers could become tools that disrupt these discourses and assist in locating new, more sustainable, categories for existing.

Writing practices from a feminist post-structuralist theoretical framework

Within the context of the research relationship, we explored different ways of writing that deconstruct the mechanisms of the 'veracity' of research practices in the field of education, particularly with narrative inquiry in education. This task involved searching for strategies that problematize the relationship between discursive teaching practices and different systems of pedagogical theory that describe, locate and normalize teachers (and by extension, children). In doing this, we took a feminist post-structuralist perspective in the field of narrative inquiry. Post-structural theorizing is a 'mode of analysis [that] shifts attention from individualism to subjectivity, from text to discursive practices, and from signifier to signifying practices. Its focus is on how language works, in whose and what interests, on what cultural sites and why' (Kelly 1997: 19).

Narrative inquiry that engages with a post-structuralist stance, 'is aware of narrative's social positioning as discourses and the problematic of subjectivity and meaning' (Squire, Andrews and Tamboukou 2008: 9). From this standpoint, some narrative researchers embrace the assumption that language, subjectivity, discourse and power relations need to be revised thoroughly (ibid). In this manner, feminist post-structuralist theories introduce the dimension of gender, ethnicity, race and sexuality as powerful constituting discourses (Butler 1997, 2004; Walkerdine 1998). These theories focus on plurality and multivocality, allowing us to question the existence of androcentric roles and blind spots that are supposedly natural and biological. They also help us understand, expose and transform the hierarchical social networks that those in power use to silence and marginalize the discourses that acknowledge gender. Finally, they offer effective tools for a local analysis of power mechanisms and a new understanding of subjectivity as multiple, precarious, contradictory, desirous and moving (Rifà 2009: 673). They portray subjectivity as constantly being reconstituted in discourse each time we think or speak (Weedon 1987: 32).

As you will see in the four narratives included in this chapter, I discuss a number of methodological movements and emerging themes which attempt to:

- Produce a narrative that avoids a naturalist and totalizing research text, instead creating one that shows the conditions in which it was produced (the difficulties, the incidents, life's vicissitudes ...).
- Disrupt specular narratives that aim to present a total comprehension of the subjects and their experiences, using fragmentation, partial vision and disassociations, fiction or anecdotes, as ways of negotiating between understanding and transgression.
- Generate critical narratives that reflect on the conditions of the production and editing process (Vidiella and Larrain 2012).

The narratives will address the following questions: How do some systems of different pedagogical models organize our perceptions, our ways of responding to the world or our desires, as teachers and educators? What material practices create our professional teaching personae, and what means of resistance do we have? What language have we created and do we use to discuss what it means to be a teacher, a researcher, a woman or an immigrant in our school system and other educational contexts? What borders have we crossed? And, what tools did we use? What price did we pay? How are children's expressions recoded, interpreted or appropriated and, what does this reveal about how they can speak themselves and say who they are? Why do we assume different positions, particularly when they may be contradictory and/or oppressive? And finally, how do our stories of teaching/researching enhance women teachers/researchers' agencies in global capitalism (i.e. crossing national, social, age and gender categories)?

Deconstructing experiences of subjection in the classroom

Feminist post-structuralism allows one to understand the processes of subjection and the kind of gendered subjectivities that are available within a particular discourse. When I started visiting Nuria at her school and spent a large amount of time in her classroom, I became particularly interested in the experience of subjection as 'the very context in which becoming is engendered' (Gibson-Graham 2006: 25). It is the experience of subjection that conditions the subject to articulate itself and express agency. In Judith Butler's terms (1997: 11), the subject is 'the linguistic occasion for the individual to achieve and reproduce intelligibility, the linguistic condition of its existence and agency.' In experiences of subjection both processes and practices of subjection take place. Processes of subjection are the lattice of subject positions, incorporated in power relations in a permanent play of complicities and resistances. They entail certain specific conditions of subject production, understood as the condition of being a subject. (Walkerdine 2000: 96). That is why, from the questions mentioned above, 'Who are we?' 'How have we become who we are?', I decided to raise more specific objectives which consisted of the review of the meanings of experiences of subjection, based on the narratives which emerged in the research relationship between Nuria and myself.

Revising what it means to be a teacher/narrative researcher through gendered experiences of subjection also entails focusing not only on our visions of education and pedagogy, or on the practices which have authorized them, but also on the uses of the terms ('primary school teacher', 'good teacher', 'professional', 'student,' 'woman', 'researcher', etc.) which are not as easily controlled as the efforts to disassociate them from current meanings.

During my first stay in Nuria's school, a variety of writing strategies emerged, in large part conditioned by different situations that occurred in the classroom. The aim in writing these narratives consisted in making the experiences of subjection in the classroom visible. Specifically, (a) to review the mechanisms which tell us how to be and act, as well as the regulations and surveillances in the research process, and (b) to review the knowledge we assume to be an absolute truth.

Locating *The Vulnerable Researcher*

> (. . .) 'DON'T PEE ON THE FLOOR!'
>
> Each word coming out of Nuria's mouth, with a sharp and dry tone unknown to me, echoed powerfully on the classroom walls, and the space felt bigger to me, more intimidating.
>
> 'I'M NOT GOING TO CLEAN UP YOUR PEE!'
>
> Manuel had to clean up his pee with a sheet of kitchen paper.
>
> 'THIS IS NOT COMPLETELY CLEAN!'
>
> The child was moving silently, dutifully.

> (...) 'Clean, very clean.'
>
> Nuria took Manuel's arm and holding it firmly started to help him. Her body had transformed and now she looked as if she had the physical force of a sumo wrestler. On their knees, Nuria and Manuel cleaned up the pee stain, turned now into a deep well full of pride. 'Don't ever pee on the floor again.' But Manuel had also peed in the corner of the restroom, next to the classroom.
>
> And there I was, with a pencil and a notebook writing down every word so I didn't lose anything, showing no emotion when I would hear the dry voice strike another time.
>
> (Excerpt from the *Scene, The Vulnerable Researcher*)

I was raised in Chile during the military dictatorship, whose objective was 'not just to combat and conquer the left but also to transform Chilean society' (Acuña 2005: 15). As a girl and adult coming from a middle-class context, I learnt well to emulate, without questioning, the Virgin Mary's model and not to speak openly or reflect on my experiences of being a woman who is to be capable of 'doing everything'. I learned to be patient, comprehensive, nurturing and, especially, not to shout or lose control in front of my students (or anyone else). Doing this was a signal of being a bad teacher and a hysterical woman. Bearing in mind my own history, the confrontation between Nuria and Manuel seemed extremely violent to me. As teacher and woman, it was difficult for me not to judge her as a 'bad teacher' and as a 'hysterical woman'.

Living complex situations in the field affects the way in which research is performed, as well as the relationship between participants. This provokes complex questions that are difficult to answer, like: 'What happens with our emotions during observation?' 'How does one account for them?' From this pondering, *Scenes* that describe a critical incident like the passage included above were born. Defining what would be a *Scene* led to recuperating dilemmas or uncomfortable situations lived in the research process. *Scenes* are meticulous descriptions of the events that happen in the classroom and they allow for narrating situations related to experiences of subjectivity (Hernández 2010: 19). The events chosen are situations that frequently occur in the classroom or that are meaningful because of their special singularity. One *Scene* becomes important when it is part of the day-to-day routine, such that it is almost invisible, or, alternatively, when it interrupts the routine and introduces conflict, generating new ways of doing and relating (Hernández 2010). *Scenes* are always constructed from the researcher's partial and subjective perspective. As *Scenes* are *edited*, they open up the process of text production and the discourse behind them is uncovered. By using *Scenes* in research, we can confront problematic ethnographic descriptions as representations of realities that are far from objective. The school where I carried out my first observation, in 2004, is the centre where Nuria had spent most of her professional life. In recent years, this centre had become a border between a middle-class neighbourhood and a marginalized one containing Roma, South American, Moroccan and Sub-Saharan families. On my fifth day observing in Nuria's classroom, the *Scene* I described earlier, and which I was implicated in, took place. We both knew that it would be hard to act as if nothing had happened, if we were trying to have a conversation about her experiences in the classroom. Therefore, I reconstructed the events in the form of a *Scene*.

Constructing a *Scene* based on a situation that seemed both physically and verbally awkward lent a framework to my subsequent observations in the classroom and the decisions I would take regarding how to position myself in the relationship I was beginning to establish with Nuria, as well as a way of recounting what I observed. The incorporation of the concept of the *vulnerable researcher* into the epistemological framework of this study was a great help. This notion allowed me to adopt a way for writing the *Scenes* that could account for the difficulties in describing complex situations 'from the outside', bringing to light the incomplete view one has of what is happening, and the difficulties of managing one's feelings.

The concept of vulnerability, as presented by Ruth Behar (1996) in her book *The Vulnerable Observer*, was an important reference point. I was struck by the way she resorts to the condition of *vulnerability* in order to refer to the ambiguous position she often felt as an anthropologist in the field. This ambiguity was produced during research when sharing, interpreting and making meaning together implied setting aside the authority which the research position confers. Setting aside the authority one has as researcher goes beyond exposing oneself so that the subject of investigation and the reader can discover our fears, insecurities and weaknesses and identify (or not) with them. It is more than allowing oneself to be vulnerable so that others can respond in kind. Rather, it entails thinking of the narrative produced as a reconstruction, revealing on the one hand, the porous, fragmentary and contradictory elements of the interpretations, and on the other hand, the power/ knowledge relations in/out/within the research, through questions like: What does the validating research context and academic authority expect of me?

Narratives which interrogate the *Scene: The Vulnerable Researcher*

NURIA: The first sensation, like, intuition, or the first sensation I had was, 'Wow'. How it affects us, right? And more, how it affects me. With sincerity, and even taking responsibility for it. Taking total responsibility. Because I think, of course, if you read this, and you read it of another person ...

VERÓNICA: You are a monster ...

NURIA: Or 'she's tough, very tough'.

VERÓNICA: Of course, of course. (...) I have seen that a big challenge in this school is the diversity. I wonder if some of what happened with Manuel has to do with how to cope with this diversity, this cultural, sometimes unknown, unexpected heterogeneity that questions traditional models of teaching and learning.

NURIA: Diversity is an issue that mixes up some teachers' preconceptions, it mixes up my own beliefs about how to construct a relationship with students. It is complex, because my points of reference, my life, my biography are very, very far away from those that the children have. In the case of Manuel … for me it's very easy to use the argument of saying 'well, it's just that I don't have the time to redefine this relationship', I'd like to make it up with him at some point. (…)

VERÓNICA: You know, when I worked as a teacher in Chile, what I had to do was pretty clear: I had to 'introduce' students to the dominant culture, following a middle-class educational model. But I should recognize that I didn't see this cultural domination, probably because diversity wasn't so evident or explicit like in your school, and it was easy to ignore difference.

NURIA: In my case, I think I have reinforced Judeo-Christian middle-class values with my attitude. I'm sure of this. All my self-assessment work comes to mind, the idea of bringing to light the contradictions between what I think and what I do. My school has many philosophical beliefs that I don't share. For example, their concept of teaching and learning, or some of the ways they sanction children's behaviour. But sometimes my actions seem to agree with this philosophy. Recently I've been doing a lot of thinking. I've been asking myself questions that I don't have the answer to. I'll tell you some of them, for example: What emotions do I allow into the classroom? What personality characteristics do I value and give my approval to? What type of relationship with boys and girls do I prioritize? What knowledge do the children and their families bring to the school, and how do I read, listen to, and interpret what they say? (...)

(Excerpt from *the fictional dialogue, A Revealing Conversation*)

An important aspect of the *Scene The Vulnerable Researcher* is the search for the validation of my research experience. Such validation would serve as a source of authority in my fieldwork, and my search is evident through the plot, and the rhetoric and arguments I used. As James Clifford has pointed out, a narrative in which the researcher explicitly shows how she/he is affected by what takes place and identifies with 'his/her' research subjects is not necessarily an intersubjective or dialogic narrative. Accounting for 'my' experience can exclude 'ours' or 'yours' (Clifford 1988).

Based on our conversations regarding the *Scene* – which were recorded and transcribed – Nuria and I made a joint fictional dialogue (Clough 2002) in order to subvert the authority of the research experience within the research text. In order to craft this fictional dialogue, we first recorded our conversation when we discussed our opinions about the *Scene*. Then, when we were transcribing, we remade the conversation, adding or taking away different concepts or issues. We situated the conversation in time and space: in the evening, seated at Nuria's kitchen table, this quotidian space used for meals, which had been the site of the majority of our encounters. This type of writing had three objectives. First, it sought to articulate the meaning that Nuria was giving to her work and to her professional identity at a time of particular tension in a marginalized school, which was living the complex reality of immigration. Second, it sought to legitimize her position in the knowledge production process, based on an analysis of her teaching practice. Lastly, it sought to increase her presence as author of the interpretation. Thus, the partial viewpoint of the *Scene* was nuanced, giving us a situated understanding of the experience which is seen together with the Other, without claiming to be the other.

The role of language in the production of subjectivities

> At assembly time the boys and girls gather round the big table to talk about their feelings towards each other (…)
>
> Jordi is very restless. He makes faces and gestures that make his classmates laugh. He constantly interrupts the conversation that Nuria is trying to have with some of the boys and girls. He goes on like this for some time, interrupting, responding stupidly to the questions which Nuria is asking the group in order to make them speak about certain relationship difficulties which have arisen recently in the classroom. She gets tired of this and asks him if something has happened at home to make him behave like this.

Jordi : No
Nuria: I reckon so. If you are like this at nine in the morning it is because something has happened. We'll talk later.
Jordi continues to make faces, laughing and moving.
Nuria: Ah, so you want people to look at you.
Jordi: Yes
Nuria: And how long do you want them to look at you for? A short time, an hour, a day?
Jordi: All week

> The rest laugh and start to chant 'Jordi, Jordi, Jordi.' Jordi stands up and waves his arms as if he were conducting an orchestra. Nuria takes the ones enjoying the fun the most (Ismael, Borja, Diego and Ivan), by the arm and puts them in front of the class. She says to Jordi, 'These are the people who are going to watch you play the fool.' Nuria puts them all in a corner near the door, so that Jordi can do his 'performance' and she says 'Jordi, now you can play the fool' (…) We look at each other, not knowing whether to laugh or keep a straight face, as if to say 'this is important'.
>
> (Fragment from the *anecdote Jordi Plays the Fool*).

An *anecdote*, as Jane Gallop (2002: 2) explains, is usually defined as 'a short account of something interesting or humorous incident'. But anecdotes, despite how they could be seen as diametrically opposed to the seriousness implicit in theory, can be used to generate new knowledge and produce theory with a better sense of humour (Gallop 2002). This is what she calls *anecdotalizing theory*, by 'insisting on the occasional, on the event, the moment, as the site of productive thinking' (ibid: 5). *Jordi Plays the Fool* is an example of our desire to theorize from a place where humour cohabits with the deconstruction of the metaphysical and rhetorical structures which are at work in a narrative (Derrida 1974). It is also an example of 'how theory is lived by the theorizing subject' (Gallop 2002: 11). Anecdotes need to be re-read for the theoretical insights they afford.

Different approaches to narrative inquiry have frequently taken the view that stories can represent an authentic and genuine experience of the subject and therefore can be a gateway to interior selves. From other perspectives, as I have discussed in this chapter, narratives can be understood as political praxis. As Chris Weedon says, 'The most significant theoretical shift made by post-structuralist feminism is the deconstruction of the unified subject and of the transparency of language' (Weedon 2004: 55). In agreement with this perspective, the four examples I include here take the view that language is not transparent and that the way we speak and write reflect the power structures in our society. Language is a productive, constitutive force, and while its meaning is never permanently or irrevocably fixed, it is limited by the codes of intelligibility we have at our disposal (Lather 1992: 11) Thus, language can be deconstructed to show how 'the real' or 'the norm' is created through a binary format (normal/pathologic). By paying attention to our language and our 'rituals of speaking', and by making discourses visible, we can revise what we take to be natural, or common sense, and thus, unquestionable (Weedon 2004) and begin to think the unthinkable (Britzman 1995).

In the school context, language serves as a mechanism that builds and regulates everyone and everything that coexists in classrooms. For Judith Butler (1997), subjects become subjects not only through the control of their speech, but also through the control of the circumstances in which things can be expressed. Thus, students and teachers are constituted by language 'through a selective process in which the terms of legible and intelligible subjecthood are regulated' (Butler 1997: 41).

In the 2005–6 school year, Nuria was hired by a new school in a middle-class neighbourhood in Barcelona, whose core curriculum was organized around the work project as a new strategy to approach a construction of the complex thinking (see Hernández 2000). On the school's webpage it states: 'The function of the work project is to favour the development of strategies for organizing school knowledge around: learning to make decisions, processing information; transmitting information; and, evaluating what has been learned'.[1] This change in Nuria's professional life was not unexpected. Instead it was planned months in advance. She knew several teachers that worked in the new school who shared her vision of project-based learning. When I called her in October 2005 to schedule a number of visits, I was surprised to learn that she was going through a difficult time with the children in the class she had been given, in the first year of primary school. I got the impression that the students were quite different from the image Nuria had had, for years, of children who had been doing project-based learning. I observed Nuria's classes until the end of the school year, averaging approximately two visits a week, except in April when I travelled to Chile. My field notes during this period went in a different direction.

I thought that, somehow, the words and phrases used in the classroom, such as the phrase 'play the fool', could give an account of the mechanisms involved in the construction and control of subjects in the classroom. Phrases like this led me to question how ideas underlying different pedagogic models condition the way Nuria and her pupils perceived and responded to the world, and how they saw themselves. When I wrote this anecdote, which we decided to entitle *Jordi Plays the Fool*, I took into account those words or phrases which Nuria and the children used to produce an effect, or to reaffirm a particular state of being.

Paying attention to the role of language in the struggle for power and in the production of subjectivities made it possible to locate the meaning of subjectivity. In this sense, not only in relation to those discourses and practices which are in operation during Nuria's process of becoming a specific type of teacher, but also in locating the meaning within the group and in the relationships between students.

Reviewing her practices and experiences in relation to her pupils enables Nuria to ask herself questions from her point of view as a middle-class teacher, such as: Who is authorized to speak in the classroom, and under what circumstances? What underlies the idea of *appropriate behaviour*? And, how capable are pupils of becoming active agents in their learning process, and in forging relationships with other people? On the basis of these questions, Nuria was able to reflect – through different stories – on the effects of having, and wishing to have, authority over what is and what is not correct (in terms of what is considered pedagogically and professionally normal). The visual, physical and affective frames of reference in the space in which subjectivities are constructed (e.g. in the assembly) provide an example of this. In this respect, listening and affection as pedagogic actions, linked to care and emotional empathy, are constituted and gain validity within these frameworks. Another way of framing the Other textually within the language of the sayable (Britzman 2002) was produced through the idea of 'restraint' (of the pupil), based on certain norms (listening to the others, being quiet when others are speaking, behaving in an appropriate way, etc.).

Technologies of the female self: The Correfoc Rap (to the tune of *Rap A Duras Penas*, by Pedro Guerra)[2]

Now it's 5 ... in the ... morning
Was is the Coca Cola that made me feel so awake?
Or is it a Correfoc that runs through my body

Waking up the neurons
and making me relaxed ... but anxious?

I have to assume so many things
that in this Correfoc histories get mixed-up
A group of little people, when I listen to them
I fall in love ...
but so many times ... they unsettle me
I would throw them out ... through the window
but afterwards ... I would fish for them.
(...)
But do you all want to know what/ annoys me?
I have so many things to learn
I'm not learning how to work in groups,
Sometimes I think that they/ are wasting time
Maybe I want ... to control everything?
It's complicated, being everything.

I know how to listen to ... and interpret
What they propose
About what they want ... to research
But what happens when they talk/ between the lines
and we don't pick up on it?
It's not important, why isn't it?

Interruptions annoy me
and they happen ... all the time
without reason or on purpose
What model do I propose ... for the interactions?
Is it enough, too moralist?
I'm very serious,
should I be more lucid?
These moments are hard for me,
maybe I don't know.

Sometimes common sense abandons me
And we yell ... it's not the best
But I get confused
and it doesn't make me happy
More patience?
More self-control?

Discipline, getting along, respect. Hard Words
Sometimes, it's so easy, going beyond the limits

> Self-complacency, authority, authoritarianism,
> The children's silence is not a guarantee of respect
> /Maybe they are ... submissive, afraid ... needing affection/ (...)
>
> (Fragment from the musical poem the *Correfoc Rap*, written by Nuria during her first year at the new school.)

The notion of the *technologies of the self* (Foucault 1988) was very useful for us. It helped Nuria and me situate the reflexive activity as a posteriori, as a concrete practice that demanded a specific type of relationship with the self (know thyself). The aim of *technologies of the self* is to allow the subject to become an artifice of his/her own transformation beneath a real or imagined authority of a truth system with an authorized subject. For example, in a society with a capitalist system like ours, which conditions institutions and imposes a neo-liberal political system. Or, the model of the rational Cartesian subject, symbol of modernity, which we know is nonviable nowadays but, paradoxically, is predominant in today's schools and coexists with those subject models where coercion operates through the practice of self-control.

We were interested in reading the *Correfoc* Rap in a deconstructive way. When doing so, we were attentive to how splits and overlaps can be used to look at, play with, dominate, frame ... and change ourselves. Modern educational practices, still active today, emphasize logic as a way to confront authoritarian practices. Valerie Walkerdine (2000) believes the idea of logic to be a gradual abstraction anchored in modernism, one that pragmatically opposes the idea of 'the animal', 'the primitive' and 'the wild' as embodied threats of 'the masses'; an Other that needs to be guided to reason (Walkerdine 2000: 89–90). Following this analysis, the *Correfoc* Rap could be a way for Nuria to get to know herself through reasoning. She expresses herself through the lyrics and melody of a rap song, which she uses to narrate the relational-pedagogical experience she has with her students, and which gives her teaching identity meaning. In this song, Nuria judges and evaluates what she knows, says and is, in relation to norms that fix the way things should be. Self-regulation, as a positive factor in terms of professional strengthening, can end up being very useful in moments of uncertainty. As Jennifer Gore has noted (1993: 138), it is possible that introducing the need for self-regulation increases the efficiency of subjects/teachers, particularly when they are not completely sure of what their positions, attitudes and desires should be.

However, the *Correfoc* Rap also brings to light the doubts, uncertainties and contradictions that are part of the emotions felt towards one's self and one's students. One way of coming close to understanding this relationship was through the concept of *technologies of the female self* developed by Maria Tamboukou (2003). With these technologies, the reflexive action through which the subject 'objectifies' herself, in a sort of mirroring, in order to judge herself, is articulated differently. Her mirroring has two main characteristics. The first has to do with the fact that a woman who practices such self-control techniques sees herself not as a solitary and coherent subject, but rather as part of a web of identifications and misidentifications where subjectivity is continually dispersed. The revision of one's self in women's texts that are predominantly autobiographical tends to work among binary opposites and contradictions. The second characteristic refers to the care of the self (Foucault, 1991) as a technology that can lend someone a role in a social community. As Tamboukou explains (2003) in her genealogical study of female teachers' autobiographical texts, in these cases, the care of the self becomes a priority, even though the act has been subordinated to the care of others. Care of the self and care for others alternate in the process of self-formation, not necessarily in a problematic or contradictory way, but operating on different and multiple levels that allow glimpses of gaps and uncertainties (Tamboukou 2003: 174).

Recognizing that many of the contradictions belonged to a series of available discourses, and not to a coherent, essential, solitary I, allowed us to 'examine the contradictory elements of one's subjectivity without guilt or anxiety and yet with a sense of moral responsibility' (Davies 2000: 71). We believe that it becomes extremely difficult to reconcile the politics of caring and affection, or pay attention to the bodily dimension, in patriarchal contexts that regulate mostly feminized professions like teaching. Different narratives, for example, must coexist. On the one hand, there is the idea of the primary school teacher as a profession of conscientious, heterosexual mothers, and on the other hand, discourses about professional change and the need to adapt to new times (professional recycling, continued education, teaching innovation) are articulated around the neo-liberal subject model, one who is responsible for his/her own future and present situation, and who is adaptive to new social demands.

Problematizing certainties, fracturing the unquestionable

In this chapter, I have shown a series of narratives that were created in order to explore how the professional and the personal have become profoundly interwoven and feed off each other when one tries to respond to complex questions about who we are. These narratives propose a decentring of the subject that goes against any notion of a fixed, unified, stable or homogenous identity, and pays attention to the local, partial and multiple.

I remember several times when Nuria said, 'I have always been someone who profoundly criticizes myself'. I think the phrase reveals a powerful force which relegates to the background, or eclipses altogether, certain ideas about education, pedagogy, sexuality and the condition of being a woman (Butler, 1993). I am convinced that the group of social practices and institutional devices that sustain the classification and construction of the female teacher are closely tied to the production of neo-liberal citizens and, furthermore, are embodied, material and symbolic. However, certain categories like 'teacher' also depend on the discursive conditions of possibility, available in concrete moments and places (Lather 1992: 12).

These discursive conditions are dramatically changing in Spain with the dismantling of the Welfare State, influencing how things are ordered. Since 2008, Spain has suffered a major economic crisis. National spending cuts introduced in the past two years are already being felt in classrooms and are affecting the employment status of teachers. All regions of the country have cut money from their education budgets in order to meet the 10,000€ billion reduction in social spending ordered by the current government. In the context of primary and secondary education there still remains, for the meantime, an impression of 'stability', while job offerings and placements continue at an average rate. However, the effects of these cuts can already be seen: salaries have not increased and bonuses have been suspended; the minimum teaching time went from 18 hours per week to 25 hours at the primary level and to 20 hours at the secondary level; the student-teacher ratio has increased from 27 to 30 students in primary, 33 to 36 in secondary and up to 43 in upper high school. Teachers' working week will remain the same, at 37.5 hours, but they will have less time for other things, mainly activities related to the quality of teaching: training activities, team-teaching, lesson preparation, time with students' families or covering for an absent colleague.

The debate over whether these cuts are necessary, however painful they are, in light of Spain's economic situation and market pressure, has many sides and it is impossible to settle this conflict with a simple yes or no. Therefore, arguments claiming that these cuts will not have an impact on the work of teachers and the quality of their teaching practices are scarce. These topics are closely linked with how teachers are perceived as such, within post-Fordist regimes of work which requires them to master 'good practices'. This logic regarding how identity is established is paradoxical because it involves a tension between the interest and the desire to learn, to serve others, to train, and the docile and voluntary subjugation to (usually under-recognized) conditions of instability, precariousness (on the rise), self-exploitation, permanent flexibility and the renunciation of desire and affection. This is an issue that concerns me, because it is very difficult to reconcile the policies of care and affection, or the attention paid to physical and material dimensions, in patriarchal and post-Fordist contexts that govern mostly feminized professions such as education and care-giving.

In this context, the methodological approach presented in this chapter could bring to educational research a way of seeing and exploring aspects regarding pedagogical practice, like the meaning of being a woman teacher, knowledge that the formal logic of economics or dominant research models marginalize (for instance, the failure to foreground gender and ethnicity in the analysis of immaterial and affective labour within the frame of post-Fordist regimes of production, McRobbie 2011). I am not referring to the benefits of narrative inquiry that we already know about, like the opportunity it gives to teachers to position themselves as authors in a politically charged social context, or the way it facilitates the understanding of something as intensely personal as teaching, as well as the social, technological, economic, cultural and political context in which it is practised.

I believe that narrative inquiry from a feminist post-structuralist theoretical framework, allows us to explore aspects such as which voices are heard in dominant educational discourses, and how so-called 'teachers voices' can become distorted or fictionalized as they are re-inscribed within research that aims to address the new educational realities after the economic crisis. It also provides a means for analyzing pedagogical practices that are carried about by liberal governments, and which 'are used to produce logical citizens that can be directed and controlled through self-regulating practices, through which the subjects consider themselves responsible for their own regulation' (Walkerdine 2000: 105)[3].

By attending to the fictions that bring together social practices and institutional devices, we can explore the complexity involved in becoming what these practices regulate (and silence). In this way, post-structuralist feminism entwined with narrative inquiry gives us the opportunity to (re)think and develop our teaching and researching practice from different places. These other parameters allow us to become involved in change, and experiment with forms of resistance that subvert dominant practices in education and research.

References

Acuña, M. E. (2005) Embodying memory: Women and the legacy of the military government in Chile, *Feminist Review*, 79: 150–61.

Andrews, M., Squire, C., and Tamboukou, M. (eds) (2008) *Doing Narrative Research*, London: Sage Publications.

Behar, R. (1996) *The Vulnerable Observer: Anthropology that Breaks your Heart*, Boston: Beacon Press.

Britzman, D. (1995) Is there a Queer Pedagogy? Or Stop Reading Straight, *Educational Theory*, 45 (2), 151–65.

—(2002) 'La Pedagogía Trasgresora y sus Extrañas Técnicas', in R. Mérida Jiménez (ed.), *Sexualidades trasgresoras. Una antología de estudios queer*, Barcelona: Icaria, pp. 197–228.

Butler, J. (1993) 'Critically Queer' In *Bodies that Matter: on the discursive limits of 'sex'*, New York: Routledge: 223–42.

—(1997) *The Psychic Life of Power: Theories in Subjection*, Stanford: Stanford University Press.

—(2004) *Undoing Gender*, New York, London: Routledge.

Clifford, J. (1988) 'On Ethnographic Authority' in *The Predicament of Culture*, Cambridge, MA: Harvard University Press, pp. 21–54.

Clough, P. (2002) *Narratives and Fictions in Educational Research*, Buckingham: Open University Press.

Davies, B. (2000) *A Body of Writing*, Oxford: Rowan & Littlefield.

Derrida, J. (1974) *Of Grammatology*, Baltimore: Johns Hopkins University Press.

Foucault, M. (1988) 'Technologies of the Self', in L. Martin, H. Gutman and P. Hutton (eds), T*echnologies of the Self*, London: Tavistock, pp. 16–49.

—(1991) 'The Ethics of Care for the Self as a Practice for Freedom', in J. Bernahuer and D. Rasmussen (eds), *The final Foucault*, Cambridge, MA: MIT Press, pp. 1–20.
Gallop, J. (2002) *Anecdotal Theory*, Durham, NC: Duke University Press.
Gibson-Graham, J. K. (2006) *A Postcapitalist Politics*, Minneapolis: University of Minnesota.
Gore, J. M. (1993) *The Struggle for Pedagogies: Critical and Feminist discourses as Regimes of Truth*, New York: Routledge.
Haraway, D. (1991) *Simians, Cyborgs and Women: the Reinvention of Nature*, London, New York: Routledge.
Hernández, F. (2000) Los Proyectos de Trabajo: la Necesidad de Nuevas Competencias para Nuevas Formas de Racionalidad, *Educar*, 26, 39–51.
—(2010) 'Narrativas en torno a las Experiencias de Subjetividad en la Escuela Primaria' in F. Hernández (coord.), *Aprender a ser en la escuela primaria*, Barcelona: Octaedro, pp. 9–26.
Lather, P. (1992) El Postmodernismo y las Políticas de la Ilustración, *Revista de Educación*, 297: 7–24.
McRobbie, A. (2011) Reflections On Feminism, Immaterial Labour And The Post-Fordist Regime, *New Formations*, 70 (17), 60–76.
Popkewitz, T. S. (1998) *La Conquista del Alma Infantil. Politica de Escolarización y Construcción del Nuevo Docente*, Barcelona: Ediciones Pomares-Corredor.
Rifà, M. (2009) Deconstructing Immigrant Girls' Identities Through the Production of Visual Narratives in a Catalan Urban Primary School, *Gender and Education*, 21 (6): 671–88.
Squire, C., Andrews, M. and Tamboukou, M. (2008) 'Introduction: What is narrative research?', in M. Andrews, C. Squire, and M. Tamboukou (eds), *Doing narrative research*, London: Sage Publications, pp. 1–21.
Steyerl, H. (2004) 'La política de la verdad. Documentalismo en el ámbito artístico', in *Ficcions documentals*, Barcelona: CaixaForum, 22–3. Available at: http://www.springerin.at/dyn/heft.php?id=36&pos=1&textid=1353&lang=en
Tamboukou, M. (2003) *Women, Education and the Self. A Foucauldian Perspective*, New York: Palgrave Macmillan.
Vidiella, J., and Larrain, V. (2011) 'La (De) Construcción de la Identidad Docente', working paper presented at the research *IDENTIDOC. The Identity Construction of Primary and Pre-school Teachers in the First Years of Labour*, University of Barcelona, 27 February 2012.
Walkerdine, V. (1998) *Counting Girls Out*, 2nd edn, London: Falmer.
—(2000) 'La Infancia en el mundo Postmoderno: La Psicología del Desarrollo y la Prepración de los Futuros Ciudadanos', in T. T. Da Silva (ed.), *Las pedagogías psicológicas y el gobierno del yo en tiempos neoliberales*, Sevilla: Publicaciones M.C.E.P. Sevilla, pp. 83–108.
Weedon, C. (1987) *Feminist Practice and Post-Structuralist Theory*, Oxford: Basil Blakwell.
—(2004) *Feminist practice and poststructural theory*, 2nd edn, Massachusetts: Malden.

Notes

1 Confidentiality measures prohibit the inclusion of the URL of the school's web page.
2 A Correfoc, literally 'fire run', is a folkloric Catalonian tradition that involves an array of pyrotechnics (torches, bonfires and tunnels of fireworks). The spectacle carries explicit associations with hell, frequently involving characters who play the devil during the ceremony.
3 Author's translation.

Chapter 10

No horror stories to tell

Critical moments in exploring the literacy practices of Jamaican-born elders in the UK

Pam Bennett

Introduction

In this chapter, I make explicit some critical emotional, ethical and methodological moments I encountered when first using narrative inquiry as part of a study that explored the literacy practices of two Jamaican elders in the United Kingdom. In order to bring into focus these critical events, I discuss their respective interviews and elements from my own story, or as I term it, 'para-narrative'. The first interview is with Annie. I undertook this structured interview (Transcript 1a) as a part of an independent research module when I was training to obtain my Post-Graduate Certificate in Education (PGCE) in 2006. The PGCE is a professional qualification that teachers in the United Kingdom (UK) are obligated to complete in order to meet the government's benchmark for teaching in further education. The second interview is a narrative interview with Ellouise (Transcript 2). This interview was conducted during my Advanced Qualitative Research Methods training at the University of Bristol two years after the interview with Annie.

Before I progress to these narratives, I provide a brief statement about Bristol, the city in England where the interviews were conducted. I then set out the way in which the project was conceptualized and how I position myself in the macro-narrative. This is followed by a profile of Jamaica, which incorporates a pen-sketch of its history and social development, as it relates to children and their education. I present a summary of the social perspective of literacy before moving on to the women's respective narratives and finally, I engage with the tensions of using narrative inquiry to explore the women's literacy practices.

Bristol

Bristol is the sixth largest city in England. In 2009, it had an estimated population of 441,000 (Bristol City Council, 2012). Demographics, based on estimates from the Office for National Statistics (2009), indicate that 86.5 per cent of the city's population describe themselves as White, 5.2 as Asian or Asian British, 3.4 as Black[1] or Black British, 2.4 as Mixed Race[2], 1.5 as Chinese and 1.1 per cent as 'other'. Figures from Bristol's Equalities Unit (Bristol City Council, 2011), indicate that an estimated 73,826 of its population are aged 60 or over. With former links to the transatlantic slave trade, Bristol continues to be a large and important seaport (Bristol.org.uk).

Jamaican elders as literacy learners

In 2005, when I started teaching a literacy group in a small community centre in Bristol, I noticed that the majority of learners were Jamaicans. This was by no means a worrying observation, but rather one that aroused my curiosity. Among the group were four or five pensioners – hereafter, 'elders'. As an African-Jamaican-born woman and teacher, these elders were of particular interest to me for a number of reasons. First, we shared the same racial and ethnic background. Second, I was interested in knowing why they constituted the majority of learners in the lowest literacy group. Third, why two of them, John and Annie, a husband and wife couple, were the least confident readers and writers in the group. These questions evoked a fourth, more practical thought. That is, how do such elders, without the apparent ability to write their addresses, or to read [what could be seen as] the most basic of information, negotiate their way through the daily turns of using literacy in our society? These questions would remain dormant until a year after I began my professional training to become an adult education teacher.

Memories elude me

At this point, it may be helpful to provide a glimpse of my own background, so that I situate myself more clearly in this emerging macro-narrative (Holliday 2007). I begin with a quote from Gregory and Williams (2000: 72) who state 'memories of learning mingle with other memories of life'. I want to include this quotation because it is a potent reminder to me, that, in order to get the detail, I must first consider the whole. At the same time, as Trahar (2009) points out, recall is not always as reliable as we may believe it to be. The absence of detail in my para-narrative, therefore, relates to a number of things which not only include the previous two comments, but also time and the purpose of this chapter.

I was born in St Ann, Jamaica, in 1957. From my recollection, the first seven years of my childhood were spent without any real knowledge of my parents. Like so many other adults of that generation, they had left the island at different times in search of work (Manley, 1960). My father first travelled to America to work on the cotton fields and then to England, where my mother was to join him in the early 1960s. My siblings: two older brothers, a younger sister and I were left in the care of my mother's sister. I have very few memories of those years, but somehow I remember my mother coming to the village where we lived. I remember going to school only on a single occasion; I say more about this towards the end of this chapter. I remember travelling to England on a passenger ship that docked in Southampton: it was there I would meet my father for the first time. That was in August 1964.

At the age of 11, I started secondary school (high school) in north London. The school was a vibrant place with girls from the West Indies, Asia, Africa, Cyprus and England. I liked most of the subjects I studied. A few years later, my destiny was being mapped out, both at home and at school. My highest qualifications were in the subjects I seemed to have grasped with greater ease. Therefore, I was heading towards a career in nursing; at least, that was what my mother had determined and the school's careers adviser would initially prescribe.

My parents did not attend my parents' evenings, despite my pleas. With eight children to bring up, a mortgage and an extended family back home to support, they had to make decisions based on their priorities, as they saw them. As their eldest daughter and with five younger siblings, I would sometimes act as a substitute parent by attending my siblings' parents' evenings. Seeing mainly white parents coming into the school to discuss their offspring's progress, made me think that this was something parents did as a matter of course. At the age of 17, I left one secondary school to begin work in another as a science laboratory assistant. I never became a nurse. That was the lot of one of my sisters. She was the first professional among us, as siblings. I can recall the pride in my mother's voice as she announced to her friends that her daughter was a nurse.

The journey to where I now stand has been a long, and sometimes eventful one. My links with Jamaica continue to exist on an emotional level. However, it is more than those few short years lived out in Jamaica that connect Annie and Ellouise with me. I now turn to Jamaica: now and then.

Jamaica

Jamaica is the third largest island in the Caribbean Sea. It is situated between Cuba to the north and Haiti to the east. It is a mountainous country covering an estimated 11,244 sq kilometres and home to circa. 2.9 million people (Central Intelligence Agency 2012). The population is broken down into 91.2 per cent 'blacks', 6.1 per cent 'mixed' and 2.6 per cent 'other' [A reference to the Asian, Middle Eastern and European ethnic minorities, many of whom have a long historical connection with the island and see themselves as Jamaicans] (CIA 2012). Most of the poorest islanders live in rural or urban communities (Pan American Health Organization 2010).

Historically, as we see in the following section, access to education has always been a challenge for children and the adults who make up the 'marginal majority' (Miller 1999: 293).

Jamaica's colonial past

Prior to its independence from Britain in 1962, Jamaica was a part of the British Empire from 1655. At the height of colonial rule, it existed as a plantation economy: supplying sugar first, and later, banana, coffee and other natural products and minerals to Europe and elsewhere (Bryan 2000). The demand for these commodities from across the West Indies meant that the colonizers had to take measures to ensure that the market needs were met. For this, they turned to Africa.

The exportation and exploitation of black men, women and children from Africa brought with it a period of epic dehumanization (see Mazrui 1986). It is difficult to estimate how many enslaved Africans were exported to the New World (see Mazrui 1986; Jones 2007). However, enslavement, continued in different ways after abolitionists in England fought and won their bid to have slavery abolished in 1833 (Bryan 2000).

Education patterns in Jamaica: 1838–1940

There were a number of factors that influenced the quality of life for children born into working class families, post emancipation. Needless to say, children's lives continued to be fashioned in the moulds that had been created for their parents (Bryan 2000; Foner 1973). That is, they were regarded as resources to sustain local industries and support for their families, when required. In a society stratified first by race and later class, the majority of black, working class children were only expected to access a primary education (Foner 1973; King 1999; Manley 1960). Their restrictive curriculum centred on rote learning and conformity to a social structure that had kept many of their parents locked in positions they could do little to change (Bryan 2000). The fledging 'popular' education system struggled to organize a system that could accommodate its growing child population (Manley 1960). Both local government and church bodies were unable to adequately address many of the attendant issues (Foner 1973). This, coupled with the constraints facing many parents, meant that thousands of children did not go to school or only attended spasmodically (Bryan 2000; Foner 1973).

King (1999) reports that secondary education was not meant for the working class population, but for children of the middle class who had progressed from private primary schools. Nevertheless, in instances where children from a working class background were bright enough to continue their education, their parents might have still found access prohibitive 'since they could not comply with the schools ['] entry requirements of either paying fees, belonging to a higher social class or having had some exposure of secondary education' (King 1999: 30).

At the end of the nineteenth century, Enos Nuttall, Archbishop of West Indies and sometime ally of the working class majority, argued that race should not be a determinant, but that bright and aspiring children should be granted admission to secondary schooling (Bryan 2000). Beyond the sense of good will was the question of how open the door was to such children: in the late nineteenth century the Jamaican government offered a small number of scholarships for children to continue their education. However, the likelihood of a working class child gaining such a place was remote since they were won on a competitive basis and open to both primary and secondary school children: the latter may have spent a year or two in secondary education before withdrawing (King 1999).

Child shifting

Another complicating factor to the low educational rate and well-being of some children is what Roper (2006: 135) refer to as 'child shifting'. The separation of children from parents was not, and is not, an uncommon feature in Jamaican (if not West Indian) societies (D'Emilo et. al.: 2007; Manley 1960). Child shifting involves children being placed with relatives and unrelated members of their family for a number of reasons beyond economics, as we will see later in this chapter (Roper 2006). Although child shifting may have benefited some children: when they were well looked after or wanted, others were not so fortunate (Bryan 2000).

These historic events that evolved over hundreds of years and became a part of Jamaica's legacy bring to the fore a number of salient points that are pertinent to the next part of this macro-narrative. I now return to the question of narrative as method and narrative analysis, foregrounding some of the strengths and limitations, as I experienced them.

Narrative: as a personalized storyboard

As I began my narrative inquiry training at the University of Bristol, I realized that my earlier experience of educational research, though a productive expedition, lacked academic rigour and critical methodology. This feeling of 'less than' was further compounded by a growing awareness of other forms of research methodologies, methods and data analysis. I became interested in narrative as a data collection method and analyzing narratives as dialogic/performances (Riessman 2008: 105). Therefore, when the practical aspect of the unit arose, I wanted to trial these elements with a new informant, Ellouise, and to process the results of her interview with data from Annie's interview using dialogic/performance analysis. My intention was to examine their respective interviews for evidence that addressed my questions relating to the literacy practices of Jamaican elders, as stated earlier in this chapter.

In using a narrative interview as a data collection method, I recognize the contributions of Clandinin and Connelly (2000), Hollway and Jefferson (2000), Riessman (1993, 2000, 2008), Webster and Mertova (2007) and others in shaping my thinking. I also acknowledge the situatedness of my study and problematics of offering a universal definition of a narrative (Riessman 2008). Therefore, I have arrived at my own definition. That is: 'A narrative is the articulation of a personalized story-board based on the recollection of a past, present or projected future experience or event stimulated by an external or internal trigger' (Bennett 2009).

It is my view that, through the conscious or unconscious use of a variety of verbal and non-verbal signs, the narrator positions the listener or reader as an immediate bystander to the experience or event being narrated – thus creating a performance (Riessman 2008). Therefore, analysis of data using performance analysis could generate an understanding of how social structures assist in constructing our experiences (Labov 1997) and identities. On a superficial level, narrative analysis appears to be congruent with the social perspective of literacy, particularly in the ways in which the respective analysts seek to make explicit underlying ideologies (Street 1984).

Literacy: a social perspective

While definitions of literacy are highly contested (Meek 1992; Street and Lefstein 2008), there are many points of agreement among social practice theorists. The first general proposition is that literacy cannot be wholly represented as a single 'autonomous' phenomenon (Street 1984); for example, the popular view that literacy involves reading and writing to a certain level which can be assessed by examinations. The second, and more preferred proposition, is to view literacy as a social practice – something people do in context. Third, when the social context is acknowledged, then a discussion about the underlying ideology (or ideologies) is precipitated. The 'ideological' model of literacy, often denoted by its plural form 'literacies' (Street 1984), seeks to make explicit the power relations that govern each social context. Scholars David Barton and Mary Hamilton (1998: 7) use another contested term, 'literacy practice', to emphasize these less visible ideological frames, and 'literacy event' (Brice-Heath 1983: 386) to represent the more overt nature of using or creating a text. This ideological model of literacy has created a growing number of sub-genres. For example, 'prison literacies' and 'in-between literacies' (Wilson 2005), 'spatial and critical literacies' (Comber et. al. 2006), 'artifactual literacies' (Ormerod and Ivanič 2000; Phal and Roswell 2008) and 'vernacular literacies' (Barton and Hamilton 1998).

Links between contexts and ideologies suggest that narratives could inform our understanding, not just of social conditions and power relations that existed or exist, but also of how people's identities are constructed. Benton and Craib's (2001: 103) suggestion that 'A coherent narrative is a source of personal identity and connection to the wider social group' warrants some consideration, since I am interested in understanding how the women use their literacies; the meanings arising from what they do and how these assist or inhibit their personal identities.

Having briefly contextualised how I view narratives and how they might contribute to my understanding of the women's literacy practices, I now introduce both Annie and Ellouise, the processes involved in data collection and their respective interview transcripts.

Two voices, one generation

Annie

Annie has lived in Bristol since her arrival in the UK several decades ago. She is a mother and grandmother. Before her retirement, she worked as a hospital cleaner. Her formal educational history seems to have been limited to what appears to be two short periods: one in 'infant' school in Jamaica, and the second as a retiree in England.

Annie's spoken language, 'Jamaican patois' reflects a popular form of spoken (and increasingly written) communication among Jamaicans worldwide. However, views about this form of communication, in linguistic terms, remain contentious (Crystal 1995). For instance, is it a dialect of English or a language in its own right (Winer 2006; Crystal 1995)? Louise Bennett (1966, 1979), Benjamin Zephaniah, Bob Marley and Andrea Levy (2004) have helped to popularize Jamaican patois by pushing the linguistic boundaries, thus exemplifying their commitment to their form of Jamaican nationalism. Or is Jamaican patois a Creole (Cassidy and Le Page 1980; Crystal 1995; Pratt-Johnson 2006)? That is, an amalgamation of different languages.

In order to uphold the respect I have for Annie (and Ellouise) and to remain within the boundaries of 'ethical narrative research' (Riessman 2008: 199), the transcripts of her interview (and Ellouise's) remain faithful to her manner of speech. As a reader, participation in Annie's narrative begins in an 'interpretative relationship' (Smith, cited in Crossley 2000: 88). I take it for granted that her narrative, written in her original voice, presents a number of literary, if not, interpretative challenges (Bruner 1986: 6). However, I have also included a 'translated' version (T1b) of her original transcript to enable you to better engage with her story, should you feel hampered by the words she uses.

Transcript 1 (T1a), Annie: Realizing poverty

A: My father have me giving away to people. And the people them when I young. Then you know, I just wash, I cook, I clean and them don't send me a school.
P: So, as a young child growing up, you never went to school at all?
A: I know that I went to infant school.
P: Right.
A: And, like say, we go a school today.
P: Yes.
A: For the whole week we no go for say that we poor.
P: Ok. So money was a big problem in the family?
A: There quite a … seven of us.
P: OK.
A: Well, my other sister don't grow with me. (*Annie asks me not to include the next part of this statement.*) And she grow up and she die a couple years ago.

P: So when did you actually start going to school? Was it when you went? To … England or? Properly? Because you said that you went to infant school.
A: In JA. In Jamaica because where we live, infant school don't da far. So we go there. From the time I'm growing up, growing up. I da a Kingston. Da a Kingston and my auntie, him, I don't know. She, you know. She teach.
P: Yes.
A: But when he should look bout me, he go on all about schooling, go teach, come back. He a evangelist you see. So she go around. So, he don't have time for me.
P: So, you were quite young when you went to live with her.
A: Yeah, from small age. Me da a so, me da a so, me da da so, me da a so bout when a 16 or no quite 16. Me da all about. Me da Kingston. All about …. I can't talk.
P: It's just a question of us trying to find the best ways of helping you move on with your education and to try and make up for some of those years you missed out.
A: But I blame me parents. I know that is very hard when you growing up.
P: Yeah
A: It's very hard when you growing up. (*Annie asks me not to include the next part of this statement.)*
P: I know that sometimes education is not as important as putting food on the table.
A: Yeah, and sometime we no have it, me father would a go out a him way. He would a kill off the yam head[3] fi get food.

Transcript 1b (T1b): Annie's translated narrative

A: My father gave me away to different people. They made me wash, cook and clean, and they didn't send me to school. I know I went to infant school. Let's say, we/I went to school today – then for a whole week, we didn't go because we were poor. There were about seven of us. Well, one of my sisters, she didn't grow up with us … She died a couple years ago.
P: So, as a young child growing up, you never went to school at all?
A: All I know is that I went to infant school.
P: Right.
A: Let's say, we went a school today.
P: Yes.
A: For the rest of the week we/I didn't go because we were poor.
P: So, money was a big problem in the family?
A: There were … seven of us.
P: OK.
A: Well, one of my sisters didn't live with us. (*Annie asks me not to include the next part of her statement.*) She grew up and died a couple years ago.

P: So when did you actually start going to school? Was it when you ... to England or? Properly? Because you said that you went to infant school.

A: In JA. In Jamaica because where we/I lived wasn't far from the infant school. So we/I went there. From the time I was growing up, I was in Kingston. There in Kingston with my auntie. You know, she teaches.

P: Yes.

A: But when she should be looking after me, she went around teaching and would come back home. She was an evangelist, you see. She would go around – she didn't have time to look after me.

P: So, you were quite young when you went to live with her.

A: Yeah, from when I was young. I was here, I was there, I was over there. I was all over the place when I was 16, or not quite 16. I was everywhere. I was in Kingston. Everywhere ... I can't begin to tell you.

P: It's just a question of us trying to find the best ways of helping you move on with your education and to try and make up for some of those years you missed out.

A: I blame my parents. I know that things were very hard when I was growing up.

P: Yeah.

A: It was very hard growing up. (*Annie asks me not to include the next part of her statement.*)

P: I know that sometimes education is not as important as putting food on the table.

A: Yeah, and sometimes, we didn't have it [food], my father would go out of his way to get it – he would even kill off the head of the yam to get food

Ellouise

Prior to our meeting, I knew little about Ellouise's educational abilities or her background. As members of the same church, we had had occasional 'chats' about my research. Although I did not consider her to be a primary candidate for my intended project; she had had some formal education and had worked in nursing in the UK, and I felt that her visible interest in my studies offered a gateway to pilot the narrative methodology I wanted to use for my thesis. Having discussed my research assignment with her, she agreed to become a participant.

The method of data collection began without the constraints of a traditional structured interview, however, as time elapsed, I reverted to a semi-structured interview due to issues of time. The interview was audio-taped and transcribed.

Transcript 2 (T2), Ellouise: Sufficiency

E: Oh that's [school] great. Because we were self-sufficient and it was just only family live on the property. So, and everybody, we got our own ... lived on dress maker. One that did men's clothes. One that make the houses. They did everything. And mmm, yeah, we mix with people but we didn't have to live with people. Three of the most strangers that lived there. And those were people my grandmother ... come from different parish but they were alright. So, she said make your house there, work anywhere you want to and things. We have our own butcher. So, we didn't have to go to somebody for that. Even when they kill the cows, there were ... there. They did their own thing with the skins ... tan their own thing. And we have our own shoemakers, everything. You name it, and we had it.

P: Can you explain, when you say: we had ... I am not very clear. Can you explain what you mean by 'We had our own property?'

E: Yeah, that was our own grandparents' land. So, you know, we didn't have to say live by a piece of land to make it. We already have it and that is something coming down from older generation and there was four sisters. My grandmother was one. Anyway, in the end, they cut up the land that some people wanted to have their share, and some did not. Bought some of the land but there was two that would not .... And all the family that live there, they look after each other. If we kill a pig or goat, that was to share up for who live there. And ... a cow ... that now, we use some of the meat, we could not use all of it.

P: So, that's the family life.

E: That's the family life ... so, we were happy because we were living with the family cos my father died when I was three – I was three years old. I have an aunty that didn't have any children and she was close to my dad, I understand. So, because of that. After a while, since my mother had eight children. The last one born three months after my dad died.

So, three of us, the children, go and stay with the aunty that didn't have. One that didn't have any children. So, we grow up with her.

P: Can you talk a little bit about going to school and your life as a school child?

E: Well, going to school was good. One thing, I was a little bit of a fighter. Yes, I was. I was a little bit of a fighter. But apart from that, I was very good. Very good at school. One time, I was away from school for four months. Because I have some accident and cut my feet. It take a long time to heal up. So, for about four months I wasn't at school. And I didn't get work from school to do.

Because I use to read even before I start going to school. So, reading was fine.

P: Right, so all of that was happening for you before you were what age? The reading, private reading?

E: Well that happen to me at a very young age. Really young age. At about four, I would say. I could read and I was not going to school. Because you go to school at the age of seven. When I go to school, I could read and write. And to be honest, our teachers were very good. Very strict. You have to be very clean. Your fingernails had to be very clean. Because I prefect, we just help others. Helping hand. In school in Jamaica, as you know, But they are so proud when there school, when there are exams, and thing like that. It look done up as well. They really go out and really try to help. The children, because, even at our school, they use to give you lessons. And get after you leave, and some children, yeah,

P: I want to go back to a point you were saying about the teachers being very strict in your day. Now, your strictness is different from mine because before you started this interview, you said that you were never beaten as .... Not even at school. Whereas with me, I had, maybe one year, if that, at school in Jamaica when I was less than seven because I came over when I was seven. And the one memory I have of being in school is being chased by a teacher, who was chasing my two older brothers, but I wasn't even in their class. Or should I say, my brothers because we were late. So, when you talk about strict, you are not talking about being beaten.

Did that [helping to care for her guardian's children] continue after you finished school?

E: No. (Laughter)

P: OK. You laugh. Why are you laughing?

E: I'm not telling you that. (*Points to tape recorder.*)

Truth or reality?

As we have seen from these narratives, they provide, in part, a medium for sharing personal life events or accounts, but given the range of formats that can convey meaning beyond the spoken or written word, that is, artefacts/objects of visual representations – pictures and dramatic performances (Riessman 2008), how are we to determine the significance of these women's narratives? Brunner (1991), Clandinin and Connelly (2000) and Webster and Mertova (2007) argue that narratives emphasize the significance of both the temporal and socio-cultural dimensions in which they occur. That is, they are situated: temporally and contextually, somewhere in time past, present or future. As a result of their temporality, they have the potential to offer illumination on the cultural and social arenas in which they are set (Crossley 2000; Riessman 2008). Polkinghorne (1996) associates the temporality of narratives with the notion of 'plasticity'. For him, and others (Riessman 1993; Clandinin and Connelly 2000), in order for stories to maintain their currency, they have to be told, redefined and revised. This leads to the question about how they should be interpreted, given they can be fabrications, based on partial truths, metaphoric or regenerated by unrelated sources – an inversion of a ripple effect (Crossley 2000; McLeod 1997; Riessman 2008). Crossley's (2000: 103) comment is a helpful one. That is, narratives and narrative inquiry are not necessarily about the unearthing of universal truth claims. Webster and Mertova (2000) draw our attention to the idea of 'verisimilitude'. Amsterdam and Bruner (cited in Webster and Mertova 2007: 5) argue that verisimilitude implies that stories can be regarded as being 'true' – if 'they ring true'. This perspective creates a potential ethical dilemma.

Who, for instance, is responsible for determining the verisimilitude of a narrative? Let me illustrate by directing your attention to the socio-economic differences between Ellouise and Annie (and me, so as not to extricate myself from this process), and what we may know about Jamaica. How should we situate each of the stories I have shared with you? From a personal perspective, I might wish to contest the degree of verisimilitude in Ellouise's story. Perhaps I should express this differently by saying two things: first, if I were faithful to the dialogic relationship, I might wish to take my thoughts back to Ellouise for further discussion (Riessman 2008). This course of action, however, could have its own set of consequences, as Elliot (2005: 141) explains: 'deconstruction and interpretation may undermine the work being done by the interviewee to maintain his or her ontological security'. Second, who am I to deconstruct another person's truth or even their ontological security such as Elliot describes?

Arguably, the idealism of this form of verisimilitude may provide a way for accepting that a narrative is 'true', but only in as much as it is acknowledged as being the narrator's truth or ontological world view. Yet, as Bertaux (1995 cited in Riessman 2000: 19) argues, every narrative contains elements of facts (dates, names of places and so on) which are verifiable. My quest is made more complicated. For although I should not be seeking to establish 'facts' in the way a positivist might but instead attempt to engage with how each of us, as narrators, formulates meaning and our own sense of identity through the use of our narratives (Riessman 2001), I am drawn to the very elements that a positivist might wish to establish.

Objectivity and positionality

My submersion in the macro-narrative has created another discord that I want to resolve. Unlike quantitative (and in some forms of qualitative) research, where some have argued for a clear demarcation line between the researcher and the researched, in narrative inquiry there are fewer concerns about suppressing or isolating the personhood of the researcher (Hollway and Jefferson 2000; Chase 2005). Therefore, as Clandinin acknowledges, 'We become narrative inquirers only when we recognize and embrace the interactive quality of the researcher-research relationship' (Clandinin 2007: 7).

By the 'presencing' of my voice, channelled through the use of 'I' and elements of my personal para-narrative throughout the research process (Crossley 2000: 88; Hollway and Jefferson 2000), I make my subjective self an integral part of the performance. This however, does not mean that I am consumed by self, but remain purposeful in wanting to position the other women's voices above my own (Delamont 2009). The overriding importance to me is 'allowing the light to shine on their stories' (Chase 2005: 667). In order to do this, I mark our experiential similarities and differences by attempting to suppress one, similarities, and foregrounding the other, differences. By doing so, I create my own version of 'objectivity'. I can, at one and the same time, disconnect from their stories while remaining connected. In emphasizing our experiential differences, analyzing our dialogues and performances, I find some symbolic recognition that the stories these women recount are *their stories*, not mine. Let me illustrate. Ellouise, says: 'we were self-sufficient' (T2, Ln. 1), while Annie voices: 'My father have me giving away to people' (T1a, Ln. 1) and my own para-narrative, 'I was left with my mother's sister', provide a discrete sense of 'them and me' – these are *their stories* not mine. This brings me to the women's narratives.

Performing learning and literacy

Riessman (2008: 11) holds narrative analysis as concerned with interrogating 'intention and language – *how* and *why* incidents are storied', not simply the linguistic features of the narrative. She goes on to ask *who* the intended audience is and the purpose behind the telling of the story. The use of performance analysis creates a synthesis of analytical methods, which include thematic and structural elements, but at the same time avoids the deconstruction of data found in the thematic approach and the exploration of functions inherent in structural analysis (Riessman 2008). Performance analysts attend not only to the text, but also to the 'broader' fields of social and culture conventions, norms and differences, which existed at the time or may no longer exist (Riessman 2008: 13).

Working on the presupposition that a narrative is a type of dramatization, intended to sway the audience into believing what has been said or enacted, Peterson and Langellier (2006: 175) note that the storyteller is also a part of the audience. By creating a performance, the narrator has the opportunity to edit the story in order to create a 'desired' self (Riessman 2008: 107). Consider Ellouise's response to my question:

P: Did that [helping to care for her guardian's children] continue after you finished school?
E: No. (Laughter)
P: OK, You laugh. Why are you laughing?
E: I'm not telling you that. (*Pointing to the audio recorder.*)

(T2, Ln. 61–5)

I sense that she wants me to know 'some' things about her, but not 'every' thing. Annie, on the other hand, specifically asks that certain pieces of information not be scripted. Both exercise their agency by withholding elements of their 'selves' (Davis and Harre 1990: 5) that they do not wish to share with their audiences – known or unknown (Riessman 2000).

As a participant in her performance, Ellouise's gesturing to the audio recorder (during the interview) helps to engender a level of curiosity and my mind has already started to speculate about this 'mysterious' piece of information: I believe that she would have been more forthcoming had the conversation not been recorded. Equally, even though I wanted to know, I was not prepared to step out of my researcher role to have my curiosity satisfied by turning off the audio recorder. Riessman (2008: 191) maintains 'Providing descriptive evidence of the precise words spoken or written by narrators strengthens persuasiveness.'

Voicing the 'unvoiced'

Reflecting on the analytical process, what I find most striking about the narratives shared with me is what I term the 'unvoiced' voices that infuse our stories. It is generally accepted in literacy as social practice that literacy practices are underpinned by less visible elements, such as attitudes and ideologies (Barton and Hamilton 1998). I draw on Bahktin's (cited in Vice 1997: 112) notion of 'polyphony' – having many voices – as a metaphor to position the non-audible voices, here ideologies that permeate any performance. Thomas (1993: 20) reminds us that 'all knowledge and concepts are metaphorical in that they provide icons and mapping techniques for interpreting and speaking about the social world'.

Therefore, I want to know more about the unvoiced voices embodied in our stories. It is clear that my original intention of exploring the ways in which the women use their literacies is being counterweighed by ideological voices which bubble up from beneath the surface of their narratives (Bruner 1986; Thomas 1993). For instance, in Ellouise's narrative she tells us that she did not live with her birth mother:

> I have an aunty that didn't have any children and she was close to my dad, I understand. So, because of that. After a while, since my mother had eight children. The last one born three months after my dad died.
>
> So, three of us, the children, go and stay with the aunty that didn't have. One that didn't have any children. So, we grow up with her.
>
> (T2, Ln. 26–30)

Whereas Annie states, 'My father have me giving away to people' (T1a, Ln. 1), I present the barest fact: '[I was] left in the care of my mother's sister'. There is a common thread throughout our respective narratives that connects and disconnects us, despite our ages and social situations. Within each of our narratives there is the common element of child-shifting (Roper 2006). On a superficial level, the rupturing of our family units appears only to have benefited one person, Ellouise, who is cushioned by her grandmother's wealth: 'We were self-sufficient' (T2, Ln. 1). Annie's experience presents a very different picture.

> My father have me giving away to people. And the people them when I young. Then you know, I just wash, I cook, I clean and them don't send me a school.
>
> (T1a, Ln. 66–7)

It would be remiss to think that we were displaced from our respective families for the reasons I stated earlier. Here, I ask a number of different questions. First, how do the ideologies, which underpin the writing of our racial history, configure in the way we/children were, and are, moved within and without the immediate care of parents/parent? Second, how are we to understand the role of agency in relation to the individual adults involved in our stories? Third, how have these factors influenced not just how we learn or use our literacies, but more importantly, our perceptions of our 'selves'? These are difficult questions, which may or may not be helpful to explore, particularly as I had originally intended to examine the women's literacy habits and activities.

These aside, I am drawn to Annie's narrative because of the connections with stories I have heard from others within my friendship circle, and perhaps I allow myself to acquiesce to my subconscious self and the stories which were dormant within me. The commonalities in her story act as powerful leverages on my subjective self (Hollway and Jefferson 2000), despite my best efforts to suppress them. Gregory and Williams (2000: 72) remind me that 'memories of learning mingle with other memories of life' and that the two are inseparable. Therefore, to presuppose that Annie will align herself with my literacy agenda is to create a mirage that she is not ready to enter. Her storytelling initiates a topic she believes to be important (Trahar 2009). Although the story she is telling is not necessarily the type of 'ruling passions' literacy theorists Barton and Hamilton (1998) might have anticipated when they conducted their ethnographic study and described the literacies that participants spent much of their time doing, she is telling me something that I should become more attuned to. But still, it was not what I was expecting. Having said this, I quickly became aware that I may have unwittingly opened a proverbial can of worms. I do not want her to think that I have used my position as her tutor to become another oppressive force (Thapar-Bjorkert and Henry 2004). Noticing the direction the unfolding drama could take; I attempt to re-navigate our positions to safer waters.

P: So when did you actually start going to school? Was it when you came to England or? Properly? Because you said that you went to infant school.
A: In JA. In Jamaica because where live, infant school don't da far. So we go there. From the time I'm growing up, growing up. I da a Kingston. Da a Kingston and my auntie, him, I don't know. She, you know. She teach.
P: Yes.
A: But when she should look bout me, she go on all about schooling, go teach, come back. She a evangelist you see. So, she go around. So, she don't have time for me.

(T1a, Ln. 14–22)

While Annie may not have much to say about her schooling or her literacies, she has shed a great deal of light on the social arena which may seemingly have precluded her from going to school (Barton and Hamilton 1998). Her childhood, at least from my initial reading, is fragmented: being passed from one family member to another, coupled with her expressions of neglect. In the next part of reawakening her childhood memories, her storytelling takes on a different art form. Listen to the lyrics as she sings them:

A: Yeah, from small age... Me da a so, me da da so, me da a so bout when a 16 or no quite 16. Me da all about. Me da Kingston. All about .... I can't talk.

(T1a, Ln. 24–26)

As the participant in her story, her words and their articulation evoke an array of emotions in me. But I am not the only one affected; Annie herself is also moved to the point where she appears to be overwhelmed and concludes with 'I can't talk'.

Conversations with family members, friends and data from the wider research community indicate that the socio-economic well-being of many West Indians in the first half of the nineteenth century was far from that shared by Ellouise (Foner 1973; Gordon 1963; Curtin 1955). It was only as a young adult that I came to appreciate the historic social divisions so many Jamaicans (including my family) had to endure. Yet, unlike others in my family and the Annie in the narrative, I have no horror stories to tell.

Annie's account of her early years: 'I know that I went to infant school' (T1, Ln. 4) and her schooling: 'For the whole week we no go for say that we poor' (T1, Ln. 8) leads me to think she is stuck in a memory of yester-year. I begin to feel uncomfortable. I again attempt to find something that focuses her attention on literacy. I try to bring her back to the present time, to a more familiar reality. I draw her attention to her current education.

P: It's just a question of us trying to find the best ways of helping you move on with your education and to try and make up for some of those years you missed out.

A: But I blame me parents. I know that is very hard when you growing up.

P: Yeah,

A: It's very hard when you growing up. (*Annie asks me not to include the next part of this statement.*)

P: I know that sometimes education is not as important as putting food on the table.

A: Yeah, and sometime we no have it, me father would a go out a him way. He would a kill of the yam head fi get food.

(T1a, Ln. 31–37)

Annie's commentary appears to be fixed. Her schooling and the family's apparent lack of resources prompt me to mediate between the economic climate in the late fifties/early sixties. In order to do this, I delve into my own para-narrative and present it to her, as though it were a peace offering. Couched in my response are all the basic things that the young girl and adolescent in me had to forego because my parents were trying to find ways to put food on our table. This seems to appease her mood. She is able to see her father not as an aggressor, but as someone who would use whatever resources were available to feed his family. 'He would a kill of the yam head fi get food' (T1a, Ln. 37) – even if this meant reducing the yield for the next harvest.

Ellouise's seemingly privileged life lacks the austerity evidenced in Annie's story:

> **E**: So, she [her grandmother] said make your house there, work anywhere you want to and things. We have our own butcher. So, we didn't have to go to somebody for that. Even when they kill the cows, there were ... there. They did their own thing with the skins ... tan their own thing. ... And we have our own shoemakers, everything. You name it, and we had it.
>
> (T2, Ln. 7–11)

> **E**: Well, going to school was good (T2, Ln. 32)
>
> **E**: Because I use to read even before I start going to school. So, reading was fine (T2, Ln. 38)

In Ellouise's narrative, she refers to the teachers being very strict 'And to be honest, our teachers were very good. Very strict. You have to be very clean' (T2, Ln. 45–46). The word 'strict' and her definition strike a chord in my mind but my experience of it does not match the way she qualifies it. Her interpretation of 'strictness' does not relate to my experiences or understanding of strictness as a child growing up. Strictness, in my para-narrative, is a euphemism for the way in which corporal punishment was meted out, both in this country and in Jamaica (Bryan 2000). My reference to my brothers and I being chased by one of their teachers (T2, Ln. 56–57) is the type of action I would have qualified as being 'strict': I offered this vignette in the hope that it would serve as a signal to Ellouise to talk about any similar incidents she might have experienced. However, no related commentary was forthcoming. I can only surmise that my experience of 'strictness' was indeed a foreign one for her.

It is interesting to note that both women's stories, and indeed my own, contain different types of child shifting but in none of them is there a suggestion that we were at liberty to go back to our parental home when we wanted (Roper 2006: 135). This, I would argue, affords the child more agency than they could ever dare to possess. The apparent divergences within our stories are clear, at least in relation to our places within our respective care units: Ellouise's suggests that she was well cared for and afforded a recognizable education. Annie's narrative, in contrast, suggests that she was treated like a commodity to be transferred and used accordingly. As for my own story, I can only rationalize my parents' limitations in the context of life in Jamaica and England during my adolescent years.

Bridging the gaps

Having briefly considered some of the critical moments in this research process, I am left wondering how much information I have gathered about the women's literacy practices. What have I learned about Annie and the reasons behind her use of reading and writing, either as a child or an adult? What have I learned about Ellouise through her performed story? When I started the process of analysing these data sources, I did not think I would encounter the emotions or the ethical and methodological challenges that accompanied each of our contributions. Nor did I think I would be drawn into the unfolding dramas in the ways I have been. Adopting the role of what I perceived to be a 'traditional' researcher who looks at the data with objectivity suggests that we can separate ourselves from the performances being enacted, but my experience indicates that this is a somewhat simplistic perspective. Narrative inquiry creates some unavoidable dilemmas. But of course, it is a question of how these are dealt with.

I find that, as someone who has gone through a university education and now engages in doctoral studies, I cannot divorce myself from the common history I share with these women. I also find myself asking the reasonable question about my ability to interpret someone else's story or version of reality with any authority (Elliot 2005; Thapar-Bjorkert and Henry 2004). Beyond my interpretative function, I believe that I am faced with a greater challenge, which seems to move me further away from my goal; that is, to find a way of giving voice to the unvoiced voices which dominate our respective narratives. Therein lays a further quandary; How do I bring these voices 'into the light'? Not in the same way as Chase (2005: 667) suggests we bring in 'socially marginalized people', but to ensure that there is some representation or recognition of the ideologies, which contribute to sourcing our narratives and identities and adult literacy learners.

From this discussion, narratives and narrative inquiry may provide several helpful resources for exploring themes, contexts and ideological frames in relation of literacy. However, from my experience, there are also several methodological tensions, some of which I have attempted to make explicit in this chapter. Perhaps it could be argued that these tensions are less pronounced in other forms of qualitative methodologies but of this, I remain equally uncertain.

References

Barton, D., and Hamilton, M. (1998) *Local Literacies: Reading and Writing in One Community*, London, New York: Routledge.

Bennett, L. (1966) *Jamaican Labrish*, Kingston: Sangster's Book Stores.

—(1979) *Anancy and Miss Lou*, Kingston: Sangster's Book Stores.

Bennett, P. (2009) *Interpreting Personal Narratives: Perspectives, Realities and Truths*, unpublished MSc assignment, University of Bristol.

Benton, T., and Craib, I. (2001) *Philosophy of Social Science: The Philosophical Foundations of Social Thought*, New York: Palgrave Macmillan.

Brice-Heath, S. (1983) *Ways with Words: Language, Life, and Work in Communities and Classrooms*, New York, New Rochelle, Melbourne, Sydney: Cambridge University Press.

Bristol.org.uk. Available at www.bristol.org.uk/about/, accessed 20 March 2012.

Bristol City Council (2011) 'Equalities Statistics – June 2011 Update'. Available at www.bristol.gov.uk/sites/default/files/documents/community_and_safety/equality_and_diversity/Equalities%20Statistics%20June%202011%20update.pdf, accessed 12 April 2012.

—(2012) *Key Facts about Bristol.* Available at www.bristol.gov.uk/page/key-facts-about-bristol, accessed 12 April 2012.

Bruner, J. (1986) *Actual Minds, Possible Worlds*, Cambridge, London: Harvard University Press.

—(1991) The Narrative Construction of Reality. *Critical Inquiry.* Vol.18 (1). pp. 1–21.

Bryan, P. (2000) *The Jamaican People, 1880–1902: Race, Class and Social Control*, Kingston: The University of the West Indies Press.

Cassidy, F., and Le Page, R. (1980) *Dictionary of Jamaican English*, 2nd edn. Cambridge: Cambridge University Press.

Central Intelligence Agency (2012) *The World Factbook: Jamaica.* Available at www.cia.gov/library/publications/the-world-factbook/geos/jm.html, accessed 28 March 2012.

Chase, S. (2005) 'Narrative Inquiry: Multiple lenses, approaches, voices', in N. Denzin and Y. Lincoln (eds), *The Sage Handbook of Qualitative Research*, 3rd edn, Thousand Oaks, CA: Sage Publications Inc., pp. 651–79.

Clandinin, D. (2007) *Handbook of Narrative Inquiry: Mapping a Methodology* Thousand Oak, London, New Delhi: Sage Publications.

Clandinin, D., and Connelly, M. (2000) *Narrative Inquiry: Experience and Story in Qualitative Research* San Francisco: Jossey-Bass.

Comber, B., Nixon, H., Ashmore, L., Loo, S., and Cook, J. (2006) Urban Renewal From the Inside Out: Spatial and Critical Literacies in a Low Socioeconomic School Community, *Mind, Culture, And Activity* 13 (3) 228–46.

Crossley, M. (2000) *Introducing Narrative Psychology: Self Trauma and The Construction of Meaning*, Buckingham, Philadelphia: Open University Press.

Crystal, D. (1995) *The Cambridge Encyclopedia of The English Language*, Cambridge, Cambridge University Press.

Curtin, P. (1955) *Two Jamaicas: The Role of Ideas in a Tropical Colony, 1830–1865*, New York: Greenwood Press.

Davies, B., and Harre, R. (1990) 'Positioning: The Discursive Production of Selves', in *Journal for the Theory of Social Behaviour*, 19, (4): 43–63. Available at www.massey.ac.nz/~alock/position/position.htm, accessed 1 November 2009.

Delamont, S. (2009) The only honest thing: autoethnography, reflexivity and small crisis in fieldwork, *Ethnography and Education*, 4, (1), 51–63.

D'Emilo, A. Cordero, B. Bainvel, B. Skoog, C. Comini, D. Gough, J. Dias, M., Saab, R. and Kilbane, T. (2007) *The Impact of International Mogration: Children Left Behind in Selected Countries of Latin America and the Caribbean.* Online. http://www.unicef.org/socialpolicy/files/The_Impact_of_International_Migration_LAC.pdf, accessed 27 October 2012.

Elliot, J. (2005) *Using Narrative in Social Research: Qualitative & Quantitative Approaches*, London, Thousand Oaks, New Delhi: Sage Publications.

Foner, N. (1973) *Status and Power in Rural Jamaica: A study of Educational & Political Change*, New York, London: Teachers' College Press.

Gregory, E., and Williams, A. (2000) *City Literacies: Learning to read across generations and cultures*, London: Routledge.

Gordon, S. (1963) *A Century of West Indian Education*, Malta: Longman Group Ltd.

Holliday, A. (2007), *Doing and Writing Qualitative Research*, 2nd edn, London, Thousand Oaks, New Delhi: Sage Publications.

Hollway, W., and Jefferson, T. (2000) *Doing Qualitative Research Differently*, London, New York, New Delhi: Sage Publications.

Hyndman, A. (1960) 'The West Indian in London', in S. Ruck (ed.) *The West Indian Comes to England: Part 3*, London: Routledge & Kegan Paul Ltd, pp. 63–151.

Jones, P. (2007) *Satan's Kingdom: Bristol and the Transatlantic Slave Trade*. Bristol: Past & Present Press.

King, R. (1999) 'Education in the British Caribbean: The Legacy of the Nineteenth Century', in E. Miller (ed.), *Educational Reform in the Commonwealth, Caribbean*. Washington, DC: Organization of the American States, pp. 23–45.

Labov, W. (1997) Some further steps in narrative analysis, in *Journal of Narrative and Life History Research*. Available at www.ling.uenn.edu/~wlabov/sfs.html, accessed 1 November 1999.

Levy, A. (2004) *Small Island*, London: Headline Book Publishing.

Manley, D. (1960) 'Migration Past and Present', in S. Ruck (ed.), *The West Indian Comes to England*, London: Routledge & Kegan Paul Ltd, pp. 1–48.

Mazrui, A. (1998) *The Africans*, London: BBC.

McLeod, J. (1997) *Narrative and Psychotherapy*, London, Thousand Oaks, New Delhi: Sage.

Meek, M. (1986) *Learning to Read*, London: The Bodley Head.

Miller, E. (1999) 'Educational Reform in Jamaica', in E. Miller (ed.) *Educational Reform in the Commonwealth Caribbean*, Washington, DC: Organization of the American States, pp. 199–253.

Morgan, P. (2004) The Black Experience in the British Empire 1680–1810, in P. Morgan and S. Hawkins (eds). *Black Experience and the Empire*. Oxford: Oxford University Press.

Office for National Statistics (2009) 'Area: Bristol (Local Authority)'. Available atneighbourhood.statistics.gov.uk/dissemination/LeadTableView.do;jsessionid=ac1f930b30d59ced1e53dcc84d8784f2c8337bdd7245?a=5&b=276834&c=bristol&d=13&e=13&g=398712&i=1001x1003x1004&m=0&r=1&s=1306549942589&enc=1&dsFamilyId=1812&nsjs=true&nsck=false&nssvg=false&nswid=1440, accessed 12 April 2012.

Omerod, F., and Ivanič, R. (2000) 'Texts in Practices: Interpreting the physical characteristics of children's project work', in D. Barton, M. Hamilton, and R. Ivanič (eds), *Situated Literacies: Reading and Writing in Context*, London, New York: Routledge, pp. 91–107.

Pahl, K., and Roswell, J. (2010) *Artifactual Literacies: Every Object Tells a Story*, New York: Teachers College Press.

Peterson, E. and Langellier, K (2006), The performance turn in narrative studies, *Narrative Inquiry*, 16, (1), 173–80.

Polkinghorne, D. (1988) *Narrative Knowing and the Human Sciences*, Albany: State University of New York Press.

Pratt-Johnson, Y. (2006) 'Teaching Jamaican Creole-Speaking Students', in S. Nero (ed.) *Dailects, Englishes, Creoles, and Education*, New York, London: Lawrence Erlbaum Associates, pp. 19–36.

Riessman, C. (1993) *Narrative Analysis*, London, Newbury Park, New Delhi: Sage

—(2000) ONLINE: http://alumni.media.mit.edu/~brooks/storybiz/riessman.pdf, accessed 10 September 2009.

—(2008) *Narrative Methods for the Human Sciences*, London, Thousand Oaks, New Delhi: Sage Publications Inc.

Roper, S. (2006) Perceptions of Children in Jamaica between 1914 and 1938, in A. Henry-Lee and J. Meeks Gardener, J. (eds) *Promoting Child Rights: Selected Proceedings of the Caribbean Child Research*, pp. 188–167. Online. http://www.unicef.org/jamaica/Pages_from_Promoting_child_Rights2.pdf. Accessed 03 March 2012.

Street, B. (1984) *Literacy in Theory and Practice*, Cambridge: Cambridge University Press.

Street, B., and Lefstein, A. (2008) *Literacy: An Advanced Resource Book*, London: Routledge.

Thapar-Bjorket, S., and Henry, M. (2004) Reassessing the research relationship: location, position and power in fieldwork accounts, *International Journal of Social Research Methodology*, 7, (5), 363–81.

Thomas, J. (1993) *Doing Critical Ethnography*, London, New Delhi: Sage Publications.

Trahar, S. (2009) Beyond the Story Itself: Narrative Inquiry and Autoethnography in Intercultural Research in Higher Education [41]. *Forum Qualitative Sozialforshung/forum: Qualitative Social Research*, 10, (1), Art. 30. Available at nbn-resolving.de/um:nbn;de:0114-fqs0901308

Vice, S. (1997) *Introducing Bakhtin*. Manchester, New York: Manchester University Press.

Webster, L., and Mertova, P. (2007) *Using Narrative Inquiry as a Research Method*, London, New York: Routledge.

Notes

1 The term 'Black/black' is used in different ways throughout this chapter. For example, Morgan (2004: 87) indicates its impreciseness and also points to it being used to describe first nation Africans and their descendants in some eighteenth-century situations. Hyndman (1960: 68), on the other hand, draws attention to 'Britain's colored population' from India, Pakistan and Africa [no doubt including black West Indians] to shows that skin color is used as the basis to categorize 'non-Europeans'. How it is used by other sources identified in this study is uncertain, but seems to align more with Morgan's (2004) interpretation.

2 I prefer the term 'Dual Heritage.'

3 'Yam head', or the head of a yam, is the part of the 'yam tuber from which the vine shoots, and from which the new tubers grow' (Cassidy and Le Page 1995: 484).

Chapter 11

Words collide, mindsets remain

A journey of cross-cultural narrative inquiry

Jane Horan

Introduction

Narrative inquiry is like walking through a garden maze, richly diverse with many twists and turns. If you walk too quickly, you will not see the texture or you will forget to make a critical turn. You will reach the end but may not remember what you saw. If you walk too slowly, you will be too close to see the thorn on the hedge and may become disoriented on which direction to go. You will reach the end but with blurred vision. Walking through the maze, the most important thing to do is watch, reflect and listen. Similarly with narrative, the ability to quietly observe, critically reflect and listen to variegated voices provides the path to the journey's end.

My goal in writing this chapter is to share my experiences of walking through the narrative maze in leadership research over a three year period to relate the stories of four Asian women leaders from Bangladesh, Japan, Taiwan and Singapore. I started this journey with extensive experience of working in the Asia Pacific region, but with little background in narrative inquiry. Along the way, I uncovered insights on leadership and the challenges of language that were uncomfortable to my under-examined mind. The written word is inextricably woven into the fabric of research, providing both insight and ambiguity, and can be enigmatic or engaging. Yet, words can be heartbreakingly insufficient in producing a story unless we have an in-depth understanding of the deeper meaning and emotional force beneath the surface.

Whether researching or working cross-culturally, these communicative differences present obstacles in understanding and appreciating local cultures. Working as the head of organizational development offered a front row seat to communication challenges, specifically during talent selection, succession planning and leadership development. Communication style differences and language nuances presented complications whether working for a US firm or with a Chinese family-run conglomerate. In both organizations, my focus was to develop and prepare the next generation of leaders. This noble objective of identifying and selecting talent was not entirely successful, given that the disproportionate view of the 'majority voices' (Cortazzi and Jin 2009: 28) inside the organization clashed with the wider constituency of the local voices and the inability of both to recognize and reconcile subtle style differences.

This chapter highlights challenges and opportunities in using cross-cultural narrative inquiry. The first challenge begins with words. Working in a globally, interconnected environment puts more emphasis on communication and interpretation. While English is the language of commerce, do we really understand one another? This research raised questions around word meaning and corresponding emotions while interviewing cross-culturally. The second challenge is about culture. To grasp meaning, I needed an understanding of my participants' culture and an appreciation of history. Yet the ubiquitous use of social networks and expanding global business gives the pretence of cultures blending and boundaries fusing, but in reality tradition and lineage hold strong. The notion of face is one example of a deeply entrenched, long standing belief across cultures in Asia. I describe and define this misunderstood concept in relation to the word 'failure'. The third challenge and opportunity is knowledge. I explore the challenges when an over-abundance of cross-cultural theory hindered my ability to recognize and value the individual.

My first interview confronted my solid foundation in cross-cultural thinking. From that point on, I navigated the labyrinth cautiously. I started off using open-ended questions to allow my participants' stories to unravel. As I listened to the stories, I realized my choice of words and my participants' inability to assimilate meaning was obvious through silence or rejection. This impasse coupled with my entrenched beliefs had the potential to block the unfolding narrative. Narrative is not easy across cultures, but reflecting on these challenges highlights the benefits in exploring social, cultural and historical aspects to create meaning from diverse perspectives. However, meaning would not be possible without reflexivity, embedded within this narrative project, providing critical self-evaluation in gathering information and writing stories. Creating narrative is a process of discovery; reviewing my notes and starting to write provided extended periods of critical self-reflection. Writing became a way of knowing my participants and their culture and finding myself in the process (Richardson 2000; Thomas et al. 2009). During this reflexive period, what I thought I knew about cultures became a specious argument. I now understand the importance of struggling between knowing with certainty and accepting uncertainty. Walking through this maze, I learned to appreciate the puzzle presented, value internal confrontations and critically reflect on situations in the process of understanding.

Why choose narrative?

As an inquisitive researcher, I wanted to learn new ideas and explore a topic that related to my work and intellectual interest (Etherington 2009). Narrative, nestled within philosophy, history and sociology, provided a viable method to understand the experiences of women leaders across cultures in Asia. In my first Doctor of Education course with the University of Bristol, I became acquainted with multicultural narrative through Connelly, Philion and He's exploration of multicultural education and narrative in Canada (2003). Earlier as an undergraduate humanities student, I read Ervin Goffman, Margaret Mead and Gregory Bateson's narratives. At that time operating under a positivistic mindset, I assumed statistics equalled research and therefore did not make the intellectual connection to qualitative research. Admittedly, I was fascinated by these early works and intrigued by Phillion's (2002) research using multicultural narrative in schools. Reading further about narrative inquiry, I discovered the connections to educational research (Clandinin and Connelly 1990), counselling and psychotherapy (Riesmann and Speedy 2007). Besides education, narrative, oral histories and storytelling have an extensive tradition across cultures and within feminist research (Maynes et al. 2008; Behar and Gordon 1995). Storytelling provides insights and reflections on culture passing knowledge down through generations (Etherington 2004).

At work, I facilitated storytelling workshops, helping leaders learn how to tell stories of identity, vision and purpose (Simmons 2001). In facilitating these sessions, I experienced first-hand the links between good storytelling and great leadership. As I realized the expansive nature of narrative inquiry, the alignment to my research with women leaders across cultures made sense. This approach offered more than a glimpse into the lives of my participants by providing a broader perspective looking into values, differences and experiences. Before embarking on this journey, I read the captivating work of Ming Fang He's (2002) inquiry into the lives of Chinese teachers, JoAnn Phillion's (2002) inquiry in multicultural learning environments and Sheila Trahar's (2005/6) research in higher education in diverse learning environments. Looking back on my work experience, there were similarities with their collective research and my life experience of working in multicultural environments. Given my work experience and research interest, cross-cultural narrative inquiry as a methodological approach offered an unencumbered platform of inquiry.

Setting the research stage

Today's global expansion of business and increasingly interconnected communities provide a sound backdrop for research exploring leadership in various cultures – specifically with women. Using narrative inquiry, I listened attentively and reflected as each narrative gathered momentum. Listening to stories triggered new questions, provided fresh and different tangential stories as well as reflective silence. The journey of discovery begins with words 'attained in and through listening to the other' (Kaminsky 1992:134) and upholding the 'other' to ensure voices are heard (Cortazzi and Jin 2009; Etherington 2009; Trahar 2009). Adding cross-cultural elements into the narrative mix presented complications representing the 'others' voice, specifically interpreting English words and meanings within and across cultures to create a uniquely personal voice and story (Thomas et al. 2009).

As I write this chapter, it is important to set the stage and outline context, experience and influence for this research and the researcher. I was born and raised in an idyllic beach community on the West Coast of Southern California, and attended both high school and university in the same area. This environment offered little ethnic or racial diversity; neighbourhoods were middle-class and predominantly white. Attending graduate school in Northern California in the late 1980's, I decided to volunteer to teach English in China. My Asia career started in Changsha, Hunan Province teaching English to graduate engineering students. Changsha had a history of civil war, battles and rebellion, and is well known in China as the birthplace of Mao Tse-tung. Land-locked, hot and still staunchly Communist, Changsha was vastly different from my world view and experiences, the first country I had lived in outside of the United States. Before leaving for China, my graduate school required complete immersion in Chinese culture, philosophy and history. Upon arrival, all English teachers were required to study Chinese for three months, six days a week and eight hours a day in Beijing. After three months, I moved to Changsha with only rudimentary communication skills in Chinese. A few years later, I moved to Hong Kong to work for a Shanghainese family-run company before moving into multinational organizations in Hong Kong, and working across Asia as the head of organizational development for a global entertainment conglomerate. From my early days in China and work tenure within multinational organizations, I experienced what I was about to study, and was deeply immersed in both the organizational and national cultures of this project.

Cross cultural labels and identity

Examining culture began with questions around identity, boundaries and belonging. This identity question appears murky both with researchers and with individuals. Asking the phenomenological question about the origins of home may answer the question of identity for some but confuse others (Sarup 1996). Interviewing a successful Singaporean business executive, Ms. Chin, I asked questions about home and culture. She replied with a quick, firm answer, 'I am Malaysian Chinese'. As she rapidly reeled off this response, we both looked surprised. She is a Singapore citizen, having lived, worked and studied in Singapore for more than 40 years. When I asked a similar question, 'where is home?' to Ms. Chow, a Taiwanese strategy consultant, she produced the thoughtful response of 'I am Chinese or (pause) I mean Taiwanese but African in my soul'. Ms. Ali, a professor from Bangladesh revealed that she is a citizen of the world, at home in any culture. For my participants, the question of identity or home is confusing; most had spent significant time away from their home countries.

Researchers might label them as global nomads, third culture adults or itinerant migrants and each tag carries a different meaning and connotations.

A 'third culture' adult has spent significant periods living outside of their home country or their parents' culture, particularly during the developmental years (Pollack and Van Recken 1999). A global nomad does not fit within one culture, but easily adapts and feels at home between two or more cultures (Schaetti 1996). For me, the word, 'migrant' conjures up farmers or the negative term, 'Okies'' used in the 1930's Dust Bowl Depression-era migratory movement in America. Today 'migrant' is attributed to the immigrant, unskilled global labour, mostly from South Asia. Obviously this connotation did not fit the highly educated, experienced women in my research. The global nomad and third culture adult have less negative connotations, but also did not accurately depict my participants. Some willingly discussed home and identity, and more importantly reaffirmed the creeping obsolescence of these labels. Working in a globally connected world, the notion of identity is blurred, remains fluid and has stretched across boundaries (Ford 2011).

Unlike my participants, I spent my formative educational years in the country of birth, attending schools in the same suburb, and my adult working years in another country. This experience does not fit within the category of a global nomad or third culture adult. This distinction is important because our formative years shape the role culture has on language and behaviour, and influence how we interpret both (Polanyi 1985). Given these terms did not fit with my experience, I borrowed Phillion's (2002) concept of Ms. Multicultural. I started this project with an understanding and appreciation for cultures. For me, the multicultural researcher demonstrates cultural knowledge and acts from a position of cultural insight (Phillion 2002). Belief in such a perspective provided a solid framework and identity for conducting research. I entered the project seeing myself as part of the community I was researching, although my physical appearance did not match the majority of the population in Asia. Through the interviewing experiences, I quickly saw that my participants categorized me as American, and [understandably] may have based such reasoning on appearance and voice. My Caucasian face cannot be erased from view. A few times I started the interview using Chinese but we quickly switched to English. As my participants were all fluent in English, it was used throughout the interviews. My spoken Chinese is not as fluent as my English or my Chinese participants' English. To allow my participants a different view of me, I repeated my story of living in China, and my work throughout Asia. While I strived to understand my participants from their view, I wanted them to see another side of me. This proved difficult, however, and the mindsets remained. In this sense, my participants viewed me as American, ignoring or not accepting my time spent working in China, Hong Kong, Singapore and Japan. I was not burdened or overwhelmed by cultural differences. I focused on and related to the similarities; that is, a professional woman interviewing professional women. Oddly enough, this notion of being culturally cognizant hindered my views and ability to accept differences, specifically when my participants' answers did not align with how I viewed their culture. Looking back, we all carried entrenched mindsets and belief systems into this research. For me, it was not the lack of knowledge, but rather *too much* knowledge that had the potential to cloud my perspective and derail their stories.

First setback

Using the Ms. Multicultural label-similar to other labels – global nomads, cultural hybrids and third culture adults – became a strait-jacket rather than springboard for me in understanding my participants' stories. Unexamined assumptions and entrenched mindsets influenced and hampered my ability to clearly see the 'other' as an individual in this research. I had to examine well beneath the surface of the cultural ideals, unchecked assumptions and unconscious bias before I was able to understand my participants' experiences (Phillion 2002). I engaged in this research as a member of the community, and an intrinsic part of the research process was not to look in from the outside. My first interview with Ms. Akiko Ito, a Japanese leader of a global non-profit organisation, uncovered my own rigid beliefs about culture and values in Japan and across Asia. I asked Ms. Ito 'Tell me about your early influences family, school, sports or any early experiences ....' Without hesitancy, Ms. Ito firmly said, 'No one.' This hearty, emphatic response hit me very strongly. Sitting in a small café, with the lunch cacophony surrounding us, I rephrased the question: 'No one influenced you? How can that be?' I wanted to explore early life experiences, influences and values. With the desire of hearing and allowing for stories to unfold, I used open-ended statements beginning with 'Tell me about a time when...' These questions were intended to surface and discuss underlying value drivers. Examining my interview notes, I had put question marks and notes of disbelief. More than notebook comments, I was struck by my emotional response. The careful planning of the interview process and how to elicit stories proved inconsequential to this response. Going back over my experiences, research and knowledge across Asian cultures, Ms. Ito's answer did not fit with my cross-cultural belief systems or my ersatz 'multicultural' self. In my notebook, and embedded in my mind, I had written 'Everyone responds to this question with, "mother or father"'. This particular incident surfaced the constraints of my beliefs and the stranglehold of Ms. Multicultural. I automatically assumed the question would result in the same answers. Simplistic as these remarks sound, I was momentarily stuck, finding it difficult to regroup and continue the interview.

Being in close proximity with my participants, I overlooked the individual in the story. I could not pull myself away from the feelings, and in this sense I was unable to create 'new and reflexive knowledge' (Etherington 2004: 81). While reflexive interviewing should have opened the door to share experiences or engage in dialogue, I remained stuck and deeply unsettled. I failed to recognize that the responses to my questions and the story itself were simply the starting point. Glancing through my notes, the individual journey was laid bare, a story waiting to unfold. It was not until I dealt with my confusion and grappled with my ideals around multiculturalism that there was a different view and new story. This reflexive period forced a revolution, turning me inward to crack open the black box of cultural constructs.

Words and (home) cultural baggage

I started this project proudly displaying my badge of cross-cultural experience and academic study in Asian cultures. As much as I embedded myself in my participants' culture, one foot remained firmly on the ground of my cultural upbringing. The strong, enduring link between both my life experiences and research provided both unifying and destabilizing elements, influencing my ability to read each interview clearly. I carried into this project a US educational mindset. Western leadership concepts and English as the medium of communication presented linguistic challenges and philosophical questions, both basic and profound. Remarkably, my cross-cultural awareness did not stop me from keeping the vestiges of some shop-worn Western ideas whilst accepting a universal framework of leadership. Similar to other researchers, the framework I selected, the words I used and the assumptions I carried with me were defined and determined by an 'Anglo-North American dominant and parochial culture' (Thomas et al. 2009: 314).

I continued along this path, not perceiving there would be challenges in discussing and using leadership concepts from the West (Ciulla 2004; Eagly et al. 2003; Eagly 2007; Helgesen 1995; Gardner 1995). Some of these leadership theories had been researched globally (Gardner 1995) specifically in China (Bass and Steidlmeier 2004) and supported my idea of universality. In addition to putting culture aside, I assumed there were global feminine qualities of leadership that were contextual, taking on a chameleon-like character to assimilate with the environment (Chinn et al. 2007; Eagly 2007). Discussions on behavioural shifts and transformational leadership were highlighted during my interviews with women in banking, technology, academia and non-profit organizations. I used a transformational leadership model because of the quantitative links to women (Eagly 2007). Some researchers argue that gender cannot be applied to leadership, while others have found riveting quantitative support 'that female leaders were more transformational than male leaders' (Eagly 2007: 5) specifically in abilities to coach, engage and encourage a loyal group of followers.

Reading literature on Confucian cultures also provided references to transformational leadership qualities and authentic motivation for the greater good (Ciulla 2004). While most of my participants had leadership capabilities described by Alice Eagly as 'transformational', they also shared experiences of shifting between styles to fit the prevailing organizational environment. Women flex between transactional and transformational styles, and both are needed for organizational success (Eagly et al. 2003; Eagly 2007). Understandably, the relevance and efficacy of a particular style depends on organizational culture and individual followers. During my interviews with these women, I heard stories of bias and entrenched mindsets within their organizations and within my research. In fact, terms used to describe leadership demonstrate 'how embarrassingly sexist the field has been' (Solomon 2004: 86).

Working in a globally connected environment and across diverse communities, the so-called feminine values of collaboration, coaching and consensus would seem to be the preferred leadership style. Following this thread, I am asserting that an ethically based, transformational leadership style inclusive of broader communities and focused on sustainability for the greater good will always be able to cut across cultures. Indeed, feminist leaders are advocates for inclusivity, empowerment and minority voices (Chinn et al. 2007). I moved forward with this narrative, using Alice Eagly's extensive research on transformational leadership, Sally Helgesen's work on building an inclusive web and Jo Ann Ciulla's study on ethical leadership as the backdrop for this project. While this model of leadership provided a framework from which to ask questions, the bigger challenge came from selecting and misinterpreting words and responses to my questions.

Challenge of words and language

Language – and specifically English – confounds and challenges. The first challenge and question is, 'If language equates to culture, how does one explain the universality of English?' The ubiquity of English gives a native speaker a false sense of being understood, assuming they are fully understood wherever they go. In order to interpret conversations we must process language through filters, but this must also reflect the culture in which we were born and raised (Fox 2009). Throughout this research project my filters, checks and gauges ran astray. An example of veering off course from a multicultural perspective begins with the word 'failure.'

As I formulated questions to ask my participants, I borrowed from Howard Gardner's book, *Leading Minds: An Anatomy of Leadership* (1995). A kindred researcher, Gardner uses a storytelling approach examining global leaders in the arts, academia, government and business. Scrutinizing these leaders, he discovered that all overcame a tragedy or failure early in life. Their stories show resilience as a significant factor of future leadership. Using Gardner's same open-ended style, I asked my participants to 'Tell me about a time when you failed...'. In response, I received blank stares, a long silent interlude or 'I have never failed at anything.' Dumbstruck, I thought 'this can't be.' Puzzled, I continued. 'Hasn't everyone failed at something at least once?' In my notes, I noted quiet disagreement, and was admittedly disgruntled. In the next column I wrote 'culture' with a question mark.

The word 'failure' was not the problem; the issue was cultural. Similarly, my disbelief of Ms. Ito's response was also cultural, but from a different perspective. While language remains an ambiguous element, the unconscious mind befuddles, creating difficulties to hear, listen and understand the individual in the process

(Rogers 2007). These two incidents reinforced the limits of my multicultural self and the elasticity of identity. Physically I moved between cultures, but unconsciously stumbled through assumptions and entrenched beliefs that arose from them. Understanding the interconnectivity and importance of family within an Asian context, I assumed that asking Ms. Ito about her early influences was innocuous, and would elicit similar responses from everyone.

I started this research seeing myself as part of this female professional community, given the similarities between those working for large organizations across Asia. In so doing, I used Western leadership theories to shape my questions. I relied heavily on my work experiences and educational background, selectively using my cross-cultural thinking. In hindsight (based on studies in Confucian cultures), I should have realized a question about failure would elicit such a response. Equipped with experience of living across Asia for two decades, I struggled and straddled both cultures, constrained by memory and conflicted by cultural insights. My world view is through an Asian prism, but my memory is coloured by cultural conditioning (Bailey 2009). The reality is the more I think I know, the less I really do know, much as this sounds like a simple cliché.

Studying my choice of the word 'failure', I have no negative emotional attachment to it. 'Failing', to me, is both a setback and opportunity to learn. Unlike North American educational systems, in China and across many cultures in Asia, mistakes are not viewed as learning opportunities (Flowerdew 1998). The crash and learn cycle of the hi-tech communities in Silicon Valley, where failure – or multiple failures – are seen as a rite of passage, do not carry the same positive feelings in some Asian cultures. This may be due to the fact that failure in Confucian cultures is not singular but multiple, impacting both present and past family lineage. In China, one reason is the notion of 'face', difficult to articulate but explored in more detail later in this chapter. Another explanation goes back to Chinese educational philosophy of the late Ming period, described as the rigorous control of a child's life that continues into adulthood. During that era, schools for wealthy boys focused on rote memorization, reading from classical Chinese texts and frequent drills culminating in state examinations in Beijing, of which much was expected from the exam outcomes. Successful results translated to a lucrative position along with limitless prestige. While family lineage and clans played an important role in aggregating wealth, education resulted in powerful government positions and increased prominence for the family (Spence 1990; Fairbank 1992). Failure was at an unusually high cost. Remnants from the past remain in educational philosophies in Asia, with its rigorous emphasis on examination excellence, rote memorization and the concentration on maths and sciences rather than liberal arts, which are not considered practical. Those scoring in the top percentile are rewarded with entry into the prestigious secondary schools and universities in China, Hong Kong, Japan, Korea, India and Singapore (Flowerdew 1998).

I considered my participants' response of 'I have never failed at anything', as a knee-jerk reaction to a question they did not want to answer instead of accepting the cultural implications. To be human is to fail, to make mistakes and get up again, the Puritan ethic borne from the United States, beliefs from a heritage steeped in reactionary declarations to colonization, embodying risk, standing up and being held accountable (Bellah et Al. 1998). Their response to the discussion on failure did not sit well with me – or was it merely my American values? Reading through my notes, their words and my comments collided on the page in front of me. I realized the word 'failure' raised a personal question of authenticity, along with the larger issue of misunderstanding cultures. I did not begin this research exploring my values (Bridges 2009), but my beliefs created confrontations, questions and hesitancy. This misunderstanding connected with emotions and feelings underlying the words. These feelings remained dormant until ignited and had a strong effect. The emotions below the surface triggered my thoughts of values, centred on authenticity. I entered this research believing I had a solid standpoint of multiculturalism and open mindedness, only to uncover constant conflicts and multiple adjustments.

To read the nuances of language and subtle shift of conversations requires an appreciation for individual style differences, along with understanding cultures. These differences are not only cultural; social and professional groups have their own language and way of knowing. Walk the hallways of any company and you will hear corporate buzz-words. Every organization has its own dialect, and some thoughtfully provide dictionaries to ease the transition of new recruits. Each dialect carries values and shared experiences, interpreted and viewed differently depending on the familiarity and knowledge, providing opportunities for new translations. But translations can be wrong (Emerson 1983). I began this project believing myself to be well versed in these cultures and the communication style differences – a few blunders along the way exposed this fallacy. Language eluded leadership insight, and instead showed unconscious thoughts and shaped new ways of thinking about culture (Emerson 1983). 'Failure' gave the appearance of producing failure, but upon reflection provided much needed insight and I was able to correct the course for my stories.

Words are imperfect and elude meaning unless we understand the context. Improving the practice of cross-cultural interviewing requires understanding word nuances and cultural connotations. Words can be menacing across cultures unless we stop to consider the experience it has on others. In Chinese, there are over 150 words defining shame and face, each with a degree of distinction and related hierarchy (Ho, Fu and Ng 2004; Li et Al. 2003). In Greenland there are multiple words for snow (Speedy 2007), and each definition requires an understanding of the cultural landscape. Teaching leadership in Vietnam and Korea, I discovered that 'ambition' conjures up negative feelings and many people there do not want such a label. Yet across the Pacific, recruiters regularly ask 'how ambitious are you?' during assessment interviews. Most Vietnamese decline to respond because they experience the word negatively. More recently, Sheryl Sandberg, Chief Operating Officer (COO) of Facebook, spoke at the World Economic Forum, challenging women to be more ambitious (Waldman 2012;

Ettus 2012). In the US, ambition is similar to failure, gains a nod of acceptance during a corporate interview and receives a badge of courage once inside the brass door. The opposite is true in Asia. In this sense, the arbitrariness of language may very well be the reason behind the chaotic disorder of researching across cultures or what is often described as 'messiness' (Gunaratnam 2003).

Language and cultural lineage

The lineage behind words runs deep inside Confucian cultures. Given that I researched with Asian women, understanding words and digging deeper into cultural aspects becomes important for cross-cultural narrative inquiry. Particularly with this research, it is important to search for insights and explanations around the concept of face and word choice. Interestingly, the words 'failure and ambition' are inextricably linked to 'face'. Outside of Confucian cultures, the word 'face' is difficult to articulate. I often hear comments on 'saving face, giving face and having face' which intuitively make sense but remain challenging to explain. Researching this term while attempting to link with Western cultural constructs, I discovered research on 'shame'. Shame embodies four distinctly different emotional responses: humiliation, embarrassment, guilt and shame (Brown 2007). Face and shame are loosely connected, as to lose face falls within these four emotional responses.

Research indicates the idea of face originates in China, (Ho 1976; Ho, Fu and Ng 2004). Face rests within Confucian beliefs but these values are spread across China, Taiwan, Hong Kong, Singapore Japan, Korea Vietnam, Thailand and Malaysia (Wang et al. 2005; Bond 1991; Rotenburg and Donough 1993; Trompenaars 1993; Flowerdew 1998). The same notion of face can also be found within the Bangladeshi culture. Although not Confucian, it relates to the patriarchal society, hierarchy and social positioning (Kirbria 1995). Unlike shame, face reaches well beyond the individual, covering hierarchy, respect, interdependent family relationships, authority and professional status. This ingrained value both impacts and hinders students' behaviours in challenging a teacher or expert for fear of losing face (Flowerdew 1998). Expanding on this cultural value, acknowledging failure and being in a position to make a mistake raises the fear of losing face, which may well ultimately impact the family.

In a Western context, we see the tangential relationship of losing face to shame. Shame may impact the individual and family, but the difference rests between emotions, values and hierarchal cultures. This notion of face has baffled scholars (Foster 2006) for years to provide an accurate definition. In 1934, Chinese scholar Lu Hsun asked 'what is the thing called face?' (Ho 1976: 867). Challenging to comprehend, face remains an important and 'delicate standard by which Chinese social intercourse is relegated' (Ho 1976: 867).

Saving private (and public) face

So what precisely is face? Face – or more accurately, losing face – is an unfortunate event resulting in the loss of position, negatively impacting the individual, community, family or group. The recent scandal surrounding Bo Xi Lai, mayor of Chongching, is a clear example of losing face and the impact on family, community and government (The Economist 2012). Face is entangled within the rigid hierarchical systems of order and power relationships. In Mr Bo's case, the higher the social order, the harder the fall. Following the hierarchical rule of order, those in superior positions serve a higher command and follow strict protocol (Earley, Ang, Tan 2006). Mr Bo's error in judgement and misdeeds are felt more harshly than his son's fall from grace. A critical element of face is maintaining social control (Ho, Fu and Ng 2004). As the father or superior person falls, the subordinates and family members must maintain a sense of decorum devoid of external emotional outbursts or expressions. The complicated interdependence of relationships requires the ability to read subtle cues and careful communication to avoid offending anyone in the extended family. Awareness and sensitivity to relative status is important. Unlike shame, face rests within the hierarchy, social position, personal character, ethics and values. Guilt, embarrassment and shame are experienced differently across cultures, but they are universal emotions. Face, on the other hand, remains deeply entrenched within most Asian cultures.

Shame can be private or publicly displayed, but losing face is a public event and both represent dejected emotions. The dysphoric spread of emotions covering anger, humiliation and guilt are the same with shame and face, but one is external and the other internal. Losing face is visual and public, but the raw emotion underlying the experiences rarely displayed. Shame and face are similar in terms of perception; what is shown to others and what is perceived by others (Ho, Fu and Ng 2004). In Western cultures, shame is the evaluation of self, accompanied by fear and humiliation (Brown 2007). Shame is a conspicuous emotion in both cultures, but in Confucian societies avoiding shame is the overarching concern, given the link with losing face. Reviewing the historical context and deep emotional attachments to face, it is easy to understand the blank stares and long silences to my question on failure. To fail is to lose face, not only for oneself, but the extended, interconnected web of relationships.

Concluding thoughts

The purpose of this chapter is to share personal experiences using narrative to explore leadership lessons of four Asian women leaders. I embarked on this journey desirous to learn leadership lessons and share stories of these experiences. In the process, I discovered the impact of collective experiences and language associations on the interview process and the crafting of narrative (Rogers 2007). Language is arbitrary, confusing and embedded within cultures. While many people speak English, the words across cultures do not carry the same meaning. I was not seeking truth, but became intensely aware of meaning (Wilson 1986). As is true with any expedition, and particularly with narrative inquiry, there is no right path or straight line to follow. I stalled, stopped, often lost my way, but with each setback reconfigured a new path.

In writing this chapter, I also stumbled over words and philosophies. Words wreaked havoc with me throughout this narrative experience. Along with the misrepresentations presented here, I stared at the words on my note pages and wondered how these could be transformed into a vivid text to engage the reader. Finding my way with these words was clouded by being part of the story. The cross-cultural elements added new textures. Similar to the Confucian notion of face, I hold a mirror on myself while writing and living through the same experiences with my participants. Narrative inquiry is a collaborative process between researcher and participants, capturing and creating stories of lived experience (Clandinin and Huber 2010). But being an integral part of the research process created difficulties in telling the story while also living the story (Hustvedt 2011).

In some ways, we (my participants and I) are on centre stage performing together. While much has been written on using performative text in narrative inquiry, the emphasis remains on innovative approaches in capturing and telling stories (Bridge 2009; Speedy 2007; Clough 2002; Sparkes 2002; Riessman 2008). Based on my experience with this research, similar methods of improvization are needed to regroup from setbacks to reflexively ask, 'what do I do with this?' and 'what have I learned from this?' My cross-cultural experience became the prism for the way I saw the world. Sometimes this prism was a vibrant gem highlighting the colourful facets of lives, and other times it was a boulder that I needed to climb around and over. Reflexivity provided a window into my soul and a new path to walk around entrenched beliefs and mental blocks. Reflexivity offered an outlet for improvization and an opportunity to see my stories differently, becoming more self aware and cognizant of cultural beliefs. I walked into this research with years of cross-cultural experiences and now have more questions and insights, setting the stage for more learning opportunities through cross cultural narrative inquiry.

References

Bailey, G. M. P (2009) 'Curriculum Narratives: the global dimension compared', in S. Trahar (ed.) *Narrative Research on Learning: Comparative and International Perspectives*, Oxford: Symposium, pp. 129–44.

Bass, B., and Steidlmeier, P. (2004) 'Ethics, Character, and Authentic Transformational Leadership Behavior', in J. Ciulla (ed.) *Ethics, the Heart of Leadership*, 2nd edn, Westport, CT: Praeger Publishers, pp. 175–96.

Behar, R., and Gordon, D. (eds) (1995) *Women Writing Culture*, Berkely, CA: University of California Press.

Bellah, R., Madsen, R., Sullivan, W., Swidler, A., and Tipton, S. (2007) *Habits of the Heart: Individualism and Commitment in American Life*, 3rd edn, Berkeley: University of Calfornia Press.

Bond, M. (1991) *Beyond the Chinese Face: Insights from Psychology*, Hong Kong: Oxford University Press.

Bridges, N. (2009) 'Learning and Changing through a Narrative PhD: a personal narrative in progress', in S. Trahar (ed.) *Narrative Research on Learning: Comparative and International Perspectives*, Oxford: Symposium, pp. 93–105.

Brown, B. (2007) *I Thought It was Just Me (but it isn't): Telling the Truth about Perfectionism, Inadequacy, and Power*, New York: Gotham Books.

Chinn, J. L., Lott, B., Rice, J., and Sanchez-Hucles, J. (2007) *Women and Leadership: Transforming Visions and Diverse Voices*, Malden, MA: Blackewell Publishing.

Ciulla, J. B. (ed.) (2004) 'Leadership Ethics: Mapping the Territory' in *Ethics, the Heart of Leadership*, 2nd edn, Westport, CT: Praeger Publishers, pp. 3–24.

Clandinin, J., and Connelly, M. F. (1990) Stories of Experience and Narrative Inquiry, *Educational Researcher*, 19, (5): 2–14.

Clandinin, D. J., and Huber, J. (2010) 'Narrative inquiry' in B. McGaw, E. Baker, and P. P. Peterson (eds) *International Encyclopedia of Education*, 3rd edn, New York: Elsevier Science, pp. 436–47.

Clough, P. (2002) *Narrative and Fictions in Educational Research*, London: McGraw Hill.

Connelly, F. M., Phillion, J. and He, F. M. (2003) An Exploration of Narrative Inquiry into Multiculturalism in Education: Reflecting on Two Decades of Research in an Inner-City Canadian Community School, *Curriculum Inquiry*, 33, (4): 363–84.

Cortazzi, M. and Jin L., (2009) 'Asking Questions, Sharing Stories and Identity Construction: sociocultural issues in narrative research', in S. Trahar (ed.) *Narrative Research on Learning: Comparative and International Perspectives*, Oxford: Symposium, pp. 27–46.

Eagly, A. H. (2007) Female leadership advantage and disadvantage: Resolving the contradictions, *Psychology of Women Quarterly*, 31: 1–12.

Eagly, A. H., Johannesen-Schmidt, M., and van Engen, M. (2003) Transformational, transactional, and laissez-faire leadership styles: A meta-analysis comparing women and men, *Psychological Bulletin*, 129, (4): 569–91.

Earley, P. C., Ang, S., and Tan, J. S. (2006) *CQ Developing Cultural Intelligence at Work*, California: Stanford University Press.

Economist, The (2012) 'Bo Xi Lai's Political Demize: Downfall, part two', 11 April 2012. Available at www.economist.com/blogs/analects, accessed 3 May 2012.

—(2012) 'The Bo Xi Lai Case: Shattering the Façade', 14 April 2012. Available at www.economist.com/node/21552575), accessed 3 May 2012.

Emerson, C. (1983) The Outer Word and Inner Speech: Bakhtin, Vygotsky, and the Internalization of Language, *Critical Inquiry*, 10, (2): 245–64.

Etherington, K. (2004), *Becoming a Reflexive Researcher: Using Our Selves in Research*, London: Kingsley Publishers.

—(2009) 'Reflectivity: using our "selves" in narrative research', in S. Trahar (ed.) *Narrative Research on Learning: Comparative and International Perspectives*, Oxford: Symposium, pp. 77–92.

Ettus, S. (2012) 'Five Ways to Close the Ambition Gap for Girls' *Forbes*. Available atwww.forbes.com/sites/samanthaettus/2012/02/02/sheryl-sandberg/, accessed 21 April 2012.

Fairbank, J. (1992) *China: A New History*, Boston, MA: Harvard University Press.

Flowerdew, L. (1998) A Cultural Perspective on Group Work, *ELT Journal*, 52, (4): 323–9.

Ford, S. (2011) *Troubling American Women: Narratives of Gender and Nation in Hong Kong*, Hong Kong: Hong Kong University Press.

Foster, P. (2006) *Ah Q Archaeology: Lu Xun, Ah Q, Ah Q Progeny, and the National Character Discourse in Twentieth Century China*, Idaho: Lexington.

Fox, C. (2009) 'Stories Within Stories: dissolving the boundaries in narrative research and analysis', in S. Trahar (ed.) *Narrative Research on Learning: Comparative and International Perspectives*, Oxford: Symposium, pp. 47–60.

Gardner, H. (1995) *Leading Minds: An Anatomy of Leadership*, New York: Basic Books.

Gunaratnam, Y. (2003) *Researching Race and Ethnicity*, London: Sage Publications.

He. M. F. (2002) A Narrative Inquiry of Cross Cultural Lives: Lives in Canada, *Journal of Curriculum Studies*, 34, (3): 323–42.

Helgesen, S. (1995) *The Female Advantage: Women's Ways of Leadership*, New York: Doubleday.

Ho, D. Y. F. (1976) On The Concept of Face, *American Journal of Sociology*, 81, (4): 867–84.

Ho, D. Y. F., Fu, W., and Ng, S. M. (2004) Guilt, Shame and Embarrassment: Revelations of Face and Self, *Cultural Psychology*, 10, (1): 64–84.

Hufstevdt, S. (2011) *The Summer Without Men*, New York: Picador.

Kaminsky, M. (1992) 'Myerhoff's Third Voice: Ideology and Genre in Ethnographic Narrative', *Social Text*, 33: 124–44.

Kirbria N. (1995) Culture, Social Class, and Income Control in the Lives of Women Garment Workers in Bangladesh, *Gender & Society*, 9, (3): 289–309.

Li, J., Wang, L., and Fischer, K. W. (2003) The organization of shame concepts in Chinese, *Cognitive Development Laboratory Report*, Cambridge, MA: Harvard University.

Lin, C. (2008) 'Demystifying the Chameleonic Nature of Chinese Leadership', *Journal of Leadership and Organisational Studies*, 14. (4): 303–21.

Maynes, M. J., Pierce, J. L, and Laslett, B. (2008) *Telling Stories: The Use of Personal Narratives in the Social Sciences and History*, Ithaca, New York: Cornell University Press.

Phillion, J. (2002) Becoming a narrative inquirer in a multicultural landscape, *Journal of Curriculum Studies*, 34, (5), 535–56.

Polanyi, L. (1985) *Telling the American Story : A structural conversational analysis of cultural storytelling*, Westport, CT: Praeger.

Pollock, D., and Van Reken, R. (1999) *The Third Culture Kid Experience: Growing Up Among Worlds*, Maine: Intercultural Press.

Riessman, C. K. (2008) *Narrative Methods for Human Science*, London: Sage Publications Inc.

Riessman, C. K., and Speedy, J. (2007) 'Narrative inquiry in the psychotherapy professions: A critical review', in D. J. Clandinin (ed.) *Handbook of Narrative Inquiry: Mapping a Methodology*, Thousand Oaks, CA: Sage, pp. 426–56.

Rogers, A. (2007) 'The Unsayable, Lacanaian Psychoanalysis, and the Art of Narrative Interviewing', in D. J. Clandinin (ed.) *Handbook of Narrative Inquiry: Mapping a Methodology*, Thousand Oaks, CA: Sage Publications, pp. 99–119.

Rotenburg, R., and Donough, G. (1993) *The Cultural Meaning of Urban Space*, Westport, CT: Bergin & Garvey.

Sarup, M. (1996) *Identity, Culture and The Postmodern World*, Edinburgh University Press.

Schaetti, B. (1996) 'Phoenix Rising: A Question of Cultural Identity', in C. Smith (ed.) *Strangers at Home: Essays on the Effects of Living Overseas and Coming Home to a Strange Land*, New York: Aletheia Publications Inc, pp. 177–88.

Simmons, A. (2001) *The Story Factor: Inspiration, Influence, and Persuassion through the Art of Storytelling*, Cambridge, MA: Perseus Publishing.

Solomon, R. (2004) 'Ethical Leadership, Emotions, and Trust: Beyond "Charisma"', inJ. Ciulla (ed.) *Ethics, the Heart of Leadership*, 2nd edn, Westport, CT: Praeger Publishers, pp. 83–102.

Sparkes, A. (2002) *Telling Tales in Sport and Activity*, Leeds: Human Kinetic.

Speedy, J. (2007) *Narrative Inquiry and Psychotherapy*, New York: Palgrave MacMillan.

Spence, J. (1990) *The Search for Modern China*, London: W. W. Norton & Company

Thomas, R., Tienar, J., Davies, A., and Merilaine, S. (2009) Let's Talk about 'Us': A Reflexive Account of a Cross-Cultural Research Collaboration', *Journal of Management Inquiry*, 18, (4): 313–24.

Trahar, S. (2005/6) Navigating Diverse Landscapes: Investigating Experiences of Learning and Teaching in an International Higher Education Community, *The International Journal of Diversity in Organisational, Communities and Nations*, 5, (3) 163–70.

—(2009) 'A Part of the Landscape: the practitioner researcher as narrative inquirer in an international higher education community', in S. Trahar (ed.) *Narrative Research on Learning: Comparative and International Perspectives*, Oxford: Symposium, pp. 77–92.

Trompenaars, F. (1997) *Riding the Waves of Culture: Understanding Cultural Diversity in Business*, London: Nicholas Brealey.

Waldman, K. (2012) 'In Defence of Sheryl Sandberg', Slate. Available at www.slate.com/blogs/xx_factor/2012/02/07/sheryl_sandberg_is_right_about_the_ambition_gap_for_women_.html, accessed 21 April 2012.

Wilson, F. (1986) Hume and Derrida on Language and Meaning, *Hume Studies*, XII, (2): 99–121.

Wang, J., Wang, G., Ruona, W., Rojewski, J. (2005) Confucian Values and Implications for HRD, *Human Resource Development International*, 8, (3), 311–26.

Index

Note: The letter 'n' following a page number indicates an endnote.